BRITISH
TRENCH WARFARE
1917 – 1918

A REFERENCE MANUAL

GENERAL STAFF, WAR OFFICE

The Naval & Military Press Ltd

Published by
The Naval & Military Press Ltd
5 Riverside, Brambleside, Bellbrook
Industrial Estate, Uckfield, East Sussex,
TN22 1QQ England

Tel: +44 (0) 1825 749494
Fax: +44 (0) 1825 765701

www.naval-military-press.com
www.military-genealogy.com

*In reprinting in facsimile from the original, any imperfections are inevitably reproduced
and the quality may fall short of modern type and cartographic standards.*

CONTENTS

This is the fifteenth in a
series of reference manuals
produced by the publishers.

Other titles in the series:

1. *Handbook of the Austro-Hungarian Army in War, June 1918*
2. *Field Equipment of the European Foot Soldier, 1900-1914*
3. *The Austro-Hungarian Forces in the Field, October 1918*
4. *Handbook of the French Army, 1914*
5. *German Forces in the Field, 11 November 1918*
6. *Handbook of the Italian Army, 1913*
7. *German Military Terms, 1918*
8. *Prothero's Bibliography of Great War Books, 1923*
9. *Handbook of German Military and Naval Aviation, 1918*
10. *Handbook of the German Army at War, April 1918*
11. *Handbook of the Turkish Army, 1916*
12. *Handbook of the Russian Army, 1914*
13. *Handbook of the German Army, December 1940*
14. *Armies of the Balkan States, 1914-1918*

CONTENTS.

CHAPTER IV.—ORGANIZATION OF A TRENCH LINE AND ACTION IN CASE OF ATTACK.

CHAPTER V.—NOTES ON THE ATTACK IN TRENCH WARFARE.

FIGURES AND DIAGRAMS.

NOTES FOR INFANTRY OFFICERS ON TRENCH WARFARE.

CHAPTER I.

Special Characteristics of Trench Warfare.

1. TRENCH FIGHTING ONLY A PHASE OF WARFARE.

The importance assumed by trench warfare and the progress made in the application of field fortification and in the science of the attack and defence of elaborate systems of trenches, have rendered necessary special instruction in the details of trench construction and trench fighting. It must, nevertheless, be clearly understood that trench fighting is only a phase of operations, and that instruction in this subject, essential as it is, is only one branch of the training of troops. To gain a decisive success the enemy must be driven out of his defences and his armies crushed in the open.

The aim of trench fighting is, therefore, to create a favorable situation for field operations, which the troops must be capable of turning to account.

2. CONSIDERATIONS AFFECTING DESIGN OF DEFENSES.

1. Three facts in particular give to modern trench fighting under present conditions most of its special characteristics. These are:

(a) The continual proximity of the opposing forces.

(b) The length of time for which they have generally occupied the same ground.

(c) The fact that neither side has a flank so long as it remains on the defensive, so that every attack must be frontal.

2. As a result of the length of time the opposing forces have been in close proximity on practically the same ground, the original trenches dug at the end of a period of maneuver operations have grown into a complicated system of entrenchments. The design and organization of these have been influenced by the nature of the artillery, up to calibers far heavier than could be utilized in ordinary field operations, which the stationary nature of the fighting has made it possible to bring up. Arrangements have been

made by a carefully thought out system of intercommunication for the maximum cooperation between artillery and infantry, both in attack and defense, and artillery has had time to register on all targets within range. Thus either side has it in its power to concentrate heavy fire at very short notice upon any selected target, and to maintain that fire for a length of time which difficulties of ammunition supply would put out of the question in maneuver operations. Consequently, the rapidity with which artillery can form a barrage to meet attack makes it necessary that the moment of the assault should come as a surprise, and the trenches from which an attack is to be made should therefore be within close assaulting distance of the opposing front line.

3. A system of trenches must therefore be designed which facilities the preparation and launching of an unexpected assault, and at the same time is adapted to meet a sudden attack by the enemy. The organization of a trench system to facilitate attack is an important point which is frequently neglected. If additional trenches have to be hastily made when an attack is intended, the intention to attack will be obvious to the enemy by aerial reconnaissance, and surprise will be out of the question.

4. Modern field fortifications owe their elaborate form to the means employed in attack and defense respectively. A general idea of what those means are is therefore necessary.

The aim of the first stages of attack is to obtain a footing in the enemy's defenses and to consolidate and extend the gain thus made. Penetration is effected by means of an infantry assault, which, as has been said, must unavoidably be frontal and depends for success on a certain measure of surprise.

The infantry attack may be assisted by any or all of the following methods:

(a) The previous destruction, by bombardment or explosion of mines or a combination of both, of the enemy's material defenses, including obstacles.

(b) The shaking of the morale and destruction of the personnel of the defending force by bombardment or by the employment of one of the new agents of war, such as asphyxiating gas or jets of liquid fire, prior to assault.

(c) Keeping down hostile fire over the area to be crossed by the attacking infantry long enough to enable the assaulting troops to reach the cover of the enemy's defenses.

(d) The isolation, by artillery barrages, of the area to be assaulted, so as to prevent the arrival of reinforcements.

(*e*) The dispersal or destruction of troops collecting for counter-attack.

5. To meet these measures the defense employs the following means:

(*a*) Constant close observation, with a view to the detection of any signs of impending attack.[1]

(*b*) Concentration of fire on any detected assembly which might be the prelude to assault.

(*c*) Concentration of fire of artillery, machine guns, and rifles, from as wide a front as possible, over any part of the zone lying between the two lines, so as to prevent the penetration of the defense.

(*d*) Obstacles to delay the assaulting troops as long as possible under this fire.

(*e*) Barrages of fire to prevent the reenforcement of, or the sending up of materials, ammunition, or supplies to, any body of troops that has succeeded in penetrating the defense.

(*f*) Disposition of works so as to localize and confine the effect of penetration at any point.[2]

(*g*) Destruction by artillery fire of any enemy troops that have penetrated.

(*h*) Immediate counterattack, to drive out the attackers before they can have recovered from the confusion of the assault and have established themselves securely in the captured area.

3. NATURE OF FIELD DEFENSES.

A consideration of the above shows that there are certain features which are essential in a system of trenches. They must be strong, to resist heavy bombardment; they must be sited and designed to favor, by the utilization of oblique and enfilade fire of rifles and, above all, of machine guns, the development of the maximum volume of fire over any part of their front; they must be protected by a strong and well-hidden wire entanglement, in order to retain attacking infantry under this fire; they must provide protection for the garrison against weather and against the effect of artillery fire. Fire and shelter trenches must be numerous in order to accommodate the additional troops to be placed in them previous to an attack on the enemy's line, and also, in the defense, to induce dispersion of hostile artillery fire to permit the temporary with-

---

[1] E. g., installment of gas apparatus, advance of saps, passages cut in enemy's wire to facilitate egress.

[2] See sections 14 and 15.

drawal of the garrison from a heavily shelled zone, and to accommodate troops for local counterattack in close proximity to the points where they may be required. Communications must be ample, to admit of the rapid reoccupation of temporarily evacuated trenches, to minimize the interference of hostile fire with reenforcement and supply, and to facilitate local counterattack. Close observation of the enemy must be provided for by listening posts in advance of the front line and by observing stations in or behind it. Finally, the system of trenches must admit of immediate readjustment of the front, so that the effect of penetration at any point may be localized and need not weaken the hold of the defense on adjacent trenches.

4. THE OFFENSIVE SPIRIT IN TRENCH WARFARE.

The attack on such a system of defenses as has been described demands in all ranks dash and gallantry of a very high order, and in the subordinate leader, down to the lowest grades, a quick perception, rapid decision, and intelligent initiative. It is more than ever the case that success depends upon qualities of leadership in subordinate commanders, upon rapid appreciation and readiness to accept responsibility on the part of the man on the spot. Much can be done in peace training to foster these qualities and to impress on even the most subordinate leaders the necessity for acting, in cases of urgency, on their own responsibility. At the same time, the state of comparative inactivity, which is the normal condition of life in the trenches, is very unfavorable to the development of these qualities in officers and men. There is an insidious tendency to lapse into a passive and lethargic attitude, against which officers of all ranks have to be on their guard, and the fostering of the offensive spirit, under such unfavorable conditions, calls for incessant attention. Minor local enterprises and constant occupation during the tour of duty in the trenches furnish the best means of maintaining the efficiency of the troops. The repair, maintenance, and improvement of the trenches furnish ample work to afford employment to the troops, who must be made to understand that this work reacts in their own favor in the shape of increased security and comfort and conditions more favorable to health. Constant activity in harassing the enemy may lead to reprisals at first, and for this reason is sometimes neglected, but, if persevered in, it always results in an ultimate mastery, it gives the troops a healthy interest and wholesome topics of conversation, and it achieves the double purpose of raising the morale of our own troops whilst lowering that of the enemy. Every effort should be made to obtain the mastery over the enemy's snipers.

5. TRAINING IN NIGHT WORK.

The proximity of the opposing lines, the progress of aeria reconnaissance, and the close and continuous watch which either side maintains over the other, have increased the importance of night work. Many of the daily operations incidental to trench warfare can only be carried out under cover of darkness. The construction of new trenches in sight of the enemy, and much of their maintenance and repair, the construction, repair, and improvement of obstacles, and in many cases the bringing up of materials and stores and the relief of the garrison, can not be carried out by daylight. The assembly of troops and many of the final stages of preparation for an attack, as, for instance, the removal of our own obstacles, can only be kept from the enemy's knowledge by carrying them out at night. The close reconnaissance of the enemy's front line and his obstacles and of the ground to be crossed by an assault is the work of night patrols, and much of the identification of the troops opposed to us—a very important duty—can only be effected by small enterprises carried out by night against the enemy's patrols or listening posts or sometimes against a small section of his trenches. Training in all these branches of night work is an important part of the instruction of troops before leaving for the front.

6. DISCIPLINE.

The hardships, discomfort, and dangers of life in the trenches make great demands upon the endurance of the troops; the frontal attack on an enemy in a position strengthened and defended by every device that ingenuity and forethought can conceive calls for exceptional resolution and determination, and the defense of trenches against an attack, preluded generally by a protracted and severe bombardment, and often by the employment of some entirely new and unforeseen agency, requires the utmost steadfastness and devotion. No infantry will possess those qualities to the requisite degree that has not a very high standard of discipline. The first and greatest aim of all training should therefore be the establishment of the strictest discipline. To attain this there is no other method than constant and precise drill, strict enforcement of march discipline, insistence on a rigid exactness in the performance of even the dullest details of camp and barrack routine, and unceasing attention to apparently trifling detail in time of training. Without such previous preparation the silent and thorough execution of work and performance of duties, in darkness and in danger, in the presence of the enemy, and often without direct supervision of a superior, which distinguish good from bad troops and spell success, are impossible of attainment.

7. TRAINING OF SPECIALISTS.

The present type of warfare in the trenches has involved the training of a proportion of men in infantry units in duties of a special nature, e. g., grenade throwing, pioneer work, sniping, etc.

A word of warning is necessary as regards the training of these men. They must be made to realize that their training in these special duties is in addition to their ordinary training as infantry soldiers and must not be allowed to interfere with their performance of the ordinary duties of infantry soldiers, except when they are required for the special duties in which they have been trained.

CHAPTER II.

SITING AND CONSTRUCTION OF TRENCHES.

8. DELIBERATE SITING OF TRENCHES.

1. The problem of selecting the position of fire trenches varies according to the circumstances under which the choice has to be made and the work carried out. The siting and construction of a trench line in the presence of the enemy and under fire is influenced by factors which are absent in the deliberate and undisturbed choice such as can be made when preparing a rear line. It is important to recognize that the two problems are distinct, and that their solution calls for different methods.

2. The first step in the case of a line which is to be constructed free from interference by the enemy, and under circumstances which make time a factor of minor importance, is a deliberate reconnaissance of the ground. This reconnaissance will usually consist of two stages. The first deals with the problem on broad lines, compares the merits of alternative general solutions, determines the general line to be taken up, and lays down certain points or localities as having special importance and calling for special treatment. Following on this, a second, more detailed, reconnaissance is made, in which are considered the form of the works to be constructed for the defense of the tactical features and localities laid down in the general scheme and the method of treating the intervals between these strong points or localities. As a result of this detailed reconnaissance, large-scale plans are produced, showing the exact siting and constructional detail of the essential works. The decision as to the general line to be taken up is the business of the general staff of the formation (division, corps, or army) concerned. The chief engineer officer will advise as to the constructional details of the line selected. In both stages of the reconnaissance due weight should be given to the questions of facilities for attack, and of securing good observation for ourselves and denying it to the enemy, cohesion in defense by mutual support of adjoining works, drainage, and concealment; the final decision arrived at is a balance between the often conflicting requirements of these different considerations. The order of importance of the works is another point decided in the two stages of the reconnaissance. Not until the reconnaissance has been com-

pleted should any work be begun and, although the close study of
the ground during the execution of the works will probably suggest
improvements in detail—in fact, a good deal of the detail should be
left to be elaborated at this stage—it will seldom be necessary or
advisable to alter any of the essential features, determined by the
reconnaissance, during the construction of the defenses.

3. Unless the ground is almost absolutely flat, the most important
question in siting trenches is whether to occupy the tops of the hills,
establishing the front line trenches on either the crest or the forward slope, or to withdraw the main front line to the reverse slope,
taking up what is known as the "back" or "retired" position.
The chief argument advanced in favor of this latter position is that
it affords greater security against hostile artillery fire. Now, it
must be borne in mind that the question of protection from artillery fire, so far as it is affected by siting, is almost entirely one of
security from observation. Any target can be heavily and accurately engaged if fire on it can be effectively observed from a point
in the occupation of the force which is carrying out the bombardment. The position of the observer relative to the gun is immate-
rial; that of the target to the gun position almost equally so. If
either side is in occupation of the hilltops and can establish an
artillery officer with a telescope and a telephone on the high ground,
its facilities for observation of fire are greater than those of its oppo-
nent, situated lower down the slopes. That being the case, the
"back position" loses the advantage of protection from artillery fire
claimed for it, unless we can deny to the enemy's observers the use
of the high ground. Experience has shown that, except in the case
of isolated features of small extent, when a concentration of fire may
effect the desired purpose, the only effective way to deny ground
to the enemy is to occupy it oneself.

Front line trenches on the crest or forward slope are certainly
exposed to view and therefore to bombardment, though this is not
so much the case as it would be if the enemy were looking down on
them, and the disadvantage can be diminished by adequate provision of material protection for the garrison. On the other hand,
the occupation of the high ground gives a feeling of superiority which
reacts favorably on the morale of the troops. Only those who have
experienced it can appreciate the depressing effect produced by
the feeling of discomfort and inferiority of position under which
troops suffer who have to occupy for some time trenches looked
down upon by those of the enemy. The forward position has the
further advantage, if the front line is not dug too far down the for-

ward slope, that supporting trenches, communications, and the works in which a large proportion of the garrison live, enjoy a comparative immunity from observation. In offensive action the forward position offers greater facilities for observation, on which the effectiveness of the previous preparation by bombardment largely depends, and for the assembly of troops for the assault, close to the front line and unobserved.

4. Special conditions may justify the deliberate choice of the "retired" position. If it is adopted, arrangements must be made to deny the enemy access to the crest of the hill, and to secure it for ourselves. The front trench line must not be too far below the crest line—50 to 100 yards will usually be far enough and is a sufficient field of fire if machine guns are well sited—and there must be an ample number of saps forward to the top to allow of continuous observation of the forward slope. With these precautions, and readiness to deliver an immediate and vigorous counter attack on the enemy if he appears on the crest, the back position may sometimes be taken up when conditions impose a temporarily defensive attitude and the local superiority in artillery is with the enemy. But if the two lines remain facing one another on the same ground for a protracted period it will be impossible to prevent the enemy indefinitely from establishing himself on the crest unless it is included in our line.

5. In deciding on both the general and the detailed trace of the line a common tendency, which is to be avoided, is towards making it too straight. An irregular line, with frequent salients and reentrants, gives greater facilities for concentration of fire over any desired area and for the most effective employment of machine guns. It will expose short lengths of trench to enfilade fire, but suitable construction will minimize the effect of this. In any case the effect is generally reciprocal; from a salient in our line some part of the enemy's line pushed forward into the adjoining reentrant will be exposed to our enfilade fire. These remarks apply with almost equal force to a large salient, constructed to include an important tactical point, and to minor irregularities in the trace of trenches. The latter should be made as a matter of invariable principle. The former should be used boldly where circumstances demand them. The determining considerations in their case are two:

(a) Whether the possession of the point in question by us would facilitate future offensive action without unduly weakening our line

(b) Whether its possession by the enemy would seriously threaten the security of our trenches.

9. SITING OF TRENCHES IN THE PRESENCE OF THE ENEMY.

1. The presence of the enemy will frequently make it impossible to select the position of fire trenches entirely on the merits of the ground. Their site will often be decided by the chance and accident of close fighting, and their general position will coincide roughly with the high-water mark reached for the moment by the attack. Troops who are unable to make any further advance will either occupy a hostile trench which has been captured in the course of the attack or start at once to procure for themselves what cover they can with the tools at their disposal, generally, for the most part, only the entrenching tool. Much can be done by officers at this stage in the way of small adjustments of position and of the distribution of their men with a view to the future development of the hasty cover constructed into the best line that circumstances will admit. Unless this is done, much of the work may be found afterwards to be useless, valuable time and effort will have been wasted, and troops may either have to try and hold an unfavorable position or be exposed again in the construction of a fresh one. Serious work will generally be impossible before dusk, unless arrangements can be made for a heavy covering fire, and after dusk it is difficult to avoid mistakes in the choice and siting of a line. Every officer, then, who finds his command unable to make further progress, should take advantage of the daylight to study the ground as far as circumstances permit, and should make up his mind exactly what line he will take up if forced to dig himself in.

2. The main problem that arises in this case is whether any of the ground won should be abandoned in order to secure a more suitable line of defense. Generally, if the check is merely temporary and it is intended to resume the advance at the earliest opportunity, all ground gained should be held except for very minor adjustments, unless some portion is clearly untenable against counter attack; if, however, strategical or tactical considerations require a temporary abandonment of the forward movement and the construction of a defensive line to be held for some time, the decision will be governed to a great extent by the same considerations as already discussed in taking up a line deliberately, and it may be advisable to give up ground on some parts of the front.

3. The satisfactory siting of a trench line constructed in these circumstances will largely depend on the power possessed by the officers on the spot to recognize during the various stages of a

battle the minor features of real tactical importance. The ability to recognize these is only acquired by previous training, and is a quality which every officer must study to possess.

10. CONCEALMENT.

The development of aerial reconnaissance has made concealment of a *position* impossible, but isolated works and gun emplacements can be hidden, and trenches in a wood may remain undetected if clearing is not overdone. But aerial observers can not only invariably locate trenches in open country but can obtain photographs showing every trench and every traverse. Good aeroplane photographs show even the wire entanglements. This is not to be interpreted as meaning that no attention need be paid to the question of concealment. Anything that tends to make a trench less conspicuous and increases the difficulty of observing fire on it for an observer on the ground is of value. If natural cover is turned to account, the existence of a trench at a particular spot may not be detected at once and it may escape the attentions of the enemy's artillery at the stage when it is most vulnerable. In siting trenches with a view to concealment the hiding of the wire entanglements and supervision and communication trenches must not be overlooked. Tracks and much trampled ground show up very clearly from the air, and may draw attention to an otherwise well hidden work. Work done to buildings themselves is easily concealed from aerial reconnaissance, but the existence of trenches round or leading into a building gives a clear indication of its occupation.

The fact that trenches can not be concealed from aerial observation makes it most important that every system of trenches should be so designed that an attack can be made from them without the necessity of constructing fresh trenches at the last moment, which would give away the fact that an attack was intended. Airmen can not see whether a trench is occupied or not without coming down dangerously low.

11. BUILDINGS.

It will frequently happen that substantial buildings are found close to the selected line of defense. The question then arises whether to occupy them or to demolish them. The decision will depend generally upon two points, whether they have cellars which can be improved into good cover, and whether it is possible to demolish them. Buildings in or near the front line invariably draw a lot of fire from artillery, and unless good cover can be constructed in connection with them are nothing but shell traps. Solid blocks of buildings, on the other hand, with cellars which can be improved to give good cover against bombardment have on many occasions proved very difficult to take. Buildings of this nature had better be included in the line if possible, as they can be converted into strong points, and if left to be occupied by the enemy might prove both a thorn in the flesh to the defense and an obstacle to attack. A building which has no cellars may be left out of the line if it can be effectively demolished so as to afford no cover to the enemy. Effective demolition is a technical job which requires the cooperation of the R. E. and demands a certain amount of time. Where it is neither possible to carry out an effective demolition, nor desirable to distort the line so as to include a building or a group of buildings, these may sometimes be held as an advanced post to prevent their occupation by the enemy. In this case they must be connected up with the main line by communication trenches and special measures to deal at the shortest possible notice with a sudden enterprise must be arranged.

12. WOODS.

1. A position in a wood affords a certain amount of concealment from observation. It is easy to conceal the wire entanglement so that accurate artillery fire can not be brought to bear on it. If the position of the line taken up is such that the enemy can establish himself inside the wood he will enjoy similar advantages. Therefore, where there is freedom of choice, the best line to take up is one which secures cover from observation for ourselves, whilst denying the edge of the wood to the enemy. The exact distance inside the wood of this position can not be definitely laid down, but experience has shown that 30 to 50 yards from the front edge usually provides ample concealment from observation. Under no circumstances should the front edge itself be occupied, as hostile artillery can obtain the range of it with accuracy. Breastworks with a parados are generally more suitable in a wood than trenches; in either case the space between parapet and parados should be made as narrow as possible to keep down casualties from splinters of shell bursting in the trees. Otherwise the siting and design of trenches in a wood do not call for any special observations.

2. If a wood can not be included in the line and has to be left unoccupied in close proximity to it, special arrangements must be made for the concentration of fire on the near edge of the wood

and on the ground between it and the front line trench, to deal with an attack by enemy who could assemble unseen under cover of the wood.

13. GENERAL DESCRIPTION OF A LINE OF TRENCHES.[1]

The front system of trenches comprises the front line and its support and reserve trenches. In front of the front line is an obstacle continuous except for narrow inconspicuous passages at intervals to serve as exits for reconnoitering patrols. The trenches may be constructed completely below ground, they may consist of a combination of trench and parapet, or the necessary cover may be provided entirely above ground level by the construction of breastworks. The first type is very seldom met with, while the use of breastworks is practically confined to positions where water makes them necessary and where time admits of their construction. The combination of trench and parapet is that most commonly met with, the depth of the trench being generally determined by the wetness of the site and facilities for drainage. The front line generally consists of two parts, the fire trench and the command or supervision trench. The fire trench may either be a continuous trench (though in no case should it be an absolutely straight one), traversed at suitable intervals to give protection from enfilade fire and to localize the effect of shell bursts, or may consist of fire bays, T-shaped or L-shaped in plan, jutting forward from the supervision trench. The latter is a continuous trench affording easy lateral communication close behind the fire bays or fire trench, and connected with them at frequent intervals. In the case of fire bays there must be a communication trench forward from the supervision trench to each bay. In the case of a continuous fire trench the best position for these communication trenches to come into the fire trench is behind a traverse, and there should be one such communication trench behind about every second traverse. (See figs. 2, 3, and 4.)

2. Emplacements for machine guns are constructed in the front line so that the whole front of the line can be swept with machine-gun fire, which for the maximum effect should be from a flank across the front covered. It is, therefore, essential that the trace of a trench should not be straight. Machine guns can also often be effectively employed behind the front line in small inconspicuous emplacements, where they may escape detection and consequent bombardment prior to an attack. The question of

---

[1] See figures 1 to 8.

machine-gun emplacements must always receive most careful attention. (See sec. 20.)

3. The support trenches (see sec. 17 (7)) accommodate the first support to the garrison of the front trench, ready for immediate reinforcement or local counterattack; they also furnish cover to which the bulk of the garrison of the front trench can be temporarily withdrawn during bombardment. [1] The support line should always be constructed as a second line of resistance, if the first line is lost, and should be protected by an obstacle. The line of support trenches may or may not be continuous, it is preferable that it should be; in any case it is connected to the front line by frequent communication trenches. In order that support trenches may not suffer from the bombardment of the front line they should not be nearer than 50 yards behind it, and the most favorable position is from 70 to 100 yards behind.

4. Behind the support trenches, and also connected with them by communication trenches, lies the reserve line, which may consist of a line of trenches but more usually of dugouts, often formed by improving the cover afforded by some natural feature. The reserve trenches or dugouts are to accommodate the battalion reserve, whose purpose is the local counter-attack. The reserve line may be from 400 to 600 yards in rear of the front line.

5. To the above are often added trenches made for a special purpose, e. g., a "bombing trench" (which is a trench dug behind the front line within easy grenade-throwing distance of it, its purpose being to enable an enemy who has captured the front line to be driven out by grenades) or so-called "slit" trenches dug off the communication trenches for the accommodation of men during a bombardment. (See sec. 19 (8) and fig. 6.)

6. A system of trenches is also usually provided with a series of works prepared for all-round defense, and surrounded with a continuous obstacle, known variously as "keeps," "supporting points," "strong points," or "reduits." Their object is to break up a hostile attack which has penetrated the front line and prevent its further development, and thus to facilitate counterattack. Their garrison must hold out to the last, whatever happens to the rest of the line. They must come as a surprise to

---

[1] Under favorable circumstances the bulk of the garrison of the front line may normally be accommodated during the day in the support trenches, leaving the front line to be garrisoned by groups of sentries only. The question of the distribution of men in the trenches is discussed later in Chapter IV. The question of the provision and position of shelter against the weather and bombardment for the garrison of the fire and support trenches is discussed later in this chapter.

the enemy, and, therefore, be carefully concealed. No definite rules can be laid down as to their number on a given frontage or their relative position with regard to the front line; this will usually depend on the facilities offered by the ground for their concealment. Adjacent works of this kind should, if possible, afford mutual support to one another.

7. Latrines are provided in all trenches, and must be in positions easy of access and protected from fire. They are usually made in T-heads at the end of short trenches leading off from the supervision trench.

Communication trenches are made to the front system from points on roads which can be reached without too much exposure to view.

14. STRONG POINTS AND DEFENDED LOCALITIES.

1. In every line there will be a certain number of points of which the loss, or their occupation by the enemy, would seriously endanger the security of the rest of the line, or would weaken the defender's hold on it. There will also probably be other points which are particularly favorable for defense. Such points should receive special treatment so as to develop to the utmost their capabilities for defense, and to enable the troops to hold on to them even after the neighboring portions of the line have been lost. In addition, if the intervals between them are great, there should be small intermediate works. The important thing about all these works is that they should be designed so as to be able to offer a protracted resistance, unsupported if necessary, to hostile attacks from any direction, flank and rear as well as frontal. The importance of the point to be strengthened, its position, and its nature generally determine the area to be embraced within the perimeter of the work. Speaking generally, large defended localities offer a less concentrated target to the enemy's guns, and are, therefore, less vulnerable, but they absorb large garrisons.

2. The small strong point referred to in last section is generally in the nature of an inclosed infantry redoubt with a continuous parapet round its whole perimeter, designed to be held by a garrison which may be anything from a section to half a company. The garrison should be kept as small as possible, and the defense provided by machine guns as far as possible. This type of work must be carefully concealed and strongly constructed, or it will become a "shell trap." Good bombproof protection for its garrison should be provided within the perimeter of the work. (See figs. 9 and 10.)

3. The more important points are better defended by a system of trenches covering a more extended area, and forming what is

better described as a defended locality. The perimeter of such a defended locality should be provided with defenses against an attack from any direction, these defenses consisting either of a continuous fire trench, or of isolated lengths of fire trench sited to cover every possible line of approach, and connected with one another and with the works in the interior of the locality by communication trenches. Small self-contained works such as have been described in the last paragraph might quite well form an element in the defenses of the perimeter or in the interior defenses of a locality. Within the defended perimeter should be the dugouts for the garrison and a series of cover and support trenches and communication trenches, many of them prepared for occupation as fire trenches. In this way the interior is cut up into compartments, and the scheme of defense is so organized that, even if the enemy succeeds in establishing a footing at some point in the perimeter, an unbroken front can still be presented to him, and the defender's hold on the locality is practically unaffected. Machine guns play an important part in the defense, and alternative emplacements should be numerous. The sitings of the emplacements should be very carefully considered, and will largely govern the general design of the defenses. A defended locality of this nature has the advantage that it does not offer a concentrated artillery target, and that its reduction by bombardment would be a difficult and lengthy operation, entailing a large expenditure of ammunition.

4. Villages placed in a state of defense make the best kind of supporting point. If the defense is properly organized, their capture has usually proved a long and costly operation. Cellars, with their roofs shored up and reinforced, form excellent shelters, and good communications entirely underground can be made by breaking through from cellar to cellar. The organization of the defense will be similar to that already outlined for defended localities. The field of fire from interior lines of resistance must be improved wherever necessary by the thorough demolition of buildings and removal or spreading of the débris.

5. These strong points or localities should, as has been already stated, be provided with a good obstacle all round them. In addition, any interior trench which may, under the scheme of defense, at any time become a line of resistance, should also be covered by a wire entanglement.

6. Unity of command is an important thing in the defense of one of these works, and they should, with this in view, be designed for a garrison of a complete unit, as far as possible.

15. DEFENSES IN REAR OF THE FRONT SYSTEM.

The defenses in rear of the front system should consist of a zone 4 or 5 miles deep, in which all points of tactical importance are fortified on the principles laid down in section 14. The intention is by the occupation of these points to break up the attack of any hostile force which has penetrated the front system, delay any further advance, and facilitate counter attack. In addition to this primary rôle, these strong points furnish a framework on which, by digging trenches in the intervals, a new line within the zone can be rapidly constructed to meet any eventuality.

A second similar zone may be prepared in rear of the first.

16. PROCEDURE WHEN CONSTRUCTING TRENCHES IN THE PRESENCE OF THE ENEMY.

1. The procedure in the case of constructing a line when hostile interference has not to be reckoned with has already been described. In the construction of a line in the presence of an enemy the first object is to get some sort of cover, as quickly as possible, for the firing line. Normally what happens is that individual men start to dig pits for themselves where they were when the advance stopped. As soon as possible these pits are joined up with one another to form a continuous fire trench. This trench may ultimately form the front fire trench, a continuous trench for purposes of lateral communication being subsequently dug behind it, or it may become the supervision trench, fresh fire trenches being pushed out at intervals from it to the front. In either case, but more especially in the former, much subsequent labor will be saved if the question of traverses in the final trench is taken into account, both in the spacing of the first constructed pits and in the joining of them up to form a trench (see details regarding traverses in section 17). If it is decided to use the trench first formed as a supervision trench, the next stage, after it is completed, is that T-heads are pushed forward from it to form the firing bays. The work of digging the individual pits will be begun by the infantry with any tools they have, generally, as has been said, mostly with infantry entrenching tools. Troops must, therefore, be well practiced in digging themselves in by night or day with these tools. But heavier tools must be got up to the firing line as soon as possible, and every plan for an advance should provide for a certain number of digging tools, other than the entrenching tool, accompanying the attack,[1] and for this number being supplemented as early as possible with every available pick and shovel. It may be necessary to wait for dark before a large

---

[1] See Chapter V.

quantity of tools can be brought up and serious work attempted, but it is sometimes possible, under covering fire from the artillery, to dig a continuous trench by day. In any case, every effort must be made to get good trenches dug as soon as possible. One of the first requirements is to get some wire in front of the trench, as this gives a greater feeling of security to the men digging. (See appendix B). During the first two or three days it may be expected that the new line will be subjected to heavy bombardment alternating with repeated counter attacks. If the front trench is constructed in the first instance very close to the enemy's position it is particularly vulnerable to counter attack and if the enemy succeeds in breaking through the line at a time when there are no defenses prepared behind it, he may force a retirement on a large front. The construction of a supporting line 70 to 100 yards in rear of the front line and of a reserve line should, therefore, be proceeded with simultaneously.

2. The following procedure, adopted in at least one instance by the Germans, may commend itself when the offensive has to be temporarily given up, and the enemy is found established in a prepared line. A line is constructed in the first instance at a considerable distance, say 500 to 600 yards, or even more, from the the enemy's front trench, the exact distance depending on the ground and facilities in the form of cover. This line is made fairly strong and complete before any farther advance is attempted. Then, under cover of night, and possibly of a heavy bombardment of the enemy's front line, a new front line is constructed at a distance of 200 to 300 yards from the enemy. From this point farther advance would usually be by sap. The advantage of this method is that, before any attempt is made to dig a line within easy reach of small counter attacks, there is a completed line ready behind the new line, to stop farther progress by the enemy if the new line is counter attacked and broken.

17. CONSTRUCTIONAL DETAILS OF TRENCHES.

1. *Fire trenches.*—There is no sealed pattern of fire trench. Various types which have been found useful are shown in figures 11–14, but the type used varies according to local conditions. Any fire trench, however, must fulfill the following essential conditions:

(a) The parapet must be bullet proof.

(b) Every man must be able to fire over the parapet with proper effect (i. e., so that he can hit the bottom of his own wire).

(c) Traverses must be adequate.

(d) A parados must be provided to give protection against the back blast of high explosive.

(*e*) The trace of the trench should be irregular, to provide flanking fire; and, if the trench is to be held for any length of time—

(*f*) The sides must be revetted.

(*g*) The bottom of the trench must be floored.

The narrower a trench is the better the cover which it affords. However, a trench which may have to be occupied for some time must allow freedom of movement. The result is that a fire trench is usually made broad enough to allow of movement behind the line of men manning the parapet. Every man must be able to use his rifle over the parapet; on the other hand people moving along the trench do not want to have to stoop down low in order to get their heads under the cover of the parapet. Therefore the trench usually has a firing step about 18 inches broad and 4 feet 6 inches below the crest of the parapet, and behind this is a deeper portion from 18 inches to 2 feet 6 inches broad at the bottom and from 6 feet to 7 feet below the crest line of the parapet (see figs. 11, 12). The firing step must have a level surface and give a firm foothold. It may either consist of an earth step strongly revetted with planks held up by well driven pickets, or of stout planks laid on low timber trestles. Sandbags are sometimes used but are not suitable, as such a firing step gets very slippery in wet weather and usually takes a slope to the rear, so that it gives a very insecure foothold. Height from firing step to crest to be frequently tested. The only test is whether the individual man can use his rifle effectively over the top.

2. *Traverses.*—Traverses are strong buttresses of earth jutting out from the front or the rear face of the trench so as to split it into a series of compartments. Their object is to decrease the exposure of the garrison to enfilade fire and to localize the effect of a shell bursting in the trench. For both these purposes they must be strong and solid. They should be made from 9 to 12 feet thick, should overlap the width of the trench by 2 feet at least, and must be strongly revetted. A traverse is described as a "forward" traverse or a "rear" traverse according as it juts out from the back or the front face of the trench, respectively. Rear traverses are generally accepted as the best for normal use, but an occasional forward traverse is useful to provide fire to a flank. Traverses add to the length of trench necessary to accommodate a given number of rifles, and, if they are too frequent, add to the difficulty of supervision and control. From 18 feet to 30 feet is the normal length of bay between two adjacent traverses. Traverses in a trench facilitate bombing attacks along its length, as grenades can be thrown from under cover of a traverse, generally into the next bay but one. As a protection against this there should be, at intervals in the line, spaces without

traverses, long enough to prevent bombing from behind the traverse at one end of the space to beyond the traverse at the other end. This length of trench should be straight and the traverses on either side of it should be loopholed for fire inward. Bombing trenches or pits behind the front line (see fig. 6) are also useful to stop an attack of this sort.

Traverses will often have to be made in a completed trench which is insufficiently traversed. To do this cut into the face of the trench opposite that from which the traverse is to jut out a recess broad enough and deep enough for the end of the traverse and the passage round it, and with the earth from this recess, supplemented if necessary by more from elsewhere, build up a wall of sandbags or of earth revetted with sandbags or other material 9 feet to 12 feet thick right across the old trench and projecting not less than 2 feet into the recess.

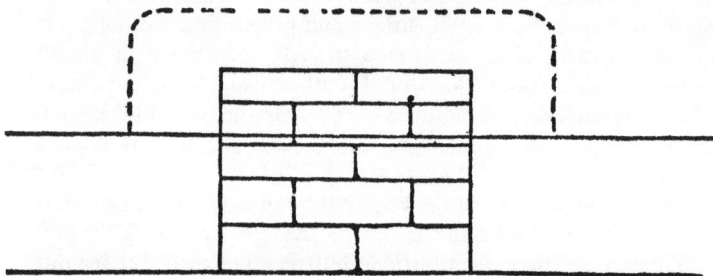

3. The sides of trenches which have to be occupied for a long time, and particularly in wet weather in a damp site, must be revetted. Hurdles or rabbit netting held up by stout stakes at frequent intervals, well driven and with their upper ends securely wired to short pickets firmly anchored in the parapet or parados, form a useful type of revetment for this purpose. Sandbags are not so suitable. High revetments (see figs. 15–19) in Flanders clay require an intermediate anchorage between the bottom of the revetment stake and the anchorage to its top, unless revetment stakes of 4 to 5 inches diameter are used. The placing of this in the solid ground forming the side of a trench is a difficult operation demanding the assistance of skilled labor. In the winter in Flanders some really solid form of revetment, such as planks or timber, or expanded metal sheets, is necessary.

The fire trench should be provided with frequent exits for the use of patrols. These exits should be in the form of tunnels leading under the parapet, whether the line be trench or breastwork, and communicating with saps.

The top of the parapet should always be irregular, as this helps to conceal men observing or firing over the parapet. Still better concealment is provided if the parados is higher than the parapet and is also irrgeular, as heads do not then show up against a sky-line.

A useful accessory in a trench line is what is known as a "bombing trench" or "bombing pits." The latter are small recesses about 5 feet square dug behind the front line and within easy grenade throwing range of it. The former is a continuous trench for the same purpose.

A tendency to be guarded against is that toward gradually increasing the width of trenches. Wide trenches are undoubtedly more comfortable to live in but they afford nothing like such good protection as narrower trenches. In repairing a trench of which the side has fallen in men are apt merely to throw the earth out which has fallen in. This should never be allowed; the débris should be cleared away, a strong revetment (hurdles, expanded metal or rabbit-netting) put up against the new face, and a sandbag wall built outside this revetment. The sandbags then support the revetment.

The question of loopholes, drainage, latrines, is dealt with later.

4. *Breastworks.*—Breastworks afford very good cover, but their construction involves much time and very heavy labor. They are therefore usually made only when the state of the ground compels it.

Breastworks are more conspicuous than trenches, but earth breastworks, if well built, do not suffer more heavily than a trench under artillery fire and are more easily repaired, while being very much more comfortable to live in.

Earth breastworks must be at least 10 feet thick at top, and have a very gentle exterior slope. The ditch excavation can be used as an obstacle and can be filled with wire. When constructing a breastwork one of the most important points to look to is that the near edge of the borrow pit in front of the parapet is far enough from the foot of the interior slope. There is a tendency on the part of the diggers to save themselves labor by digging in toward the parapet. This must be guarded against by marking with a tape a line beyond which there must be no digging, and by constant supervision to see that it is observed. To ascertain the position of this line, find by drawing the minimum width of base necessary to secure a thickness of 10 feet at top, and add at least 2 feet to provide for a berm at the foot of the exterior slope. It will save much time if wooden stretchers are made to carry the earth and plank gangways are made for the carriers. If no planks or brushwood are available, wire netting laid on the ground will serve to provide a pathway. Work once begun on a breastwork must be completed as quickly as possible, because a new work is likely to prove a tempting target for artillery fire, to which in the early stages it is very vulnerable, and also because it is important to get the work through if possible in the dry.   In the kind of site which demands a breastwork the borrow pit very easily fills with water, and under this condition work becomes very slow and arduous, and may even become impossible.   The interior slopes of parapet and parados must be strongly revetted; hurdlework or some substitute, firmly anchored, forms the best form of revetment; sandbags do not stand the weather so well.   Once the revetment has been put up, digging close to the foot of it must on no account be allowed.

The best method of constructing a breastwork is as follows: Put up two revetments of gabions or hurdles—or if using sandbags build two sandbag walls—10 feet apart; fill in between with earth; build up a bursting course in front; finally make a very gentle slope to the front.

Breastworks constructed wholly or mainly of sandbags are much more vulnerable to artillery fire than earth breastworks and are expensive of material.   They are to be avoided except for minor works, such as blocking a trench leading toward the enemy, barricading a road, etc.   They are, however, often found in the front line, when breastworks have had to be constructed in the presence of the enemy, because they can be made more silently.[1]

---

[1] In building parapets, breastworks, or revetments with sandbags the following rules must always be observed:

(a) Sandbags should be filled only three-fourths full and well beaten into the shape of a brick.

(b) Sandbags must not be built vertically on one another.   A slope of 3/1 is advisable.

(c) Breaking joint and the use of frequent headers are necessary.

(d) Each layer of sandbags must be at right angles to the face of the parapet, not horizontal.

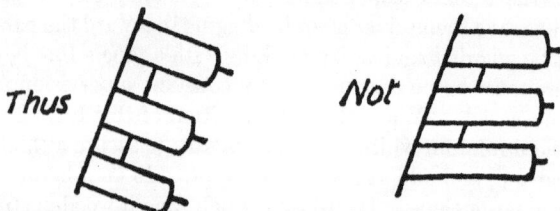

(e) Sandbags should not be filled with brick rubble; it is dangerous owing to the interstices left between lumps of brick.

They are either formed by gradually raising the parapet of a trench that has become water-logged, or they may be made by a process of sapping to join up two existing trenches or breastworks. The great fault usually in making these breastworks is to make their sides too straight and steep. The base of such a breastwork must be broader than the top or the whole wall of sandbags will collapse in wet weather.

Breastworks must be constructed with traverses in the same manner as fire trenches, and must have a firing step, to allow of every man using his rifle over the top. The necessary amount of cover for free movement along the line, 6 feet 6 inches as a minimum, can be obtained either by building up the parapet to this height, when a raised firing step will be required, or by having the firing step at ground level and digging a narrow shallow trench immediately behind it and around the ends of traverses. A parados must be constructed to protect the garrison from the back blast of high explosive shell which burst behind the line. This parados should be about 2 feet 6 inches to 3 feet thick at its base, strongly revetted on both faces. It should be as high or slightly higher than the parapet and as close to it as is compatible with free movement along the line. A path paved with brick or with floor-board gratings just behind the parados is a great convenience; it should communicate with the fire bays by openings through the parados behind at least every other traverse. The space between the breastwork and parados should be floored, and steps taken to allow for drainage from that space.

In a breastwork line filled sandbags should be stacked close behind the parados at frequent intervals, to be available for building up a gap formed by artillery fire, as a speedy temporary repair.

5. *Loopholes.*—All firing by night, and to meet an attack whether by day or by night, must be over the top of the parapet. In all fire trenches, however, a certain number of loopholes are necessary for the use of snipers to inflict casualties on the enemy whenever opportunity offers, to annoy him, interfere with his work, keep him under cover, and keep down the fire of his snipers. Usually one or two loopholes are made in each bay of the fire trenches.

Various types of loophole have been designed and are in use. It is not intended to describe them in this pamphlet,[1] but only to lay down the conditions that a satisfactory loophole must fulfill. The

---

[1] Descriptions of various types of loophole will be found in notes that are circulated among the troops from time to time.

most important of these is concealment from the front; for this reason, and to obtain if possible enfilade fire, loopholes should be placed
obliquely in the parapet.   The maximum amount of cover should
be provided for the firer, and the steel loophole plates with a metal
flap to close the loophole make probably the best form of loophole.
Loopholes should have a curtain (sandbag or some form of cloth)
hung on the firer's side, to be used in the same way as a photographer
uses a black cloth.

Observing stations and lookout posts behind the lines should be
provided with inconspicuous loopholes, but loopholes are not, as a
rule, much used for looking out from the trench, except where
special loopholes for observation with telescopes are made.   Periscopes and small pieces of mirror set up at an angle on the parados
give a better view with less exposure.

Loopholes have usually to be made in a parapet at night.   The
alignment must be carefully sited and marked by day.

6. *Overhead cover.*—Overhead cover is never used in any trench
which is to be occupied as a fire trench.   Overhead cover for shelters
and dugouts is dealt with in the paragraph on that subject.   Beyond
this the only case in which overhead protection is likely to be required is, in rare instances, over very exposed lengths of communication trench and in the form of traverse known as a "bridge"
traverse.

7. *Support trenches.*—Support trenches should be designed as
traversed fire trenches, but the supervision trench is usually omitted.
Protection against shell fire in the form of deep dugouts can be made
in the support line behind the parados, whereas their use in the
front trench interferes with the rapid manning of the trench and is
inadmissible.   The support line should be connected by numerous
communication trenches to the front line, and if there is an obstacle
in front of the support line it must be so arranged as not to interfere
with the rapid reinforcement of the front-line trenches.

8. *Communication trenches.*—To afford protection from enfilade
fire and to mimimize exposure to shrapnel in them, communication
trenches must be well bent or traversed.   The best type is the
winding one, but the curves must be sufficiently pronounced to
give real protection against enfilade fire.   If transverses are made,
the best pattern is an island traverse with the trench going round
it on both sides.   The corners of traverses should be rounded and
not square, as they are easier to pass for a man with a load or for
a stretcher,[1] and are easier to revet.   The necessary protection

---

[1] The minimum curve in winding communication trenches, so that a stretcher
can be carried round it by bearers, is 16-foot radius in a trench 3 feet wide.

can also be obtained by making the trenches zigzagged in plan, and this makes revetting easier.

Except in such soil as solid chalk, communication trenches which are required to remain serviceable for a long time or to stand wet weather must be revetted. Experience in Flanders has shown that even if the sides are given as flat, a slope as 1:1 they will fall in. A berm of 18 inches should be left between the edge of the trench and the parapet. The minimum width at the bottom should be 2 feet 6 inches, and 3 feet is better. Increasing the width reduces the protection afforded, and the width of 3 feet at the bottom should seldom be exceeded. The revetted sides must be given a slope from 4:1 to 3:1, not cut nearly vertical. The depth of the trench from top of parapet to bottom of trench or floorboard should be 7 feet, if possible; what proportion of this depth is trench and what parapet depends on the site and facilities for drainage. The question of drainage must always receive particular attention in the siting and construction of communication trenches, and they should be boarded with a drain under the boards as soon as possible after construction. Passing places and, in a long trench, occasional sidings should be arranged, and signposts should always be placed at the entrance to communication trenches, and at any branches off them, to show where they lead.

Special arrangements must be made to afford protection against the enemy's bombers working down a communication trench to attack one of the lines behind. For this purpose the enemy's bombers must be kept at a distance of not less than 40 yards from the trench to be protected. This can be done by making the last 40 yards of any communication trench, entering a support or cover or back-line trench from the front, straight and providing for machine gun or rifle fire down the straight portion (see fig. 20). A dog-leg trench will do if proper arrangements can be made for enfilading both reaches of it. Provision must be made for blocking this last 40 yards of the trench at both ends. Chevaux-de-frise ("knife rests") or other wire obstacles, placed in a recess at the point where the block is to be made, so that the last man to retire can quickly pull them down into position as he passes, will do as a temporary expedient for this purpose (see fig. 20).

Communication trenches, if prepared for use as fire trenches, are frequently of the utmost value for flank defense, when the enemy has succeeded in penetrating the front line. The best way of preparing a communication trench for fire is to dig T-heads off the trench so as to form fire bays facing in the required direction, or to cut fire trenches across a reentrant angle in the trench (see fig 10). A communication trench prepared for use as a fire trench should be protected on both sides by a good wire entanglement.

18. OBSTACLES.[1]

Front trenches and all trenches which may have to be occupied as fire trenches must be protected by an efficient obstacle. Some form of barbed wire entanglement is the most efficient obstacle and is that universally used. A wire entanglement must be broad enough not to be easily bridged or quickly cut through, must be under the close fire of the defense, and near enough to be effectively watched by night. The near edge of the entanglement should be about 20 yards from the trench, and it should be at least 10 yards broad. A height of 2 feet 6 inches is sufficient; a greater height only increases its liability to damage by our own fire. Every effort must be made to conceal and protect the entanglement; this is best done by sinking it in hollows or trenches. Where trenches are made they should be of the form shown in figure 34, i. e., sloping with maximum depth furthest from the fire trench, so as to minimize the cover which they might afford to the enemy; further, wire sunk in this manner should be carefully sited so that every portion of it is enfiladed from some point or another in the fire trench. Sunk wire is less visible, less vulnerable to artillery, and less liable to damage by our own fire.

When entanglements are at some distance from the enemy, it may sometimes be useful to construct a second belt of wire beyond the first, with its outer edge some 40 or 50 yards from the trench, to keep hostile bombers at a distance.

Good strong wire entanglements, of the pattern in figure 14, fixed to well-driven posts, should be constructed wherever it is possible. With proper training, infantry should be able to make entanglements of this nature as close as 100 yards from the enemy on a dark night. The iron posts now issued, which screw into the ground, can be placed in position without noise and strengthen the entanglement. Only when the opposing lines are too close, or as a temporary means of providing some sort of obstacle quickly, recourse may be had to portable obstacles. The best of these is that known as the "knife rest" (see fig. 36, which sufficiently explains their construction). Two or three rows of these knife rests, placed to break joint and wired together, form a fair obstacle which can be quickly and quietly placed in position. Hollow

---

[1] See figs. 23–38 and Appendix B.

barbed wire spheres are easily made up in the front trench and thrown out, and, if plentifully used, are better than no obstacle at all.

The maintenance of the wire obstacle calls for constant care. It must be inspected every night, and a few men should be told off in each company as a permanent wiring party for the repair and improvement of the obstacle.

19. PROTECTION FROM SHELL FIRE.[1]

1. Protection against loss by shell fire is afforded by details in the design of the trenches themselves, already referred to, e. g., traverses, and keeping trenches as narrow as possible, and is supplemented by the provision of shelters or dugouts. Shelters may be classified as bombproof or splinter proof, according as they are designed to afford protection against shells hitting them direct and bursting on impact, or against the splinters of shells burst over or near them. It is important to distinguish between the two.

2. The first instinct of the men is to improve the protection afforded by the trench by burrowing out for themselves hollows in the front face, under the parapet ("undercutting"). This practice must be absolutely prohibited. Unless these hollows are very carefully shored up they always result, sooner or later, in the parapet falling in, and, even if the shoring up is efficiently done, the existence of these shelters under the parapet weakens its resistance to the burst of a high-explosive shell.

3. Bombproof shelters to insure protection against heavy high-explosive shells have to be dug deep and entered by a narrow opening and steps. This means that it takes an appreciable time to get men out of them, and as in a well-planned attack the assault will be sudden and unexpected, and the fire of the artillery will not be lifted from the front trench until the leading infantry of the assaulting line is almost into it, they are usually inadmissible in the front line, except for the protection of machine guns and their detachments, and for company headquarters. Deep dugouts are, moreover, dangerous in an attack by gas.

A certain amount of splinter-proof cover should be provided in the front line, which will also serve as protection against weather. The best position, in the case of a trench, is in the front face of the supervision trench.

4. In the case of strongly constructed breastworks, dugouts giving good protection against even direct hits by the lighter

---

[1] See figs. 39–50.

natures of high-explosive shell can be made under the parapet, and are not so open to the objections which apply to dugouts in a front fire trench. The parapet over the dugout must be supported by well-made strong frames and props (see fig. 46).

5. Splinter-proof cover can also be placed behind the parados. In this case protection against back blast of shells bursting beyond the parados must not be overlooked.

6. No dugouts must ever be allowed in a trench which interfere with the use of the rifle or free passage along the trench.

7. The use of shelters proof against heavy high-explosive shell in the first system of trenches should therefore generally be confined to the position of the battalion reserves and to "strong points" or "keeps," which may form part of the front system. It is not intended to prohibit their use elsewhere, if the soil or natural features are favorable to their construction, and arrangements can be made to get men out of them quickly, but to point out the dangers that attend their use.

8. Very good protection from a hostile bombardment is afforded by "slit" trenches. These are trenches 1 foot to 2 feet wide and 7 feet deep, dug at right angles to and on either side of the communication trenches. They must be strutted at the top, or they will easily collapse. Each "slit" should be long enough to hold 10 to 12 men (see fig. 6). When they are in use a noncommissioned officer should be at the end nearest the communication trench. Control is easier when men are sheltered in these "slits" than when in dugouts. Similar provision can be made further back along the communication trenches for cover for reserves brought up to support a counter-attack.

9. A few notes on the construction of dugouts are appended. For the construction of deep bombproof dugouts, advice and assistance of Royal Engineers will usually be available.

(a) Every deep dugout must have two or more separate exits to facilitate rapid egress and in case one gets blocked.

(b) Roof timbers must always be made three or four times stronger than is necessary to support merely the load due to the thickness of roof for which they are designed. This is necessary to allow not only for the shock of the burst of a shell, but also for the possibility that a fresh garrison may take it into their heads to put another 2 or 3 feet of earth on top of the existing roof.

(c) A rectangular timber will support more weight if it stood on its edge, i. e., resting on its shorter side, than when lying flat on its longer side.

(*d*) The ends of roof timbers should never be supported on sand-bag walls or even direct on solid ground. A strong timber frame should always be used on two opposite sides of the shelter to support the ends of roof timbers (see fig. 46).

(*e*) A "burster" layer, of 6 inches to 1 foot of brick or stone, should always be provided near the top surface of the roof. Over this "burster" layer should be a layer of not less than 6 inches of earth to decrease danger from the scattering of the stone or brick by the burst of the shell. As the object of the "burster" is to explode the shell near the surface, it will be to a large extent defeated if the layer of earth above it is made more than 12 inches thick.

(*f*) Arrangements must be made for ventilating dugouts. It may occasionally be possible to combine the ventilating pipe with a periscope for lookout purposes.

(*g*) Splinter-proof cover is afforded by a layer of logs or beams, 6 inches or upward in depth, covered over with a layer of not less than 1 foot of earth. The following forms a roof proof against a 6-inch high-explosive shell: A layer of rails or beams, 18 inches of earth, a layer of brick, 2½ feet of earth, another layer of brick 6 inches to 1 foot thick, and over all 6 inches of earth. The rails or beams must have a good margin of strength over that necessary to support the load above them, so as to stand the shock of the explosion. It will be seen that this roof is fully 6 feet thick. Hence the dugout will require to be at least 10 feet deep if its position is not to be made too conspicuous.

20. MACHINE-GUN EMPLACEMENTS.

(See figs. 51-58.)

In view of the great value of machine guns to the defense, the siting and construction of emplacements for them requires very special attention and care. Machine guns should be so sited in each line that there is no part of the ground in front of it which is not under their fire. They should be arranged so as to bring a cross fire to bear in front of the trenches which they protect. In this way their power is more fully developed and also conceal-ment is easier. It is important that machine-gun emplacements should be constructed so as to be as inconspicuous as possible. Both sides are constantly on the lookout to try and locate the enemy's machine-gun emplacements, and any suspected spot is certain, sooner or later, to be made the target for bombardment.

For this reason, too, and also to protect them from damage by a chance shell in a general bombardment of the line, emplacements should be made as strong as possible. The ideal arrangement is that each gun should be in a bomb-proof shelter, with overhead cover, and in advance of and to a flank of the part of the line it is to cover. Machine guns in an inclosed emplacement may either be mounted for fire on a fixed line or so as to have a certain amount of traverse. In the latter case some form of improvised platform mounting, allowing the traversing of the gun about its muzzle and not about its center, enables the size of the loophole to be kept down to a minimum, and is, for this reason, valuable. Machine-gun loopholes, at any rate those for use by day, should be as low down in the parapet as possible. Several alternative emplacements should be prepared, some of which may be for using the gun over the top of the parapet. In particular there should be an alternative emplacement, for firing over the top, in connection with each inclosed emplacement and situated close to it. In connection with each of the covered machine-gun emplacements there should be provided a good bomb-proof shelter, preferably of the deep dugout type, to which the crew can temporarily withdraw during a bombardment. This dugout should communicate direct with the emplacement.

Concrete emplacements can generally be constructed in the reserve trenches.

21. LATRINES.

The health of the troops demands very careful sanitary arrangements and scrupulous cleanliness in trenches, which may have to be occupied for a considerable length of time. Latrine accommodation must be ample and easy of access; seats should be provided on the scale of at least 2 per cent of the troops using them. Urine tins should be provided on the same scale. The best place for latrines and urinals for the front line is behind the supervision trench in T heads at the end of short branches off it (see fig. 59). Latrines must be provided for all trenches and shelters which have to be occupied even for short periods by troops. The most sanitary system of latrines in trenches is the bucket system, buckets being removed and emptied at night.

A supply of chlorate of lime should be kept in all trenches.

22. DRAINAGE AND FLOORING. (See figs. 60–63.)

Drainage and precautions for keeping trenches dry and clean, whether they are fire, living, or communication trenches, are questions of great importance, not only from the point of view of preserving the trenches, but also for the health of the troops.

In the case of lines dug deliberately, not in the presence of the enemy, the question of drainage can be carefully studied, and it will often pay to dig drainage trenches of ample capacity before any work on trenches is commenced. Labor spent in this way will be more than repaid. In any case work on drains should keep pace with the progress of the trenches, as trouble is sure to occur if water is allowed to accumulate. For the same reason, care must be taken that the work on each section of trenches is left at an even depth each day when work ceases. Drains should be given a good fall. It will usually pay to revet the sides of an open-ditch drain. A good pattern of drain is the box drain, a rectangular channel lined and covered over with planking, laid in the bottom of a trench, which is then covered in again.

In the case of trenches dug in the presence of the enemy the above methods can not be applied. Drainage is a very difficult problem in these circumstances, even when the ground is not practically flat. Trenches on a forward slope can not be drained except to the front, and it will seldom be practicable to dig drains leading forward from the trench. Practically all that remains possible as a means of getting rid of the water and keeping trenches reasonably dry and clean is constant pumping and putting down some sort of paving or flooring. Sump pits, i. e., good deep holes, should be made at intervals to one side of the trench. They should be revetted and strutted and bridged over with plank covers. From these the water should be pumped out as often as may be necessary over the parapet or the parados, according to which way the ground slopes. If the ground falls to the rear, channels can be cut to lead off into the natural drains of the country and the water pumped into these channels. A channel along the side of the trench or down the center of it should lead the water into the sump-pits, and it must be constantly cleared. If the channel is cut down the center of the trench it can be bridged over by special flooring boards, which must be frequently taken up and cleaned. If the level of the water in the ground rises above the level of the floor of the trench, obviously no amount of pumping or digging of sump-pits will keep the trench dry. The only remedy then is to raise the floor of the trench by planks supported on short pile trestles, and then to raise the parapet accordingly. A most important point is to get some kind of flooring or paving down as soon as possible in any new trench. If this can be done before the mud has been churned up, a great deal of trouble and discomfort will be saved. Floor gratings about 6 feet long and 18 inches to 2 feet wide, made of cross pieces of $\frac{3}{4}$-inch by 4-inch plank, nailed to two longitudinal pieces of timber about 4 inches by 3 inches, on edge, are easily made up, and are a very good form of flooring for trenches.

23. DEFENSE OF BUILDINGS.

It will often happen that it is considered advisable to include substantial buildings in the front line. Experience has proved that it is extremely hard to dislodge a determined defender from a properly organized building. On the other hand, buildings in or near the front line invariably draw a great deal of artillery fire. For this reason a building should not normally be occupied by day, unless it either has cellars which can be improved to provide good bombproof cover or similar cover can be made quite close to the house and connected with it by communication trenches. Otherwise, if the building has been put into a state of defense, a garrison should be detailed who will only occupy it at the last moment in case of attack. A building is strongest for defense when it has been knocked about a bit. The defensive arrangements should be concentrated on the ground floor and cellars; time spent on work on upper stories is sure to be wasted. In the building itself the work to be done is:

(a) Reinforce the cellar roof, if possible, with concrete. It must be well shored up to enable it to carry the extra protection, and also the débris which subsequent shelling will bring down on it.

(b) Loophole the walls for rifle or machine gun fire. The nearer the loopholes are to the ground the better the protection afforded, but there is a risk of falling débris blocking them up.

(c) Thicken walls up to the height of the loopholes. This thickening may be done by throwing earth up against the outside of the building or making a wall of gabions filled with earth or of earth between hurdles, 3 feet clear of the wall of the building, to serve as a burster, but building up inside with brick rubble or earth in sandbags is better, as loopholes near ground level and cellar windows for machine guns can then be used.

(d) Block up and loophole ground floor windows and doors.

(*e*) Erect overhead cover over fire positions. This should be in the form of a false roof, preferably of concrete, otherwise of heavy rails or very stout timbers carried on very substantial timber supports or on rails or girders. This roof will protect the firers from falling débris, and the more the house is knocked about the stronger will the cover become.

(*f*) Improve internal communications by gapping internal walls where necessary.

In connection with the defense of the building there may also be fire trenches in front of it and to either flank communicating by trenches with one another and with the building, the whole forming practically a small strong point of which the house is the keep. "Slit trenches," such as have already been described, situated close behind the house and connected with it by a communication trench, form a useful adjunct to the defensive arrangements.

24. TRAINING IN DIGGING, ETC.

Infantry must be capable of the construction, repair, and maintenance, without Royal Engineer assistance, of all forms of trenches, shelters (except deep bombproof dugouts), and barbed wire entanglements. Constant practice in digging and making entanglements at night is necessary. Officers and men must be well trained in the method of marking out works to be dug at night and in extending a party silently on a task in darkness. Troops should be trained to dig, etc., fully equipped (except for their packs).

It will be found useful to have a certain number of men in each company specially trained under Royal Engineer supervision in the construction of barbed-wire entanglements, loopholes, revetting, drainage, etc.

CHAPTER III.

OCCUPATION AND RELIEF OF TRENCHES AND GENERAL TRENCH
ROUTINE.

25. SYSTEM OF RELIEF OF TRENCHES.

It is absolutely essential that in every unit a thoroughly sound system of carrying out reliefs is established. If the proper arrangements are made and the necessary precautions observed, the relief of trenches can be accomplished, with a little experience, safely and expeditiously. Carelessly conducted reliefs, on the other hand, involve not only great and unnecessary danger to the security of the trench line but avoidable loss of life and discomfort to the men.

The first essential is a careful preliminary reconnaissance. Whenever a unit is about to take over a new line of trenches, parties from it will visit the trenches previously, by day if possible. In the case of a battalion, the party should consist of the commanding officer, adjutant and machine gun officer, and at least one officer and one noncommissioned officer from each company. It will often be advisable, especially when taking over a new line and in the case of inexperienced troops, that one officer and noncommissioned officer from each company should remain a complete 24 hours in the trenches previous to the arrival of the battalion. The snipers of the relieving unit should be in the trenches for 24 hours before the relief takes place.

Detailed information from the unit to be relieved must be obtained on the following points: [1]

(a) Condition of wire entanglement, parapet, etc.

(b) Work in progress.

(c) Position of hostile machine guns, snipers, etc., so far as known.

(d) Danger points, e. g., where saps run out, portions of trench especially subject to enfilade fire, etc.

---

[1] A trench "Log book" kept up daily by each unit in the trenches and handed over to the relieving unit, is a convenient method of recording changes in the trench line and all other information of value regarding the trenches. Such a record is of great assistance to insure continuity of work.

(*e*) Position of listening posts.

(*f*) Position of small-arms ammunition reserve, bomb stores and trench stores.

(*g*) List of trench stores.[1]

(*h*) Method of communication with supporting artilley.

(*i*) Arrangements: If heavily shelled; to meet an attack; for counter-attack.

(*j*) Any arrangements for visual signaling or communication by rockets.

(*k*) Sanitary arrangements.

(*l*) Water supply.

(*m*) Arrangements for cooking and supplying hot meals.

(*n*) Route by which first line transports brings up rations at night and where rations are dumped.

A map of the trench line should also be obtained.

26. DESCRIPTION OF METHOD OF CARRYING OUT A RELIEF.

1. The following summary of the steps to be taken in the case of the relief of one brigade by another in the trench line is given as a guide to the normal procedure:

(*a*) On receiving orders to take over some portion of the line, the brigade staff obtain from the brigade to be relieved all available information regarding the line, work in progress, ammunition and stores available, etc., make what reconnaissance of the line the brigadier considers necessary, and arrange with the other brigade the details of the relief. It is important that the O. C. Brigade machine gun company should make a thorough reconnaissance of the line.

(*b*) When the brigade staff have arranged how the line is to be held they make the necessary arrangements to enable battalions to carry out their reconnaissance of the line as detailed in section 25.

It must be remembered that units of an ingoing brigade may not be of the same strength as the units to be relieved. A battalion may not, therefore, take over exactly the same frontage as is held by a battalion in the line, but may take over trenches from two battalions. This case necessitates careful arrangements as regards guides and the handling and taking over.

---

[1] Trench stores are the articles which remain permanently in the trenches and are handed over from one unit to another. They include small-arm ammunition, grenades, tools, pumps, loophole plates, braziers, etc.

(*c*) Reliefs, except in very favorable circumstances, have usually to be carried out under cover of darkness. The time of commencement of relief will depend on local circumstances and conditions, but it is generally advisable to begin reliefs as early as possible. In order to prevent the enemy from detecting our system of reliefs the intervals between reliefs and the hours at which they are carried out should be varied from time to time.

2. The brigade marches off from its billets by battalions, with an interval of about half an hour between battalions on the same road.[1] Transport accompanying units must be kept down to a minimum and a point must be fixed beyond which it is not allowed to proceed. It is usually at this point that guides from the unit. to be relieved meet the battalions. Any stores, etc., to be carried up to the trenches,[2] which may so far have been carried for convenience on the transports, are distributed amongst the men at this point, and the relief then usually proceeds by companies or smaller parties, each with its set of guides provided by the unit to be relieved.

It is usual to provide a guide from each platoon as well as guides for battalion headquarters, and for machine guns. Every guide must be in the possession of a paper showing the number or name of his trench, and the number of men in it.

3. The following notes on equipment for the trenches may be useful:

Packs are taken to the trenches, except in the case of units going to the trenches to make an attack. Men take waterproof ground sheets, but blankets should not be taken. Every man should carry two sandbag tucked into his belt.

All officers should have electric torches, and a long pole is very useful. Waterproof waders or overalls to the knee are very useful in wet weather.

27. PRECAUTIONS AND ARRANGEMENTS NECESSARY DURING A RELIEF.

The following are notes on some of the points to be observed in carrying out reliefs. It is advisable to embody some instructions on these points in Standing Orders for Trench Warfare.

---

[1] If relief takes place by day, at least two hours interval must be left between times of starting for different battalions. Relieving battalions then move up by platoons to the meeting place for guides.

[2] Rations for 48 hours and 150 rounds small-arms ammunition are usually carried on the man when going into the trenches.

(a) All units should be formed up before dark in the order in which and under the commander with whom they will go into the trenches.

(b) All parties must be kept closed up while moving to and from the trenches; the pace in front must be very slow. An officer should always be in rear. On dark nights it is often advisable for each man of a party to hold the bayonet scabbard of the man in front. Nothing causes confusion, unnecessary fatigue, and loss of morale so much as men getting lost from their parties while moving up to the trenches.

(c) Reliefs will be carried out as quietly as possible; no lights or smoking are allowed after reaching a point to be decided on by the battalion commander.

(d) Before commencing a relief every party must receive orders as to what action is to be taken by them in the event of an attack or alarm taking place while reliefs are in progress. Any retirement of troops should be avoided on principle. As a general rule, parties caught in the open during a relief should occupy the nearest trench or cover available and get into touch at once with the nearest body of troops holding the trench line.

As far as circumstances permit, and especially whenever there is a probability of attack, reliefs should be carried out gradually, so that too many men are not moving in the open at the same time.

(e) No trench or post should ever be evacuated by the troops to be relieved until the relieving troops have actually occupied it. The method of carrying out the actual relief of a trench must vary according to the nature of the trenches. The following is a usual method:

The platoon being relieved gets on the firing step. The relieving platoon files in behind and halts. On the word "Pass," which will be given quietly, being passed along, the relieved and relieving platoons change places. The new sentries, who will have been told off prior to the new platoon coming into the trenches, will take over from the old sentries, and the relieved platoon will file out. Where the trenches are too narrow to permit of above, the relieving troops must lie down behind the parados of the fire trench whilst the relief of sentries is carried out. Before dismissing the relieving platoon, the platoon commander will satisfy himself that all sentries have been properly posted and that every man can aim at the bottom of his own wire from the position allotted him.

(f) On taking over any trench the officer in charge will obtain all the information available, will take over the stores and tools in the trench, have the men told off in sentry groups and the first reliefs posted. He will ascertain at once the position of the trenches on his flanks and of the nearest supports, sending out patrols to get into touch with them and act as guides. He will insure that he has a sufficient number of guides who know the way to company and battalion headquarters.

(*g*) The completion of a relief must be reported at once—by the company commander to battalion headquarters when the relief of the company is complete, by the battalion commander to brigade headquarters when the relief of the battalion is complete, and by brigade headquarters to divisional headquarters when the relief of the brigade is complete. Both relieved and relieving units must make these reports. The battalion and brigade staffs of units relieved must remain till the relief of all the troops under them has been completed.

28. HANDING OVER TRENCHES.

Officers handing over trenches are responsible that all available information and trench maps of the locality are given to the relieving unit, and that all tools and trench stores are collected and handed over in the most convenient way and place.

A supply of Very lights and other consumable stores sufficient for at least 24 hours should be handed over to the relieving unit.

Lists of stores and reports on trenches, giving all available information, must, whenever possible, be prepared and handed over to relieving units on the day previous to relief taking place.

29. DUTIES IN TRENCHES.

The following precautions for the safety of the trench line must invariably be observed:

(*a*) By night, at least one man in every four, and by day at least one in every ten, will be on the lookout in each trench.[1]

(*b*) All men in the fire trench, and a proportion of men in the support trench, will always wear their equipment (except packs). Equipment may be taken off by order of a company commander in the case of working parties, when it will be kept close at hand. Every man will be told off to a particular post in case of attack; he will not leave the proximity of his post without the permission of his

---

[1] A good system is to work in groups of six men under a noncommissioned officer. By night, two men of each group are on sentry. By day, only one man of each group is on sentry and the number of groups may be reduced. The number of groups must depend on proximity of enemy's trenches, nature of ground, etc.

immediate commander, nor leave the trench without the permission of an officer. Bayonets will always be fixed in the fire trench during the hours of darkness, during a snowstorm or thick mist, or whenever the proximity of the enemy renders this course advisable.

All sentries are posted and relieved by a noncommissioned officer told off by each platoon for that purpose. One officer per company should be always on duty, and these noncommissioned officers report to him hourly. The officer on duty should be continually moving up and down to see that all is correct.

(c) Where enemy's lines are more than 100 or 150 yards away, a listening post should be established by each platoon in a sap communicating with the front trench and at a distance of approximately one-third of the distance to enemy's trench These posts usually consist of three men and one noncommissioned officer and are posted at dusk and relieved every four hours. All the men of the post are awake for the four hours they are on duty. The officer on duty should visit listening posts twice each night.

(d) Machine guns will be in position and ready loaded by night, by day they may for purposes of concealment be removed, provided they can be immediately placed in position in the event of an attack; one man must always be on the lookout at each machine gun, and the detachment must remain in close proximity to their gun.

(e) In every trench some form of alarm must be arranged to signal the approach of gas. Whistles should not be used for this purpose. The precautions against attacks by gas are dealt with in special instructions issued to the troops.

(f) Officers in a trench should be divided up along the trench, and must not all be together, especially at night. All the officers of a company must not live in one dug-out, as one shell might knock them all out.

Attacks prepared by artillery fire are most usually made at dawn, as soon as it is light enough for the artillery to observe, or about one hour before dusk. The former is usually the case in attacks on a large scale, or when a prolonged artillery bombardment precedes the attack, the latter when an attack on a small scale is to be prepared and carried out before dusk, and the position won then consolidated under cover of darkness.

Units (including reserves) should stand to arms about one hour before dawn and before dusk.

30. USUAL ROUTINE IN TRENCHES.

1. Rifles must be inspected twice daily, morning and evening, and every precaution must be taken to keep them and all other equipment in good order.[1] Men should be required to produce their oil bottles at rifle inspection.

2. The chief problem to be faced in the ordinary routine of trench work is to insure that the maximum amount of work is done daily toward the subjection and annoyance of the enemy and the improvement of the trenches, consistent with the necessity for every man to get a proper amount of rest and sleep. This can only be done by a good system, a definite program and time-table of work being arranged and adhered to as far as possible. Some notes on the system of work in trenches are given in the next section.

3. Rations for 48 hours should be taken into the trenches on the man whenever possible, in order to save the labor of bringing up and distributing rations to the trenches every night. A quantity of sandbags and other stores and material have usually to be carried up to the trenches every night, and the arrangements for carrying parties require careful organization and forethought The principle to be followed is that parties are detailed from behind to carry up rations or stores to troops in front, so as to avoid troops in front line having to send back parties and thus weaken their line. Thus the battalion reserve supplies carrying parties up to the front line trenches, and the brigade reserve may have to find carrying parties up to the battalion reserve or to the front trenches. Usually it will be possible to bring stores as far as the battalion reserve on pack animals or improvised handcarts. Ration parties and carrying parties must always be armed, wearing the rifle slung.

4. The system by which a unit in the trenches obtains the material required for the construction and repair of the trenches is as follows: In every brigade a "brigade workshop" is usually formed, the necessary personnel (from 12 to 20 men) being found from men in the battalions who are carpenters and artificers by trade. The "brigade workshop" is administered by the staff captain of the brigade, with a reliable noncommissioned officer in charge. It is established as near the trench line as possible, consistent with the men being able to

---

[1] Every care must be taken to prevent loss of equipment, etc., of which a great and usually avoidable waste may occur through lack of supervision, especially by junior officers. All rifles, ammunition (including fired cases), equipment, tools, trench stores, etc., found lying about within the area held by a unit must invariably be collected at a prearranged dumping ground, special parties being detailed by units for this purpose, if necessary. A list of articles so collected by any unit should be sent to brigade headquarters, who will issue instructions as to their disposal.

work in reasonable safety. Its functions are to make up the material obtained from the Royal Engineer into shapes and sizes suitable for carrying up to the trenches, to construct any simple device required for use in the trenches, and to carry out the distribution of the material. The brigade workshop makes up, for instance, barbed-wire "knife rests," box loopholes, rifle rests, floor gratings, grenade boxes, signboards for communication trenches, etc.

Each unit in the trenches sends in daily to brigade headquarters, as early in the morning as possible, a request for the material required to be brought up that night. The staff captain arranges for its preparation in the brigade workshop and for sending it up to battalion headquarters, who arrange for its further distribution to companies.

31. WORK IN TRENCHES.

1. The importance of working on a definite system and with a definite program has already been emphasized. The essential requirements for a fire trench are given in section 17, and must always receive first attention—the barbed-wire entanglement must be at least 10 yards wide, and concealed as far as possible.

The following points come next in order of importance:

(a) The provision of good loopholes for snipers, at least one per section of men in the trench.

(b) The construction or improvement of communication trenches; there should be one per platoon from the support line to the fire trench, if possible. From the support line to the reserve line, two per battalion will suffice.

(c) Listening posts, one per platoon, pushed well forward.

(d) The construction of bomb-proof or splinter-proof shelter. (See sec. 19.)

(e) The provision of small-arms ammunition and grenade stores should be two small-arms ammunition reserve stores,[1] and one grenade store per platoon. Both small-arms ammunition and grenades should be stored in depth; i. e., a proportion should be stored in the support and reserve lines as well as in the front line. Suitable positions for these stores are at the points where communication trenches run into the various lines. (See figs. 64–66.)

(f) An inspection trench (behind parados) and bombing pits or trenches (see p. 27) may be made, if required.

---

[1] In addition to the small-arms ammunition carried by the men (150 rounds), a supply equivalent to 120 rounds per man should be kept in the trenches and a reserve of 10 to 20 boxes at battalion headquarters.

2. When sandbags are to be filled for any work in the trenches, they must not be filled by taking earth from holes made indiscriminately in the ground behind the trenches, as this practice makes this ground difficult to walk over and often interferes with the construction of fresh trenches. A trench which will serve some useful purpose should be made when earth for filling sandbags is required. When filled sandbags have to be carried for any distance, it is preferable to have separate parties for filling and carrying.

3. It will be found convenient to have in every company a proportion of men specially trained under Royal Engineer supervision in making loopholes, laying out barbed wire, revetting, etc. All men must of course be practiced in these duties, but a specially trained squad for the more technical work will be found a great assistance.

4. As a rough guide to the number of men available for work in the trenches, it may be assumed that a company in the trenches will number about 160, leaving out signallers, machine gunners, orderlies, etc. Of these there will be by day about 16 to 20 men engaged in observation and sniping and another 16 to 20 ready to relieve them. This will leave about 120 available for work, and it should be possible to arrange for them to do two hours' work in the morning and two in the afternoon. By night 40 sentries will be required, and the next relief of 40 must not be required to work before going on duty. The number of sentries by night may be reduced, if parties are working out in front of the trench.

5. The above notes are to be taken as a guide only. Local conditions vary the order of importance in which work should be undertaken. In some trenches it is impossible to do much work to the trenches by day.

The infantry must always be prepared to assist any Royal Engineer and miners working in their section of the line.

32. OBSERVATION AND SNIPING. (See figs. 67–71.)

1. A good system of sniping and observation is of the utmost importance in trench warfare. Usually every battalion has a special detachment of trained snipers working under a selected officer or noncommissioned officer. Their duties are to keep the enemy's lines under constant observation, note any changes in the line and any new work undertaken by the enemy, keep the enemy's snipers in check, and to inflict casualties on the enemy whenever opportunity offers.

2. The following are the chief essentials for a successful sniping organization:

(*a*) Careful selection and training of snipers.

(*b*) Well-chosen and well-concealed posts or loopholes.

(*c*) A good system which will insure all parts of the enemy's line being kept under constant observation.

(*d*) Good discipline, which will prevent posts being given away by carelessness.

(*e*) Care of equipment.

(*f*) Individual ingenuity in using disguises, masks, dummies, and other devices.

3. The following notes on the above points may be found of use:

(*a*) *Selection and training of snipers.*—Men selected must be intelligent and well educated, besides being good shots. Observation and the ability to describe what he has seen are most important qualifications in a sniper.

The following are the chief points in which he should receive training:

Shooting at vanishing and moving objects.

Judging distance.

Observation of bullet strike.

Use and care of optical sights.

Use and care of telescopes, field glasses, and periscopes.

Use of natural and construction of artificial cover.

Assimilation of color to surroundings.

Construction of all types of loopholes and bullet-proof cover.

Value of immobility and silence and necessity of patience.

Map reading.

Writing of simple reports.

Eyesight training.

Location by means of flash and sound of hostile riflemen.

Snipers should be kept well informed; they should be shown aeroplane photographs of the enemy's position, and any information of interest to them from intelligence reports, examination of captured prisoners, etc., should be passed to them.

(*b*) *Choice and concealment of positions.*—No definite rules can be laid down as to the best positions for snipers. It must be left to the ingenuity and enterprise of the sniping officer or snipers to discover suitable places and to utilize them skillfully. Many excellent places will be found for observation and sniping in rear of the firing line. The best time to reconnoitre for such points is during the evening light, when the enemy can not see any distance, but while it is still possible to see whether they command the view required.

The building of loopholes so as to make them secure, invisible, and convenient for observing and firing at definite points is an art in itself and gives endless openings for originality. Loopholes usually have to be let into the parapet by night and this must be practiced, as the work has to be done quickly so as to be completed by daylight. The concealment of loopholes is made much easier if the outer face of the parapet is irregular. The Germans in many places take great pains to give an irregular outline to their parapet, using beams, timber, bolsters, mattresses, and all sorts of rubbish piled up against it. A tunnel through the parapet, if the opening is carefully concealed, may form a good sniper's post.

The use of veils and coats of a color to match the background is useful. If near sandbags, an empty sandbag worn over the head is a good disguise. Against an earth background a brown gauze veil, against grass a green one, are both difficult to detect. Grass, weeds, wood, or branches may give concealment.

Dummy loopholes are of great value to attract enemy's fire.

(c) *System.*—Posts should be so arranged that the whole front of the enemy's line opposite the battalion sector is under observation from dawn till dusk, each post having a definite front to watch. Snipers should work in pairs, one observing while the other is in readiness to shoot. Four men in two reliefs should be told off to each post.

Each post should be made to render a report daily under the following headings:

Any new work done by the enemy.

Machine guns, trench mortars, snipers, observation posts, new loopholes, etc., located during the day.

Germans seen, place, uniform, apparent age, physique, equipment.

Any of the enemy fired at, any evidence to show they were hit.

Any other information of interest.

All rifles and optical equipment must be carefully cleaned on coming off duty, and should be inspected daily by an officer.

Snipers should not usually be required to do any night work, the duty of constant observation by day is a trying one, and, with the cleaning and care of the equipment, a sniper's time will be fully occupied.

(d) *Discipline.*—Good discipline is necessary to prevent carelessness in giving away posts by exposure or by wild and unnecessary firing. The battalion snipers are apt to develop into "scallywags" in habit and appearance unless good discipline is strictly enforced.

(e) *Care of equipment.*—This has already been mentioned above. It must be remembered that telescopic sights are most delicate instruments and require testing and adjustment by an expert if good results are to be obtained.

4. When a battalion is taking over a new line, the battalion snipers should, whenever possible, spend 24 hours in the new trenches with the snipers of the battalion to be relieved, in order to obtain all the information available from them and to become acquainted with the new line.

5. If a line is taken over in which the enemy's snipers have been allowed to get the upper hand, the first task is the location of the hostile snipers' posts. The enemy's loopholes should be searched for systematically all along the parapets, together with any likely sniping places in rear. The trees, sandbags, etc., in our own trenches should be searched for rifle bullet marks which may show the direction of the hostile snipers. Sentries should be warned to try and discover from what point sniping is coming, and to watch for any flashes at night. When all possible has been done to locate the enemy's sniping, a system of loopholes should be decided on by which every part of the enemy's line can be observed and fired on from some secure position.

6. Cooperation between neighboring units is essential. Often the best position to observe and fire on a certain portion of the line is in the sector of the battalion on the flank.

7. Fixed rifle batteries for keeping certain points or localities under fire by night are often extremely useful as a means of hampering the enemy's work and causing loss.

33. COOPERATION WITH ARTILLERY.

1. *Arrangements for intercommunication.*—A certain force of artillery is detailed for the support of each infantry brigade holding a portion of the line. Batteries are allotted to sectors, and the points on which guns are normally laid [1] are selected by the infantry brigade commander in consultation with the artillery. The zones of fire allotted to adjacent batteries should overlap, if possible, at specially dangerous or important points.

The following system of communication between infantry and artillery has been found to answer well:

---

[1] Usually known as the "night lines."

A code number or letter is given to each place on which guns are laid and a sketch showing the code is kept by the company commander in the trenches, by the battalion commander, at the battery observation post, and the battery. A direct line is laid from the trenches (at some selected company headquarters) to the battery. When fire is required at night on any particular point it is sufficient to telephone down the code letter or number, and the gun concerned opens fire at once. If fire is required on any other place it should be described with reference to one of the selected points. If this system is used, careful instructions as to the occasions on which artillery fire may be called for and a good understanding on the point between the infantry and artillery are necessary. Infantry must understand that firing by night is apt to give away the gun positions, so unnecessary requests for fire must be avoided; on the other hand, frequent opportunities arise of doing the enemy damage by artillery fire at night and can only be taken advantage of if there is close cooperation between the infantry and artillery.

In order not to give away permanent gun positions, it has been found to be a good plan to lay out night lines for single guns from positions to be taken up by night to deal with any special target.

The arrangements for the action of the artillery in case of an attack by the enemy are dealt with in section 41, Chapter IV.

2. *Aggressive action.*—In order to obtain full benefit from aggressive artillery action, close cooperation between infantry and artillery is essential. Every means must be used to induce the enemy to man his parapets or come out and expose himself and then to catch him with infantry and artillery fire. Various schemes will suggest themselves, and can be worked out between infantry and artillery commanders.

It is a good thing to have a number of schemes both of retaliation and of aggressive action worked out and communicated to all concerned, so that they can be put into force at once by a message—"Scheme No. —."

3. *Information.*—The artillery require all the assistance they can get as to location of targets and the effect of their fire. Every endeavor should be made by the infantry to assist, and artillery observing posts should be connected to the front trenches for this purpose.

Infantry officers should be instructed in artillery methods of describing the position of targets, and it is a great advantage both to infantry and artillery if arrangements can be made for every infantry officer in turn to spend a few hours in the artillery observation station overlooking his part of the line. It helps him to know the country from an artillery point of view.

In describing targets, reference should always be made to points in the enemy's line, not to portions of our own line. The same names should therefore be given by infantry and artillery to prominent objects in the enemy's line.

The following rules should always be observed in reports sent by the infantry to the artillery:

(a) The time and the observer's position must be accurately stated.

(b) If reporting on enemy's artillery fire it must be stated whether shrapnel or high explosive. The direction from which the shells are coming should be given as accurately as possible.

The fuzes of German shells frequently furnish valuable information to the artillery. They should be sent at once to the nearest artillery unit, with a statement as to where they were found.

4. *Artillery observation posts.*—Careful instructions are necessary to prevent artillery observation posts being given away by infantry approaching them without precaution. On the other hand, artillery have been known to draw fire on infantry positions by approaching headquarters, reserve positions, etc., without concealment.

34. SANITATION AND CARE OF FEET.

In view of the length of time during which the same line of trenches frequently has to be occupied, special precaution must be taken to keep trenches in a clean and sanitary state. A latrine system of buckets or tins must be arranged whenever possible. A supply of chlorate of lime will be kept in each trench and used daily. Places for burying all tins and rubbish should be carefully chosen as far from the trench as is practicable and should be marked.

Bodies of dead men will be taken right away from the trenches to be buried.

The disease known as "trench feet" is caused by prolonged standing in cold water or mud and by the continued wearing of wet socks, boots, and puttees. It is brought on much more rapidly when the blood circulation is interfered with by the use of tight boots, tight puttees, or the wearing of anything calculated to cause constriction of the lower limbs. It can be prevented by:

(a) Improvements to trenches leading to dry standing and warmth.

(b) Regimental arrangements insuring that the men's feet and legs are well rubbed with whale oil or anti-frostbite grease before entering the trenches, and that, so far as is possible, men reach the trenches with dry boots, socks, trousers, and puttees.[1]

(c) By taking every opportunity while in the trenches to have boots and socks taken off from time to time, the feet dried, well rubbed, and dry socks (of which each man should carry a pair) put on.

(d) By arrangements to give the men some exercise daily so as to maintain the blood circulation.

(e) By the provision of warm food in the trenches when possible, and by the provision of warmth, shelter, hot food, and facilities for washing the feet and drying wet clothes for men leaving the trenches.

It is important to keep 50 extra pairs of boots in a battalion, so that men whose boots need repair can be given another pair while theirs are being mended. This can be done by battalion or brigade arrangements, a small shoemaker's establishment being kept up, which can go on working while the battalion is in the trenches.

35. COMMUNICATIONS.

Communications in the trench line are established by telephone, but it must be realized that in the event of heavy shelling all telephonic communication is likely to be interrupted, and an efficient alternative system of visual signalling and a service of orderlies must be arranged and tested.

The adjutant is responsible for the communications of his battalion. Battalion signals are responsible for all communications from battalion headquarters forward. The brigade signal section is responsible for communications from brigade headquarters to battalion headquarters.

It is the duty of all ranks to assist the signal service in the following ways:

(a) Reporting breaks in lines to the nearest signal station.

(b) Taking care to prevent damage to lines by troops or wagons, even if lines are badly laid.

(c) Taking into the nearest signal section any telephone equipment found lying about.

(d) Preventing any unauthorized persons interfering with lines; anyone seen interfering with cables who has not a blue and white armlet should be asked his business and sent to the nearest head

---

[1] Long gum boots are issued for use in the trenches and should be put on while the men's feet are still dry. Gum boots should not be kept on longer than absolutely necessary, as owing to lack of ventilation, men's feet sweat freely and the inside of the boot becomes wet.

quarters if his answers are not satisfactory; any civilian seen touching lines should immediately be arrested.

Where telephone lines cross roads or tracks used by troops or communication trenches, etc., they must be buried or put up at such a height as not to impede movement. All telephone lines should be labeled at frequent intervals.

An efficient system of communication by orderlies must be arranged, and long messages, unless urgent, should, whenever possible, be sent by orderly to avoid congestion of telephone lines. Within a brigade, each battalion details two permanent bicycle orderlies, who remain with brigade headquarters for the purpose of taking messages to their battalions. Battalions are responsible that they always have at least two orderlies (in addition to the permanent brigade orderlies) who know the way to brigade headquarters. There must also be at battalion headquarters guides to every trench held by the battalion.

Men should constantly be sent with messages at night so that they may know their way about. They should be able to describe accurately the position of their trench to the persons to whom they take the messages.

Headquarters should never be changed unless absolutely necessary, as it causes dislocation of the signal arrangements. Any unit which changes its headquarters must at once inform the unit above, and send an orderly to it to act as a guide to the new headquarters.

The signal service is responsible for giving the correct time, and watches should be set by signal time.

36. REPORTS.

Periodical situation reports are required from units in the trenches at stated hours, usually at morning, noon, and evening. The direction of the wind should be given in situation reports, as this affects the possibility or otherwise of a gas attack by the enemy.

Any unusual occurrence is, of course, reported at once, and any important change of wind should also be reported.

A casualty report and fighting strength return are required daily from units as soon after noon as possible.

A list of material required for the trenches should be rendered as early as possible in the morning (see p. 47).

Staffs must avoid burdening units in the trench line with unnecessary returns and correspondence; units, on the other hand, must remember that delay or carelessness in rendering reports and returns causes unnecessary work to the staff.

CHAPTER IV.

ORGANIZATION OF A TRENCH LINE AND ACTION IN CASE OF ATTACK.

37. GENERAL CONSIDERATIONS.

The importance of organizing a line of trenches, and the distribution of the garrison within it, on a definite scheme and with a definite object, is sufficiently obvious. There is, however, a tendency, due usually to a lack of guidance from above, and also to the frequent changes of units in a line, to lose sight of this and to remain content to make the best of what is found existing. In such circumstances the defensive line becomes a haphazard collection of trenches, and the organization of their defense or of an offensive movement from them is a matter of great difficulty.

The objects to be sought in the organization of a system of trenches are:

(a) To render the front line invulnerable to any small assaults by the enemy, and to create behind it a defensive zone of such depth as will not only make it impossible for an attack, in whatever strength it is made, to penetrate the whole of our defensive system, but will cause the enemy such loss, and so disorganize his attacking forces, as to enable our reserves to inflict on them a decisive defeat.

(b) To enable an attack on the enemy's defenses to be made under the most favorable conditions and with the minimum of warning to the enemy. To this end our front line of trenches should be pushed within assaulting distance of the enemy's front line, and the arrangement of the trenches be such that the attacking troops can be distributed under the best conditions.

(c) In the normal periods of trench warfare, to reduce, by the improvement of the trenches and an economical distribution of the garrison, the wastage in our own forces, both from battle casualties and from disease; and by skillful sniping and constant small enterprises to harass and inflict loss on the enemy.

Local conditions will largely determine the relative importance of the foregoing considerations. In a line of such length as now exists there will be certain portions in which there are no objectives of sufficient importance to make an attack on a large scale either by ourselves or the enemy probable; on such portions of the front the aim is by good organization of the defense and minor offensive enterprises to compel the enemy to keep as large or a larger garrison than ourselves, and to increase his rate of wastage compared to our own. On other portions of the front there may be some objective which is likely to be the aim of a hostile attack, whereas an advance on our part would result in no commensurate gain; in such a case the organization of the defense is of paramount importance. Or, again, these conditions may be exactly reversed.

On a small scale, the same considerations apply to a brigade or battalion front. Certain features are of tactical importance, while certain lengths of trench offer no particular advantage to either side. Thus the distribution of the garrison and the construction of the defenses must be founded on clear tactical ideas and not on a uniform distribution of so many men to so many yards of front.

38. DISTRIBUTION OF MEN IN TRENCHES.

By day, provided there is a good obstacle in front covered by the cross fire of machine guns, and supports can be moved up rapidly, the front line should be held lightly, in order to minimize loss from shell fire and the enemy's snipers, and to enable the majority of the men to obtain better rest and shelter in the support and reserve lines. By night, the front line must be held in sufficient strength to repulse raids by the enemy, and to prevent his reconnoitering patrols from penetrating the front line; and also because in a line held thinly by night the men are apt to become "jumpy."

The question of the number of men placed in the front line of trenches is, however, to a certain extent, affected by the question of upkeep of the trenches. Experience has shown that trenches can not be kept from falling in unless continuous work on their repair is carried on. In order, therefore, to keep a line of trenches habitable, it is often necessary to keep constantly in them a sufficient number of men to do the necessary work.

The distribution of a battalion in the trenches will usually consist of two or three conpanies in the front line finding their own supports and two or one companies in battalion reserve. Battalion headquarters should be close to the position of the battalion reserve, and will be connected by telephone to headquarters of companies.

It has been found by experience that in trench warfare it is advisable to make each company self-contained, i. e., each company should have its own trained grenadiers with a sufficient supply of grenades, its own snipers, and men trained in laying out barbed wire, making loopholes, etc. There may be in addition a party of battalion grenadiers or battalion snipers, specially trained and organized for any special work.

39. MACHINE GUNS.

1. *Distribution.*—The extra fire power now placed in the hands of brigade and battalion commanders by the increase in the number of machine guns enables men to be economized in the front trenches and a larger force thus left available for counter-attack.

A natural tendency is to place every available machine gun in the first line trenches, in order to establish an impassable curtain of fire in front of them. In the case of a bombardment, these trenches are liable to be very badly damaged and most of the machine guns may be destroyed. Any which have been located will certainly be put out of action. This tendency must therefore be suppressed.

The object to be aimed at is to place machine guns in such a way that if, after a bombardment or by the use of asphyxiating gas, the enemy succeeds in penetrating our lines, his infantry, at every step of their advance, will be met with fire from machine guns which have been previously echeloned in depth, and will thus be compelled to stop.

It is not so necessary to cover a large area with fire as to arrange for flanking fire from well selected positions; this fire will sweep away the waves of hostile infantry as they try to push forward.

Commanders must therefore divide their machine guns between the front line and the ground in rear of it, and in each particular case must see that the emplacements blend with the surrounding ground and fit in with the general scheme of defense.

The commander of the brigade machine-gun company must always make a careful study of the whole sector held by the brigade, with a view to insuring that the guns are placed to the best advantage. Cooperation must be arranged on the flanks of the sector with the machine-gun companies of the neighboring brigades.

2. *Protection and concealment.*—A really bombproof emplacement for machine guns requires considerable thickness of cover, and in the open this fact will render it liable to be easily located

by the enemy, who will be able to destroy it if he thinks it worth while.

Bomb-proof emplacements must therefore only be placed in positions where the enemy can not observe them, such as on reverse slopes, or where their relief conforms to the folds of the ground, or in woods, etc.

The importance of keeping machine guns invisible in places where a bomb-proof emplacement can not be concealed necessitates the firing emplacements being made outside the shelters, but they must be near enough for the guns to be brought into action at a moment's notice. The shelters are only to be used to protect the teams, and can therefore be dug as deep as required and so have an almost invisible relief.

Firing emplacements must be as near the shelters as possible. They can either be protected against splinters by light overhead cover, or be in the parapet without any head cover at all.

Firing emplacements can also be prepared in holes in the open in front of or behind the fire trench. These holes should be connected with the shelters by underground passages. The gun should be mounted at the last moment on the extreme edge of the hole, either without any protection at all, or, preferably, masked by a shield or gently sloping parapet. If the hole and its surroundings are carefully disguised, it will certainly escape observation by the enemy. Such emplacements should be frequently used behind the first lines (see fig. 58).

When a fire trench is dug on a reverse slope, a very useful method when the amount of work involved is not prohibitive is to dig such holes in front of the ridge and connect them with the trench by underground passages running under the ridge itself.

Machine guns can also be placed in trees in the same way as observation posts.

In order to insure invisibility, all communication trenches leading to the emplacements must be constructed as blinded saps. It is also essential to prepare a large number of emplacements in order to avoid firing daily from those which are specially constructed for the purpose of repelling an attack.

Machine gunners must never abandon their position in any circumstances. If necessary they must allow themselves to be surrounded, and must defend themselves to the last. A lost position has on many occasions been recaptured quickly thanks to the tenacity and heroism of a few machine gunners. In order to render such a desperate resistance possible, machine-gun emplacements must fulfill the following conditions:

(a) They must be surrounded by irregular barbed-wire entanglements, made as invisible as possible.

(b) There must be several emplacements in case one should be rendered useless.

(c) The teams must be provided with protection against gas, and have plenty of food, water, and ammunition.

3. *Lewis guns.*—The Lewis gun differs from the Vickers or Maxim by its greater mobility and its inability to sustain a rapid rate of fire for any length of time. Lewis guns should be used in a defensive line to economize infantry and to supplement the Vickers or Maxim guns of the brigade company, not to take their place. They can be used in cooperation with the machine guns of the brigade company to sweep depressions, covered approaches, etc., on which these guns can not fire. Lewis guns fire over the parapet and can therefore often sweep ground invisible from a machine gun emplacement, which is usually sited near ground level and therefore has a low command. There must be the closest cooperation between the battalions and the commander of the brigade machine-gun company over the choice of the positions and tasks for Lewis guns.

As Lewis guns are company weapons, their number in the front line will usually be determined by the number of companies holding it; it may, however, occasionally be advisable to take the Lewis guns of supporting or reserve companies, if thereby the number of men in the front line can be reduced, and if those companies do not require their guns for other purposes.

Owing to the mobility of the Lewis gun and the absence of a fixed platform, emplacements, in the ordinary acceptation of the term, are not required. The Lewis gun can be fired off its light mounting over any portion of the parapet with very little preliminary preparation, and its fire can be brought to bear on an object very rapidly; a much greater liberty of action can therefore be allowed to this weapon than to the Vickers or Maxim gun. Although emplacements are unnecessary, definite "firing places" must be prepared, either by means of loopholes or in depressions in the parapet, defiladed from the front if possible.

In allocating Lewis guns to a portion of the defense, certain fronts should be given to them, and the teams should be thoroughly familiar with their "firing places," and the ground to be swept from each.

It is just as essential to keep Lewis guns under cover during a bombardment as it is to keep machine guns and their teams. In the case of the former weapon, however, as there are no definite emplacements, greater choice is possible in the selection of the spot for the shelters, provided the guns can come into action without delay.

40. ACTION IN CASE OF ATTACK.

1. The measures taken by the defense to meet an attack have already been outlined at the end of section 2 (p. 9). The main principles are:

(a) To stop any attack from the outset by a concentration of artillery, machine gun, and rifle fire, the moment the enemy is seen issuing from his front trenches or collecting in them for an attack.[1] To this end careful arrangements must be made for observation and for communicating to the artillery by telephone or signal the moment the enemy's attack commences.

(b) It must be understood by all ranks that, should the enemy succeed in gaining a footing in our trenches, a counter attack made at once, and without hesitation, will almost always be successful, even if made by inferior numbers. Counter attacks by grenadier parties, especially from the flanks, are often particularly effective. On the other hand, if a counter-attack can not be launched before the enemy has had time to organize and establish himself, then it becomes necessary to wait till an attack with adequate artillery preparation can be organized.

(c) Strong points and keeps organized for all-round defense must be held to the last, even though surrounded, and whatever happens to the rest of the line. They will break up the enemy's attack and give time for a counter-attack in force to be organized.

(d) An attack on any large scale will be preceded by a very heavy bombardment, which may last several days and result in the partial obliteration of portions of the front system of trenches. During such a bombardment, special instructions may be issued by the higher commanders for the temporary withdrawal of the bulk of the garrison from portions of the front line. But strong points and localities organized for all-round defense must always be maintained.

2. All formations and units will have schemes made out for the defense of the portion of the line for which they are responsible. These schemes must always lay down the points of special tactical importance which it is essential to hold. Arrangements should be made so as to be in a position to launch immediate counter-

---

[1] A frequent method of attack by the Germans is to send on at first a few men only, and if they are successful to follow up with large numbers.

attacks, organized beforehand, to recapture any of these points which may be lost. If the important tactical points are correctly chosen, their recapture should make untenable any intermediate portions of the line which may have fallen into the enemy's hands. As far as battalions and brigades are concerned, schemes of defense are based on the following principles:

(a) The front system of trenches is the main line of defense. Should the enemy, following a heavy bombardment, succeed in penetrating into our line, he must be driven out immediately, before he has time to establish himself there, and our front system of trenches regained by counter-attacks directed against the points of tactical importance.

(b) It is the duty of the immediate supports, without waiting for orders, to reinforce the front line of trenches if required, and if any trench is captured to counter attack at once without hesitation, and if any trench is blown up to occupy the crater at once, or prevent the enemy doing so by occupying our side of the crater and placing obstacles in the hole.

(c) The battalion reserve is to be used offensively to maintain the front system of trenches by counter-attack. Should the attack be on such a large scale that the battalion reserve is obviously insufficient to attempt the reestablishment of the line, it will be used to occupy a position to check any further advance by the enemy till a counter-attack by the brigade reserve can be organized.

(d) The brigade reserve will be used on similar principles to the battalion reserve.

The brigade scheme of defense will therefore include:

(a) A definition of the sector for which each battalion in the front line is responsible.

(b) General instructions as to how the line is to be maintained in case of attack, with special reference to protection of the flanks should the enemy succeed in breaking the line to the right or left.

(c) The distribution of the machine guns of the brigade company, and the manner in which they are to be used.

(d) Arrangements for communication with the supporting artillery, to insure fire being opened on the enemy's front line immediately.

(e) The state of readiness to be maintained by the brigade reserve, arrangements for instant communication of an alarm to it, and for its action.

The brigade reserve is usually in billets, or shelters, 1 to 2 miles behind the front line. The defense scheme should arrange for it to move at once up to some position near the line of the battalion reserves by the routes most sheltered from enemy's observation and artillery fire. These routes must be reconnoitered by day and night by the brigade reserve, and guides must know them. While the brigade reserve is falling in, a mounted officer from it should go to brigade headquarters. The position to which the brigade reserve will be directed in case of attack, and the time it should take to reach it, should be known to battalions in front line. Arrangements to communicate with the reserve when it has reached this position must be made.

(f) Arrangements for action of any guns of the brigade machine-gun company which are in reserve.

(g) Orders for first line transport.

Battalion defense schemes should include:

(a) Arrangements for alternative methods of communication if telephone lines are broken.

(b) Action of battalion reserve, and arrangements for cooperation with neighboring battalions in case of counter-attack by battalion reserves.

(c) Orders to officers in charge of strong points or keeps.

(d) Special arrangements for the action of grenadier parties, if necessary, and for keeping up the supply of grenades.

3. The precautions in case of an attack by gas are given in special instructions issued.

41. ACTION OF ARTILLERY IN CASE OF ATTACK.

To meet a hostile attack by night, in a fog or under cover of smoke and gas, the important thing is to waste no time, but start the guns firing at once. Every gun should be normally laid on its "night line" (see p. 51) when not otherwise engaged, and, on receipt of a pre-arranged signal, will open fire at once on this line, "sweeping" a certain amount where necessary. The officer at the battery then endeavors to ascertain the situation, but, if the wires have been cut, he must use his own discretion as to continuing fire.

An alarm signal is necessary, and the occasions on which it should be used must be clearly understood. Every precaution should be taken to prevent it spreading needlessly to neighboring units. A visual signal, in case telephone lines are cut, must be pre-arranged.

It is advisable to test the alarm signal arrangements occasionally, but this should only be done by the brigade or division commander in consultation with the Commander Royal Artillery. The telephone communications between the artillery and infantry should be frequently tested by day and by night, and at least once every 24 hours a round should be fired by the artillery, on a pre-arranged signal, to test the time taken between the sending of the message and the bursting of the shell.

CHAPTER V.

Notes on the Attack in Trench Warfare.[1]

42. NEED FOR CAREFUL PREPARATION.

Success in an attack on a line of trenches depends on the training of the troops and on the thoroughness of the preparations made.

Confusion is apt to occur in any assault; it is specially to be expected when attacking a maze of carefully prepared positions, and is the most frequent cause of failure. Unless it can be prevented or minimized by careful preparation and training, the enemy, whose counter-attacks will have been planned and be taking place over familiar ground, will probably succeed in driving the attackers back again.

Time for preparation is available, and full use must be made of this. The attack can, therefore, be said to begin weeks before the day fixed for the assault.

43. INFANTRY PREPARATION FOR ATTACK.

1. *Reconnaissance.*—Units in occupation of a system of trenches must always consider their line and the enemy's defenses from the point of view of attack. Constant observation and patrolling will be required to add to the information available. The ground between the opposing front lines must be accurately reconnoitered so that no unsuspected obstacles, such as sunken wire or ditches, may hold up an assault. Every effort must be made to locate machine gun emplacements or strong points in the enemy's line, so as to be able to assist the artillery in the bombardment of the hostile defenses. The whole of the enemy's system of defenses over which the assault is to go must be made familiar to all ranks. A great deal of information is available from the excellent trench maps compiled from aeroplane photographs and a study of the photographs themselves.[2]

---

[1] This chapter is not intended to be exhaustive and does not touch on very many most important preparations and arrangements which have to be made in the case of an attack on a large scale. It is intended to serve as a general guide as to the arrangements necessary on the part of brigades and battalions.

[2] The use of a magic lantern to throw aeroplane photographs on a screen has been .ound of great value.

2. *Plan of attack.*—In the plan of attack the following are the chief points to consider from the point of view of infantry units (brigades and battalions):

(*a*) The distribution of the attacking infantry, i. e., the number of lines or "waves" required for the attack, the points opposite which the assaulting lines must be strongest to deal with important objectives, the detailing of parties for special tasks ("clearing" parties, carrying parties, parties to dig communication trenches back to our front line, etc.). Definite objectives must be allotted to each body of men down to sections.

(*b*) The use of machine guns and trench mortars to support the attack, and arrangements to send forward a proportion of these behind the attacking infantry.

(*c*) The employment of grenadier parties.

(*d*) The protection of the flanks, and arrangements for cooperation with, and assistance of, neighboring units.

(*e*) Arrangements for communication.

(*f*) Arrangements for supply of small-arms ammunition, grenades, tools, etc.

3. *Training.*—Before taking part in an attack, troops that have been a long time sedentary in the trenches will require special training to fit them for the assault. They will require marching and exercise to harden them. The enemy's defensive lines should be reproduced to actual scale somewhere well behind our lines, and the troops be practiced in the assault, with and without officers, till every man knows his rôle in the attack. The cooperation of grenadiers with the rest of the infantry must be practiced.

Signalers will require practice in visual signaling.

4. *Preparation of trenches for attack.*—All possible preparation of the trenches should be done long before the attack takes place, otherwise our intention to attack will be made plain to the enemy. Therefore in every system of trenches dispositions for an attack must be considered, and only minor additions should be necessary previous to the actual attack. It should be the aim of every commander to push his front line trenches before an assault as close to the enemy as possible or at least to within 200 yards. This may be done by sapping and then joining up the heads of saps.

Advantage can sometimes be taken of a dark night and a new trench be dug in front of our old front trench during the night. In this case the party must be large enough to insure getting cover the first night. This method will also only be possible if the troops holding the line, by stopping the enemy's patrols moving about, have established a superiority in the "debatable ground."

Assembly trenches must be prepared so that the successive waves of assaulting troops can be launched at the required time. These trenches should be prepared gradually. As far as possible use should be made of the existing trenches. A stereotyped form can not be laid down for assembly trenches. The requisites are:

(*a*) There must be easy egress both above ground and by communication trenches.

(*b*) The assaulting troops must be close enough up.

(*c*) The general line must be perpendicular to the line of advance.

In arranging assembly trenches care must be taken to provide forming up places for the various special parties, such as grenadiers, working parties, etc.

Sidings will probably be required for reserves. These can be suitably made off the "up" communication trenches.

Communication trenches must be provided in sufficient number to avoid congestion. One for up and one for down traffic per battalion frontage at least will be required, and between the last lines the number will require further increase, so that finally there will be one trench leading into the front line about every 50 yards.

Signboards will be required on all communication trenches showing which are for up and which are for down traffic. Care must be taken to make those intended for evacuation of wounded wide enough and with sufficiently easy curves to allow a stretcher to pass.

Saps should be dug forward to be converted into communication trenches to the enemy's front line when captured. These should be tunnelled under the parapet, and when time allows be continued underground instead of above ground.

Exits from trenches must be prepared. These can either be made out of sandbags or by means of ladders. If ladders are used, all the ladders in one bay should be nailed together top and bottom by planks to prevent a ladder falling. Care must be taken that the tops of ladders do not protrude over the parapet.

In short, the preparation of trenches for assault entails the careful selection of the position of every man prior to the assault, and then the preparation of forming up places to suit.

Our own wire must be cut by parties detailed from the assaulting battalions. It should be cut during darkness the night before the assault.[1]

---

[1] The fact that our own wire has been cut can be disguised by cutting transverse gaps or by écheloning the original wire thus _____ _____.

Bridges will have to be made over our trenches at certain points to provide for the advance of the artillery.

5. *Small-arms ammunition, grenades, food, water.*—Stores of small-arms ammunition, grenades, food, water, tools, and Royal Engineer material must be established in the trenches. They must be conveniently placed for carrying forward to the captured position. One man should be in charge of each store. Special carrying parties will require to be detailed to carry the stores forward. Dumps of stores should be arranged in échelon, so that those in the trenches can be easily replenished.

44. EQUIPMENT.

Assaulting troops should be as lightly equipped as possible, but it is difficult to reduce the weight carried below the following scale: [1]

200 rounds small-arms ammunition.

One day's rations (in addition to iron ration).

Two sandbags.

One pick or shovel to every third man.

Extra wire cutters, flares, smoke candles, etc., will be carried by a proportion of the men.

The equipment of grenadier parties is dealt with in the pamphlet on "Training and Employment of Grenadiers."

Grenadiers carry rifle and bayonet and 50 rounds small-arms ammunition.

45. PRELIMINARY BOMBARDMENT.

The artillery will prepare the way for the assault by battering the enemy's defenses and destroying his obstacles. It will be the duty of the infantry to assist the artillery by continually reporting information gained about the enemy's line, and by observing the effect of the artillery fire mainly as to whether strong points or machine gun emplacements are being suitably dealt with, and the success or otherwise of the wire cutting. It is also necessary for infantry officers to make certain that they and the artillery commanders are in agreement as to the places where the wire is going to be cut.

This bombardment will probably take a long time, and during that time the garrisons of trenches should be reduced to avoid the casualties from the enemy's retaliation.

The enemy must be prevented from repairing his obstacles and trenches after they have been damaged by artillery fire by keeping

---

[1] Arrangements for storing packs of troops taking part in an attack must be made. Each man's name should be marked on his pack.

the damaged portions under fire of trench mortars, rifle grenades, machine guns and rifle.

Definite tasks must always be allotted to trench mortars, in co-operation with the artillery.

46. THE ASSAULT.

The bombardment is kept up till the moment fixed for assault, when the artillery lifts, and the assault is launched.

The assaulting troops will consist of successive waves, each wave consisting of men extended at about one man every two yards, and with about 50 yards between waves. The number of waves will depend on the distance from our front trench of the final objective. The pace will be moderate, and on no account must a wild rush be allowed. The assault must be pressed on above ground till its objective is reached, special parties being detailed to clear up the trenches over which the assault passes. These "clearing" parties accompany the assaulting waves, but remain behind in the trenches which they have been detailed to clear, while the assaulting troops press on to the final objective without entering them. "Clearing" parties will be composed largely of grenadiers.

The assaulting troops, on gaining the final objective, proceed to consolidate. Royal Engineer parties and carrying parties to take up the tools and material required must be detailed beforehand. It may be impossible to take up material till after dark.

Parties must also be detailed to consolidate tactical points in rear of the assaulting troops, as they are gained. They will be assisted by the "clearing" parties, when these have finished their task of disposing of the enemy.

Generally speaking, then, attacking troops will consist of:

(a) The troops detailed to carry through the assault to the final objective.

(b) The clearing parties who dispose of any enemy left behind in the trenches over which the assault has passed.

(c) The parties detailed for the consolidation of tactical points behind the assaulting troops and parties to carry up to the assaulting troops the material required to consolidate the positions won.

Special arrangements will have to be made, and special bodies of troops detailed to form a defensive flank on each side of the front assaulted, and also to attack isolated or semi-isolated strong points encountered on the flanks of assaulting troops. (See Figs. 73–76.)

The relative strength of the various parties can not be laid down. They vary according to circumstances. The important principle is that every body of troops has a definite task assigned to it and knows what that task is.

47. ACTION OF ARTILLERY DURING THE ASSAULT.

At the moment fixed for assault, artillery fire must "lift" from the actual places to be assaulted, but must be kept up on the immediate flanks of the attack. Once the assault has been launched, the duty of the artillery is:

(a) To keep down the fire of the hostile artillery. This is done by the counter batteries.

(b) To prevent the enemy bringing up supports and reserves, by keeping up a steady fire on his communication trenches and other lines of approach and places in rear where troops might collect for a counter-attack.

(c) To give continuous support to the infantry during their advance and to deal with obstacles, strong points, etc., which may be holding them up.

The difficulties of this latter task are almost entirely those of observation and intercommunication. It is often impossible owing to smoke, dust, etc., to see exactly where the infantry have got to, and what is stopping their progress. The obtaining of timely information from the advanced troops presents great difficulties, and will depend largely on the efficiency of our counter-battery work. If the enemy's guns are not silenced, they will form a barrage behind our attacking troops which will make the sending back of information exceedingly uncertain.

The measures to be taken to insure, so far as possible, continued artillery support to the infantry during the advance are as follows:

(a) A proportion of field guns dug in close to our front trenches are useful to cover the flanks and give close support to the infantry.

(b) Battery commanders must place themselves where they can best see the general situation and keep touch with their batteries, and must be prepared to act on their own initiative, in the absence of information and orders from above.

(c) Each battery must have a forward observing officer, whose duties are to keep in touch with the infantry commander whom the battery is supporting, to keep the battery commander informed as to the exact position of the infantry, and to assist him in ranging on to anything that is checking the progress of our infantry.

The forward observing officer must be provided with telephone and signalling equipment. In selecting his position he must remember that his business is to assist the battery commander, not to join in the infantry fight, and that his information is of no use unless he can get it through to the battery commander. His best position will normally be the farthest point forward to which good communication has been opened up. He must keep the battalion commander informed of his whereabouts. It is then the duty of the infantry to let him know their requirements, and the measure of support they receive will depend largely on their reports being clear and intelligible to the artillery. For this reason it is very necessary that infantry officers should understand what information the artillery require.

Some form of light signal, visible to aircraft and artillery through smoke and mist, is required to let everyone know when the infantry have gained a certain objective. It should be sufficiently portable to be carried by every man. Flags and screens have been used, but they often get left behind and are then very misleading.

A proportion of light trench mortars should be brought up behind the infantry as soon as possible, and it may sometimes be possible to use them against some point which is checking the advance.

48. EMPLOYMENT OF MACHINE GUNS.

The rôle of machine guns in the attack is—

(a) To assist the artillery in the preparation of the attack if required.

(b) To cover the assaulting infantry with their fire and to keep down flanking fire.

(c) To fill up gaps that may occur either laterally or in depth.

(d) To assist in the consolidation of the position and repulse hostile counter-attacks.

It is most important that all machine guns are allotted a definite task and given definite orders. The guns of the brigade company may be allotted as follows:

(a) Some to cover advance by firing on the enemy's parapet, keeping down fire against flanks of attack, and sweeping ground in rear of enemy's first line, till masked by the advance of the infantry.

(b) Some to follow up the assaulting infantry. A proportion of these guns should accompany the parties detailed to consolidate tactical points in rear of the assaulting troops. Usually, Lewis guns only will go forward with the assaulting infantry at first. But some of the guns of the brigade company must be brought up as soon as possible after the assault has reached its final objective. These guns should not fire before the advance; the line of advance of each gun should be carefully selected beforehand.

(c) Some may be detailed to fire from positions in rear on points where enemy are likely to collect for counter-attack.

Lewis guns, owing to their mobility, are very suitable at the opening of an attack to provide covering fire from the front. Under cover of darkness, smoke, or artillery bombardment, Lewis gunners can creep out in front of the trenches and establish themselves in shell holes, ditches, long grass, etc., where it will be difficult to detect them. They may thus be able to cut wire which the artillery have been unable to cut and to fire on hostile machine gun emplacements, loopholes, and parapet.

Lewis guns will accompany the assaulting troops, but not in the first line, and will assist to keep down the enemy's machine-gun fire, cover the reorganization of the infantry, consolidate the ground won, protect the flanks, and repel counter-attacks.

49. USE OF GRENADIERS.

Grenadiers will principally be employed in clearing trenches, after these have been successfully attacked, and also to check and destroy hostile bombing parties attempting to counter-attack. They will be required to clear a portion of a trench from the flanks when its capture from the front has failed.

Full instructions on hand and rifle grenades and their employment are to be found in the "Training and Employment of Grenadiers." Emphasis may here be laid on the necessity of new units arriving at the front with thoroughly trained grenadiers, and also on the necessity for organizing with great care the supply of grenades during an attack.

50. COMMUNICATIONS.

Buried telephone wires will previously have been installed in our front-line system. These should be carried on up to the front line, and wire be ready to run across to the hostile line when captured. These wires will, however, be very exposed and can not be relied on.

Visual signaling and runners will therefore often be the only means available. The issue of disks, rockets, flares, or other improvised signals and their use must therefore be arranged. Receiving stations for visual signaling must be arranged for in our trenches, and these must be suitably protected.

APPENDIX A.

Winter Avenues.

BREASTWORK COMMUNICATION TRENCHES.

1. The "winter avenue" is primarily designed for construction in winter in ground where deep communication trenches are impossible and the difficulties of digging are increased by the soil clinging to the shovel and preventing a long "throw."

2. *Trace.*—The trace is designed to reduce labor by combining protection from enfilade fire with passing places. A change of direction is made about every 60 yards to safeguard the avenue from being swept from end to end. Each arm is broken twice in its length at the passing places. Those are made sufficiently wide to permit of stretchers passing the angles. The breaks are right-handed to enable a man to fire down the trench while keeping most of his body covered. In the arm nearest to the trench whence the communication starts, part of the inner breastwork of the passing places is omitted so that each section of the arm can be enfiladed from the parapet.

The avenues and borrow pits are flanked by means of short breastworks projecting from the elbows of the parapet.

3. *Profile.*—The height of the parapet will depend on depth below the surface of the ground at which the trench gratings will be clear of the subsoil water. Six feet of cover at least must be provided, and the more of this there is below ground the less the labor required for the parapet. But even if submerged, the gratings, being wired to the transoms, give a good foothold; and they can always be raised by putting another transom on the trestle, the parapet being heightened correspondingly.

A trench is, however, always advisable, even if the gratings are to be at ground level, as it acts as a drain and supplies some earth for the parapet. The sides of the trench should be revetted by slipping planks, brushwood, or netting between them and the trestles, stakes being added if necessary.

The borrow pits should be as far as possible from the breastwork consistent with the power of "throw" in the particular ground. A 2-foot berm is the absolute minimum.

72

4. *Time of construction.*—The avenue can be made in from 10 to 12 hours by two to three reliefs, and so can be completed in one night.

5. *Preparation.*—The most careful preparations must be made, materials calculated out beforehand, and transported to the nearest convenient place under cover. There they must be laid out in such a manner as will insure rapid and easy issue in the dark.

Working parties must be carefully calculated and divided up into small gangs.

The officers and men for each relief should be carefully practiced by rehearsal by day in their rôles in the operations on which they will be employed.

It will hasten the work and prevent confusion if the avenue is started from both ends, and a stores dump is made at each of them.

It is generally inadvisable to extend a working party of 100 men from one point at night. The line of the proposed avenue should be divided into sections by marking stakes or other means, and each party led direct to its starting stake by its officer.

6. *Tracing and reconnaissance.*—The Royal Engineer should reconnoiter the ground at dusk on the preceding night, and mark out with tapes the lines along which the hurdles are to be placed.

If there is any danger of the tapes being observed by the enemy during the day, tracing must be done at dusk on the actual night.

The infantry officers in charge of parties should accompany the tracing officer and should familiarize themselves with the approaches to the dumps and starting points.

7. *Men and tools and materials.*—The men and tools and materials are as follows:

First relief (5 hours).

	Per 4-yard run.	Per 100-yard run.
Royal Engineer	2	50 (2 officers, 5 noncommissioned officers).
Infantry	8	220 (5 officers, 20 noncommissioned officers).
Shovels	8	220.
Picks	8	200.
Pliers	2	50.
Measuring rods	1	25.
3-foot hurdles	4	100.
5-foot pickets	8	200 (3 inches diameter).
Wire (14 steel wire gauge) (2 extra for first hurdles.)	(¹)	(²)
3-foot rabbit netting	......	

¹ 1,056 feet (18 pounds), 8 yards.   ² 26,400 feet (450 pounds), 200 yards.

Second relief (5 hours).

	Per 4-yard run.	Per 100-yard run.
Royal Engineers.................	(1)	
Infantry...........................		
Tools...............................		
18-inch hurdles.................	4	100.
15-inch rabbit netting....yards..	8	200 yards.
Sandbags........................	70	1,750.
Wire (14 steel wire gauge).......	(2)	(3)

[1] As in first relief.
[2] 264 feet (4½ pounds).
[3] 6,600 feet (112½ pounds).

Third relief.

	Per 4-yard run.	Per 100-yard run.
Royal Engineers............	2	50 (1 officer).
Infantry....................	4	110 (2 officers, 10 noncommissioned officers).
Shovels.....................	4	110.
Picks.......................	4	100.
Trestles....................	3	76.
8-foot gratings..............	[1] 1½	38.
Planks for revetting........	[2] 48	1,200.[2]
Mauls.......................	½	12.

[1] Special gratings for passing places to be calculated and 8-foot gratings to be decreased accordingly.
[2] Square feet.

NOTE 1.—The length of third relief depends on whether the full amount of digging has been carried out in the first and second reliefs. If the full amount has been done there is no necessity for a third relief, as the trench gratings can be laid by the Royal Engineers next morning.

NOTE 2.—No mauls in first two reliefs on account of noise.

NOTE 3.—Reliefs are reckoned from time of leaving dumps.

8. *Organization of working party.*—The most convenient unit of organization is a squad consisting of two Royal Engineers and eight infantry. This unit is completely equipped with tools and materials as in column 1, paragraph 7, and does 4 yards of avenue.

(*a*) Every five squads as above should be formed into an officer's party, with four noncommissioned officers and four spare men, and does 20 yards of avenue, or just the length between the breaks for which special squads could be provided if necessary.

(b) If the tactical situation permits, the infantry should leave their equipment at the dump, and carry rifle and cartridge slings only.

(c) In the first relief each infantryman carries pick and shovel slung. Slings of spun yarn or cord should be attached to these beforehand by the party preparing the stores. In addition, a hurdle is given to every two infantrymen.

The two sappers carry the measuring rod, pliers, pickets, wire, and rabbit netting.

NOTE.—Netting being in rolls would usually be carried down by the four spare men in every officer's party.

(d) In the second relief four infantrymen in each squad carry the light hurdles and the other four carry the sandbags. Royal Engineers carry the wire and netting (but see note to c). Tools are taken over from first relief on the ground.

9. *Extension.*—(a) A squad should march to its work in regular order.

The men are numbered and the hurdles lettered for purposes of reference.

(b) When the leading squad reaches the farthest forward end of the section allotted to the party, the hurdles are placed on the ground netting downward and feet to the tape.

The men lay their arms 5 yards from the tape.

(c) The Royal Engineers then measure the distances of the picket holes from the tape. The infantry then dig holes with the picks for the pickets and hurdle feet.

While the infantry are making the holes the Royal Engineers prepare the wire.

(d) When the holes are complete, hurdle feet and pickets are put in them and the earth pressed down. (If the earth is so hard as to necessitate hammering, mauls must be brought and muffled, but only in circumstances of a very special nature must hurdles be mauled in, as the process strains them.)

(e) Nos. 1 and 7 then hold the hurdles, the Royal Engineers put on the first two wires and the rabbit netting, assisted by the remaining infantry. The work will be greatly accelerated if the infantry have had previous practice.

(f) As soon as the netting and the first two ties are fixed, the infantry begin to dig. While they are doing so the Royal Engineers fix the other ties, and see that the borrow ditch is kept 2 feet or more as ordered from the netting stakes.

(*g*) When filling in the parapet, care should be taken to keep the weight of earth against the rabbit netting greater than that against the hurdles, in order to avoid forcing the latter over toward the trench.

10. *Tasks.*—In the first relief the number of cubic feet of earth in the parapets of the squads' task is 360 cubic feet (i. e., 4 times 6 feet by 5 feet by 3 feet). This will be too much for the men to do in the time at their disposal after completion of wiring, etc., but they should be able to fill up to a height of 2½ feet.

In that case:

Parapets=300 cubic feet.

Two men in the trench dig 30 cubic feet each=60 cubic feet.

Five men in borrow ditches dig 40 cubic feet each=240 cubic feet.

In the second relief there are 60 cubic feet of the lower part of the parapet to be done (as above), and the top parts of the parapets amount to 210 cubic feet, a total of 270 cubic feet. This should easily be completed by the eight infantrymen in four hours, including filling the sandbags.

11. *Action of reliefs.*—At the end of the first relief the infantry stand at their tasks. The second relief extend beside them and take over their tools. The first relief then put on their equipment and file off. Not until after they have gone will the second relief lay down their rifles and equipment.

Royal Engineers hand over tools and duties in similar manner.

12. The work should be easily completed in one night if careful preparations have been made and if not greatly interrupted by fire.

Until the end of February a third relief is always possible before dawn. It should be provided. At the end of the first relief it can easily be seen if the third relief will not be required, and message to that effect sent.

APPENDIX B.

Rapid Wire Entanglements.

The following are two methods of putting up wire entanglements, when rapidity is essential.

First Method (used by French).

Bays of wire fencing about 90 feet long are prepared beforehand, using light posts 7 feet 6 inches apart with horizontal top and bottom wires and diagonal wires. For the top wire and one of the diagonals barbed wire is employed, plain wire about 0.15 inch thick for the others. Each bay is then rolled up and weighs about 90 pounds; it can be carried easily by two men if a stick is passed through it.

To put up the entanglement, unroll the bays along the front at 90 feet intervals and drive in the posts. This gives the front row of the obstacle. In rear of it unroll and place more bays, zigzag fashion, so as to form a series of equilateral triangles with the original line. In this portion two rolls of fencing are required for each roll in the front row. Repeat the same process to form additional sections.

Light posts are necessary from consideration of weight, but as there are three posts alongside each other where the straight and zigzag portions meet (except in the front and back row of fencing, when there are only two) a strong support is formed if the posts are bound together.

Second Method.

See figures 30, 31, 32, which sufficiently explain the method used.

As a variation of this method, work may be commenced by making the fence on the front line of posts first (work of Nos. 5, 6, 7, 8), then joining the first line of posts by criss-cross wires to the second (work of Nos. 1, 2, 3, 4,), and lastly making the fence on the rear posts. The advantage of this alternative method is that the working party then has the obstacle between them and the enemy the whole time they are working, instead of having to carry stores and work in the second stage in front of the obstacle erected by Nos. 1, 2, 3, and 4 in the first stage.

APPENDIX C.

The lighting up of the foreground and obstacles at night is of great importance.

The usual means adopted for this purpose is the Very light, of which a liberal supply is now available, but occasions may arrive when the undermentioned methods will prove of value. These lights should be so arranged that they can be put in action instantaneously when the enemy approaches the obstacle; they must illuminate the whole of the obstacles and the foreground while leaving the defenders in shadow.

BONFIRES.

Bonfires are effective when fuel is to be had. They may be built close to the line of the obstacle, with screens behind them.

A bonfire should be so built that it can not easily be pulled down by the enemy. A stout post may be fixed upright in the ground, and the fuel built up round it in the form of a cone. Or three posts may be erected, 3 or 4 feet apart, with sticks nailed to them horizontally so as to form a cage, and the fuel piled inside. A heap of shavings or dry leaves should be placed at the bottom, and means of lighting arranged in connection with it. For this purpose a length of instantaneous fuze may be used, with one end in a small bag of gunpowder, under the heap of shavings, and the other inside the work. But the fuze must be kept in thoroughly good condition. Friction tubes form an excellent means of ignition. They can be fired by the release of a weight which is attached by wire to the eye of the pin. The tubes must be rigidly fixed, and strong wire used for suspending the weight. The blast from a friction tube being considerable, the end of the instantaneous fuze nearest the tube should be 1 inch away from it. Both ends of the fuze may be packed with quickmatch to insure ignition. Another method is to arrange a match under the shavings so that by a pull on a cord the match will be rubbed against an igniting surface. The shavings must be enough to make a bright flame at once, and petroleum or pitch should be added to them if available. Materials for renewing the bonfire should be kept at hand. Small pieces of canvas should be fixed over the firing arrangements to protect them from weather.

LIGHTS, ILLUMINATING WRECK.

Lights, illuminating wreck are articles of store. They can be lit with either instantaneous or safety fuze. Instantaneous fuze should be stripped at the end to insure good contact with the light. They illuminate a circle of about 100 yards diameter and burn for about 20 minutes.

ALARMS AND FLARES.

Where night attacks may be expected, automatic alarms and flare lights are useful adjuncts. They are usually combined with the obstacle. One of the simplest alarms is a row of tin pots, each containing a pebble, hung on a wire fence so as to rattle when the latter is disturbed. A piece of tin 2 inches to 3 inches in diameter, such as the top of a jam pot, may be bent around the wire and will answer the same purpose. Trip wires can be arranged to fire a rifle, or to fire a cartridge, which in its turn will ignite a flare.

It must be borne in mind that flares lighted within a few yards of the perimeter of a camp, or close to a parapet, are difficult to screen effectively and are likely to be a source of greater danger to the defence than to the attack; they should therefore be used with great caution. At night troops have a tendency to concentrate their fire on any brilliantly illuminated area. A number of flares capable of burning from two to five minutes are preferable to one or two bonfires; a better effect is obtained from flares by placing them at some height above the ground. Convenient trees may be used for this purpose.

Arrangements for automatic alarm signals, in connection with entanglements or intermediate fences, generally have to be improvised on the spot with whatever materials are available.

A trip flare that has been found to work satisfactorily consists of a balanced board fixed in a trench having at one end the flare and at the other a heavy weight which is temporarily supported. The trip wire having been pulled, the support beneath the weight is withdrawn, and the end of the beam falls. By this means the flare appears above ground, and the jerk given to the beam fires a friction tube attached to the flare by instantaneous fuze, and so lights the flare.

The flare is composed of a mixture of nitrate of potash, sulphur, and orpiment (Lights, G. S., long, Mark III).

A similar device for the firing of a mine or bonfire outside the pit, composed of straw, dry wood, etc., is readily set on fire by a small 1-ounce cartridge composed of five parts white sugar and four parts chlorate of potash, inclosed in grease-proof paper, fired by either instantaneous fuze or electrically by No. 14 fuze, with metal cap with the meal powder removed.

DIAGRAMS.

TRACE OF TRENCHES.

(Diagrammatic, it should not be too straight.)

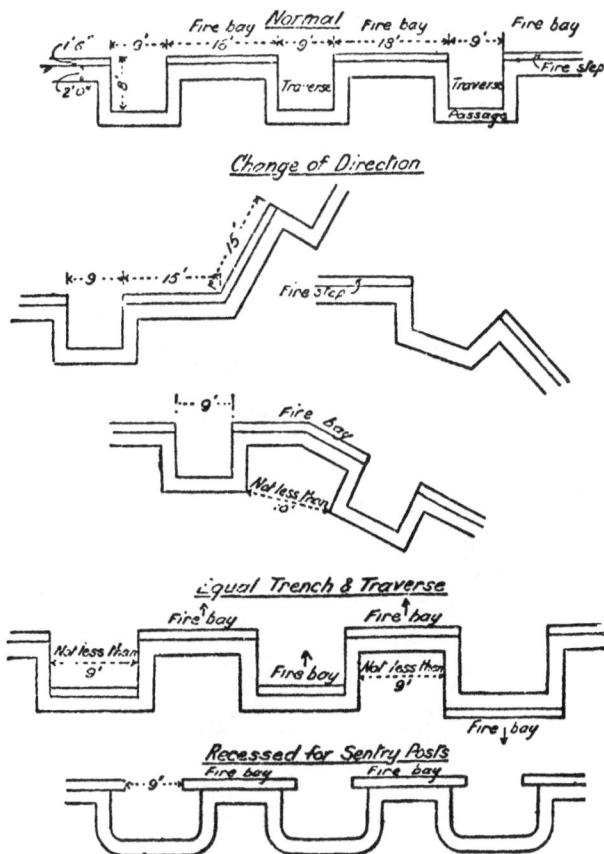

Normal

Change of Direction

Equal Trench & Traverse

Recessed for Sentry Posts

For sections see Figs. 9, 10, 11 & 12.

FIG. 1.

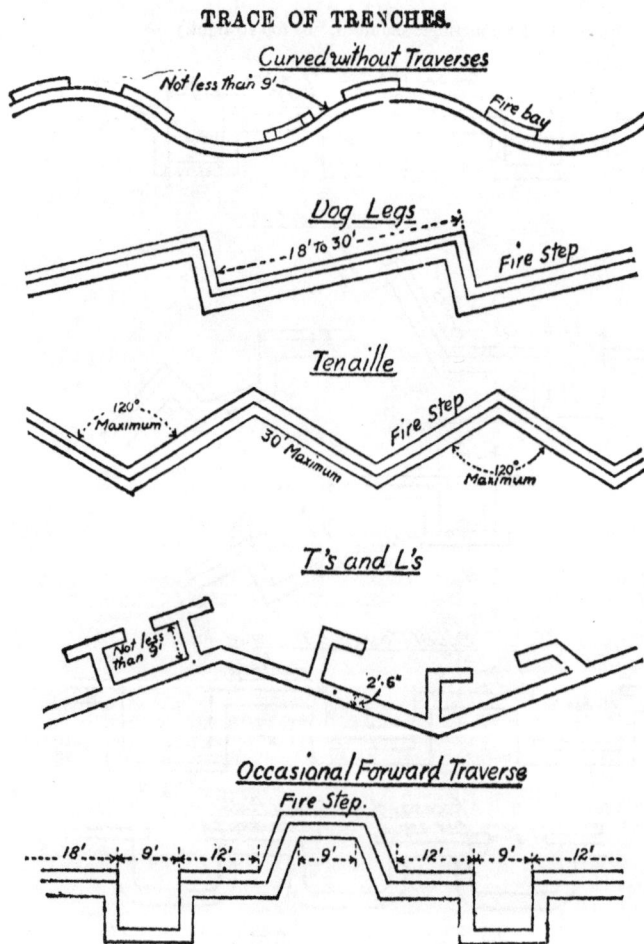

TRACE OF TRENCHES.

Curved without Traverses

Not less than 9'

Fire bay

Dog Legs

18' to 30'

Fire Step

Tenaille

120° Maximum

30' Maximum

Fire Step

120° Maximum

T's and L's

Not less than 9'

2'.6"

Occasional Forward Traverse

Fire Step.

18' 9' 12' 9' 12' 9' 12'

FIG. 2.

TRACE OF TRENCHES.

Flanking Pedam.

Bastioned.

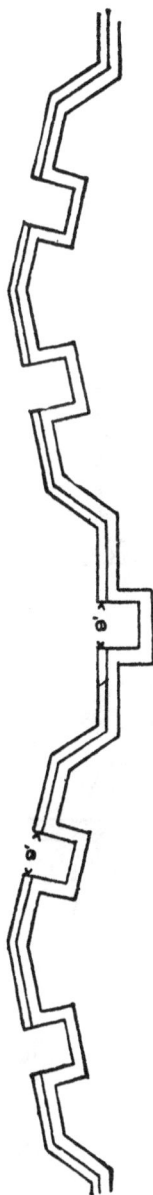

Dummy Trench or Trench to be Enfiladed. not less than

FIG. 3.

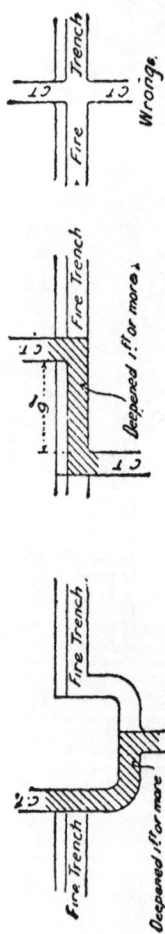

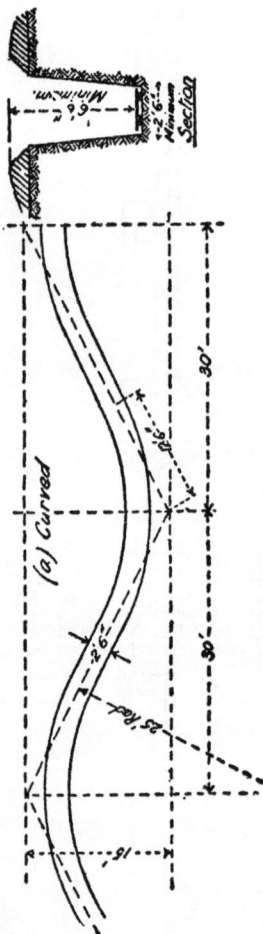

FIG. 4.

COMMUNICATION TRENCHES.

Plan depends on the ground; the length of legs should **never be** shorter than 9 ft. and not longer than 60 ft.

Short—downhill towards enemy; long—uphill.

(*b*) Zigzag.

(*c*) Elbowed or Saw.

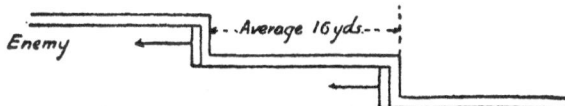

(*d*) Traversed.

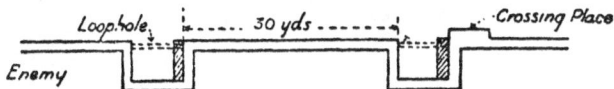

(*e*) Island Traverses.

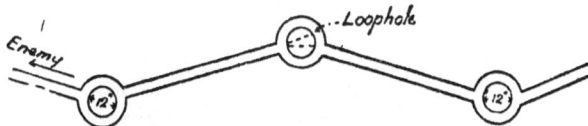

(*f*) Bridge Traverses.
(A trench may be blinded continuously in this way.)

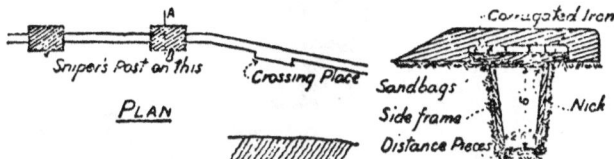

(*g*) Tunnelled Subway.

Fig. 5.

DIAGRAMMATIC SKETCH OF PORTION OF A FRONT LINE, WITH SUPERVISION TRENCH, LIVING DUG-OUTS AND SHELL TRENCHES.

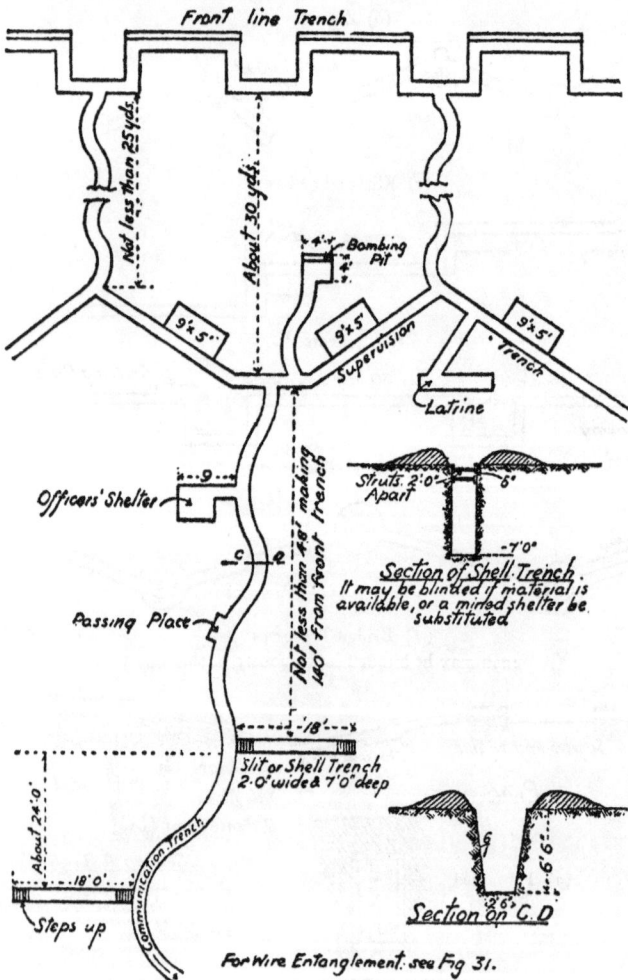

Front line Trench

Not less than 25 yds.

About 30 yds.

4'4" Bombing Pit

9'x 5'

9'x 5'

9'x 5'

Supervision Trench

Latrine

Struts 2'0" Apart

5'

7'0"

Section of Shell Trench.
It may be blinded if material is available, or a mined shelter be substituted.

Officers' Shelter

9

c e

Passing Place

Not less than 4'6" making 140' from Front Trench

18'

Slit or Shell Trench
2·0" wide & 7'0" deep

6'

6'6"

Section on C.D

2'6"

About 24'0"

18'0"

Steps up

Communication trench.

For Wire Entanglement see Fig 31.

FIG. 6.

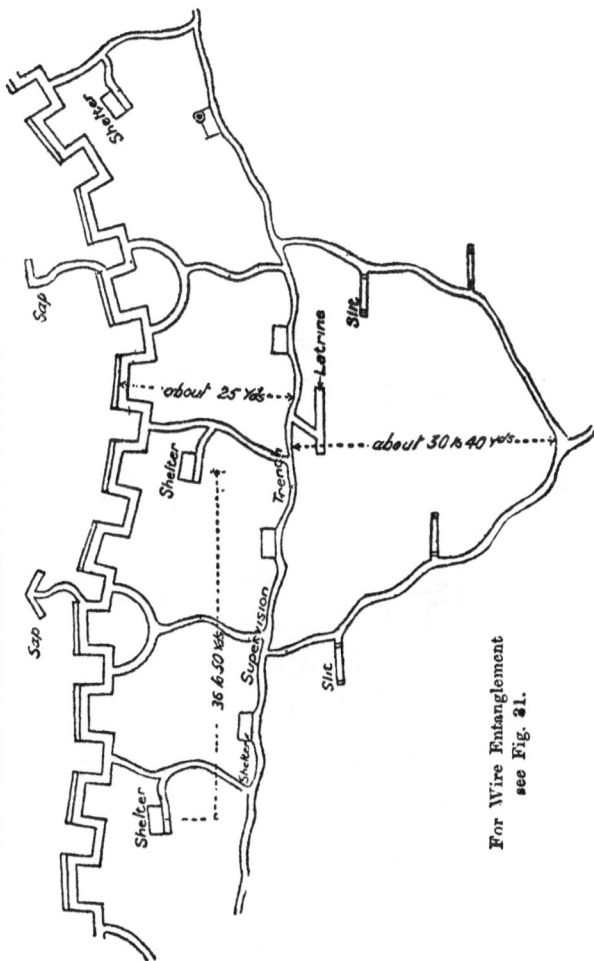

ALTERNATIVE DIAGRAMMATIC ORGANIZATION OF A FRONT LINE.

FIG. 7.

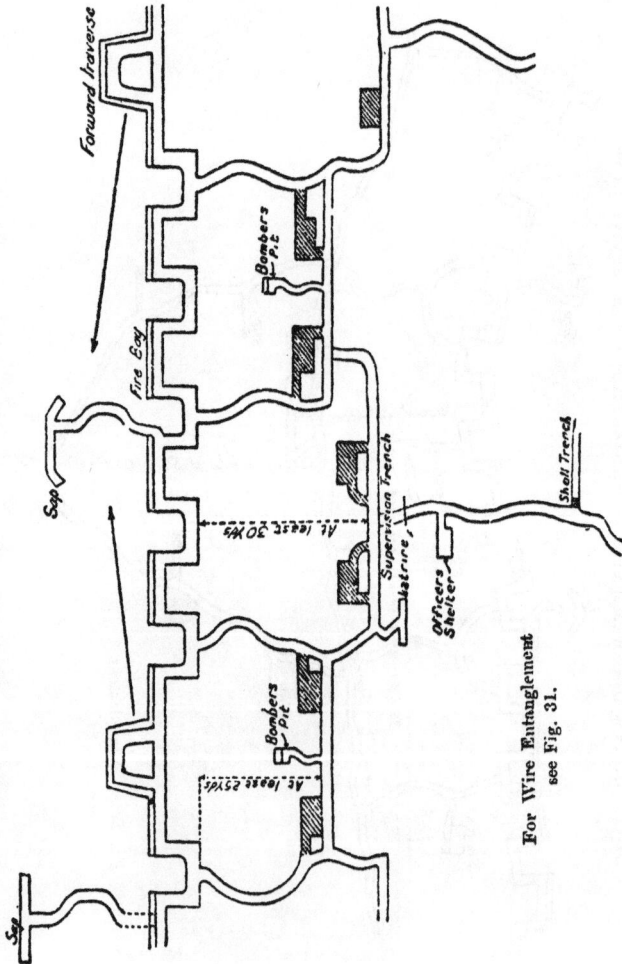

ALTERNATIVE DIAGRAMMATIC ORGANIZATION OF A FRONT LINE.

Forward Traverse

Fire Bay

Sap

Bombers Pit

Supervision Trench

At least 30 Yds.

Latrine

Officers Shelter

Shell Trench

Bombers Pit

At least 25 Yds.

Sap

For Wire Entanglement
see Fig. 31.

FIG. 8.

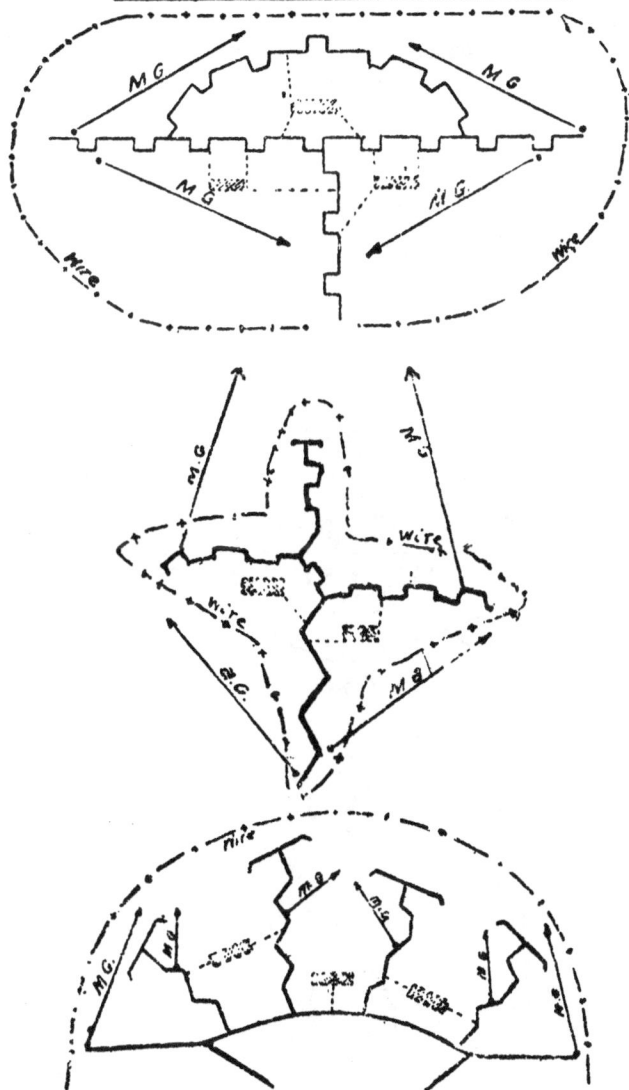

Fig. 9.

Type of Trace for Strong Point

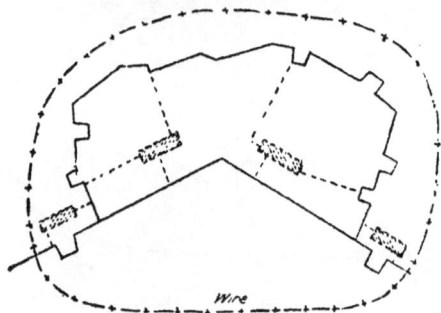

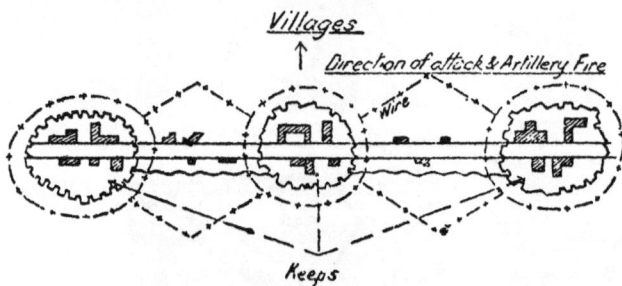

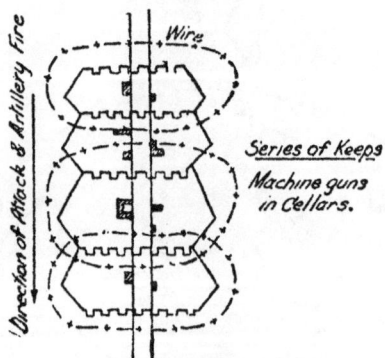

Villages

Direction of attack & Artillery Fire

Wire

Keeps

Wire

Direction of Attack & Artillery Fire

Series of Keeps
Machine guns
in Cellars.

FIG. 10.

SECTIONS OF FIRE TRENCHES.

(1) *Names of parts of a trench.*

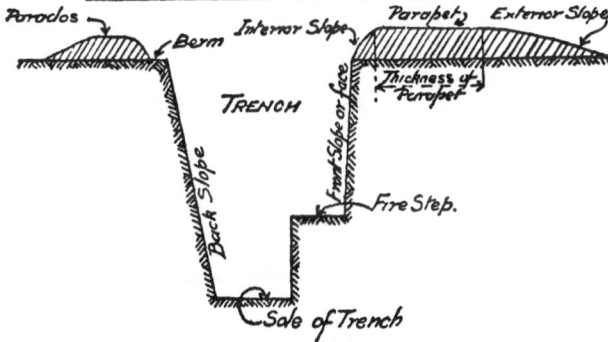

Parados — Berm — Interior Slope — Parapet — Exterior Slope

Trench

Back Slope — Front Slope or face — Thickness of Parapet — Fire Step.

Sole of Trench

(2a) *First Stage in Dry Ground.*

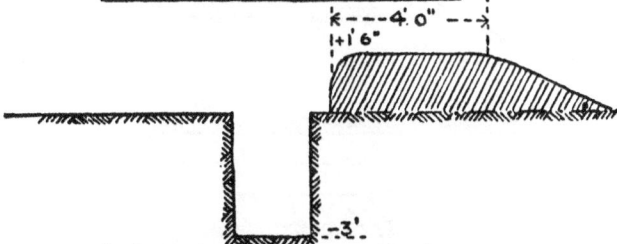

— 4' 0" —
1' 6"
— 3'

(2b) *First Stage in Dry Ground (Alternative).*

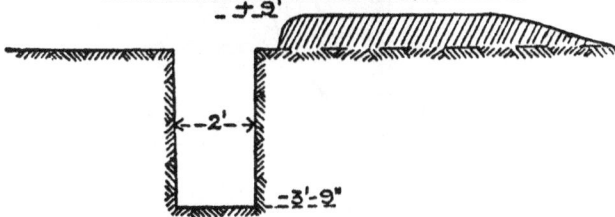

— 1' 2"
— 2' —
— 3' 9"

FIG. 11.

SECTIONS OF TRENCHES.

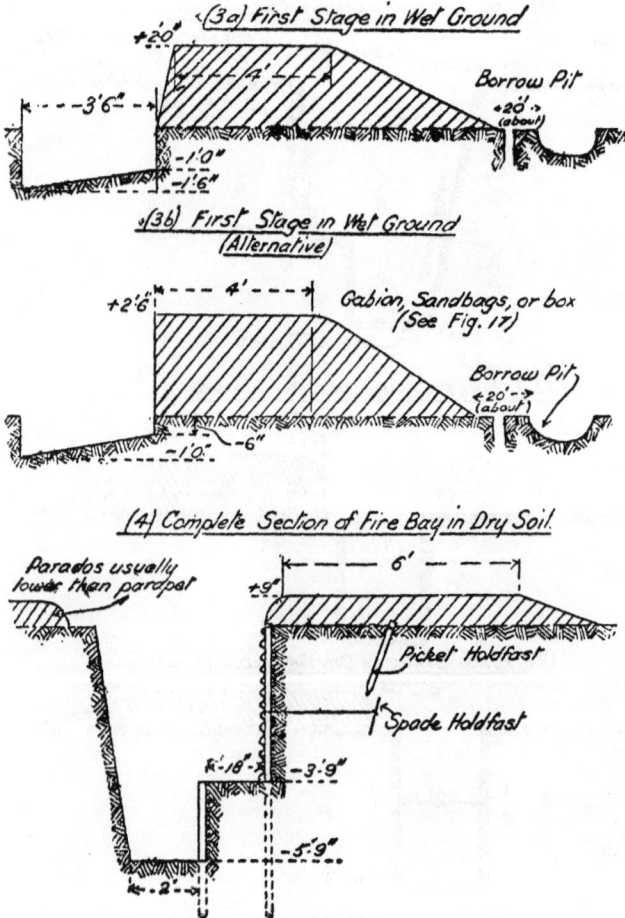

(3a) First Stage in Wet Ground

+2'0"

3'6"

'1"

Borrow Pit

2'0" (about)

-1'0"

-1'6"

(3b) First Stage in Wet Ground
(Alternative)

+2'6"

4'

Gabion, Sandbags, or box
(See Fig. 17)

Borrow Pit

20' (about)

-1'0"   -6"

(4) Complete Section of Fire Bay in Dry Soil.

Parados usually lower than parapet

6'

+9"

Picket Holdfast

Spade Holdfast

8'-18"   -3'9"

-5'9"

2'

Fig. 12.

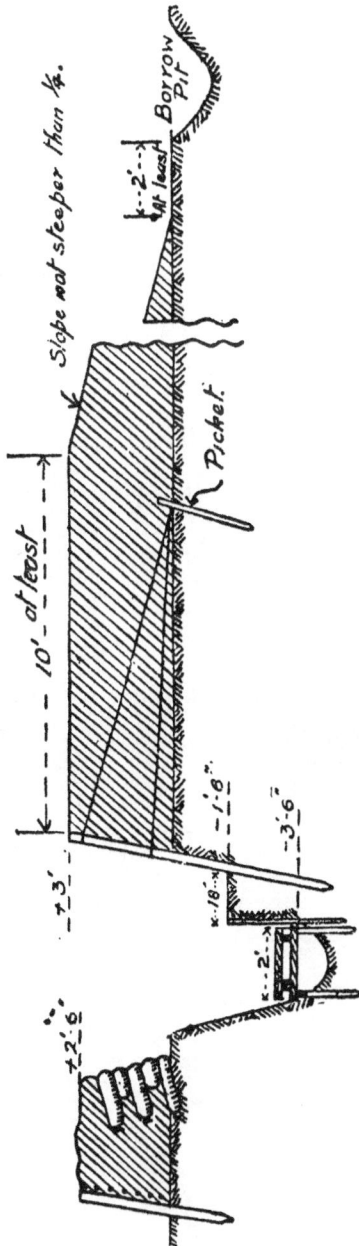

SECTIONS OF FIRE TRENCHES.

(5) SECTION OF BREASTWORK IN WET SOIL.

The Breastwork should be formed if possible on a nucleus of boxes, gabions, etc., filled with earth.

FIG. 13.

SECTIONS OF TRENCHES.
(6) Section Round Traverse.

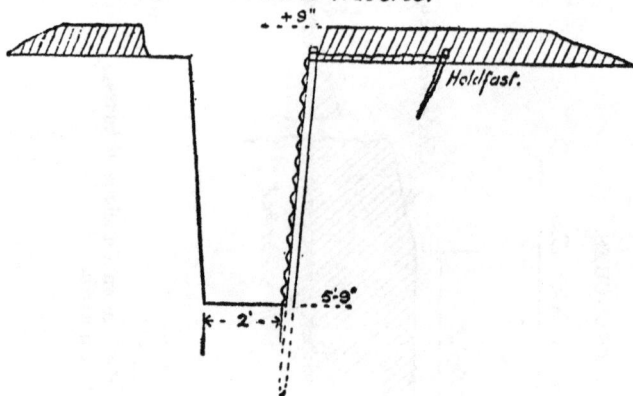

+9"

Holdfast.

5'-9"

- 2' -

(7) Section of Communication Trench.

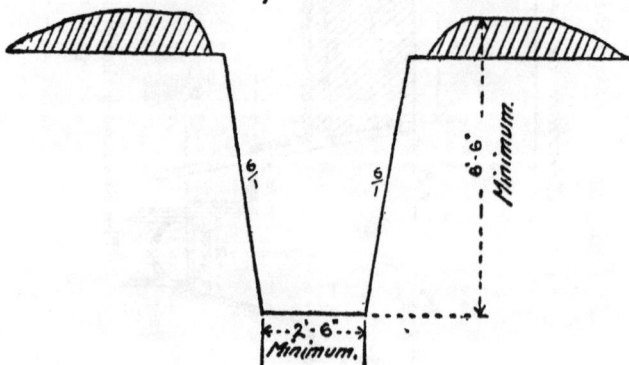

6/1

6/1

6'-6"
Minimum.

2'-6"
Minimum.

FIG. 14.

REVETMENTS.

TRENCH FRAMES FOR USE IN SOFT GROUND.

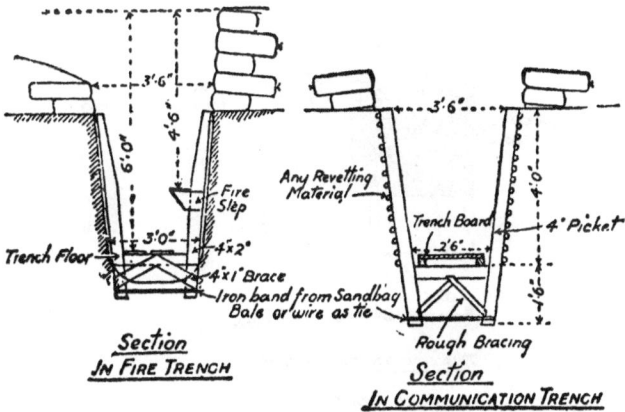

FIG. 15.

REVETMENTS.

EXPANDED METAL OR WIRE HURDLE FOR CORNERS OF TRAVERSES

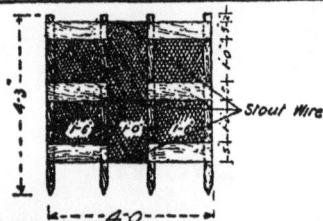

HURDLE MADE FROM OLD CEMENT CASKS.

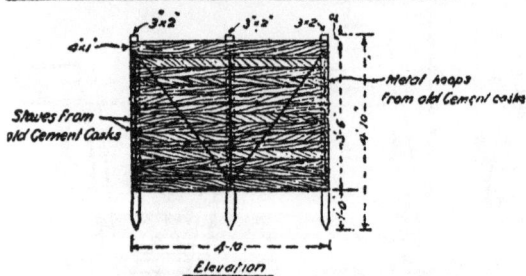

Elevation

This side against parapet

ROUGH HURDLE

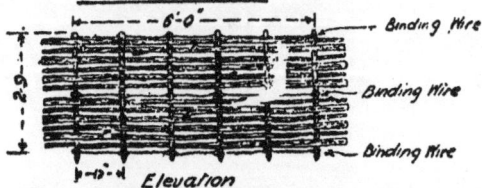

Elevation

Plan

(Shewing Pickets & Binding Wire)

Or the pickets may be driven in and brushwood packed between them
and the parapet to be revetted.

FIG. 16.

ANCHORAGES IN BREASTWORKS.

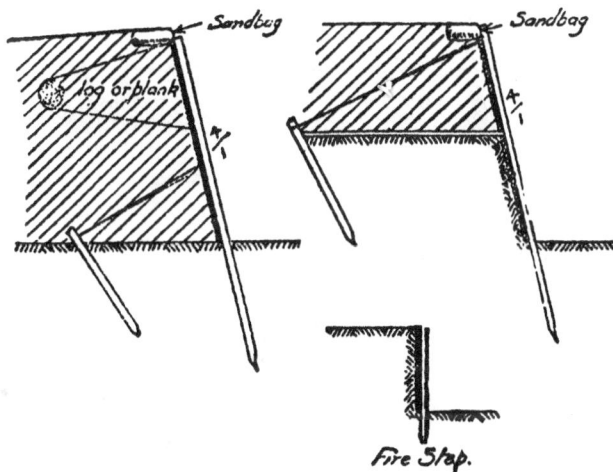

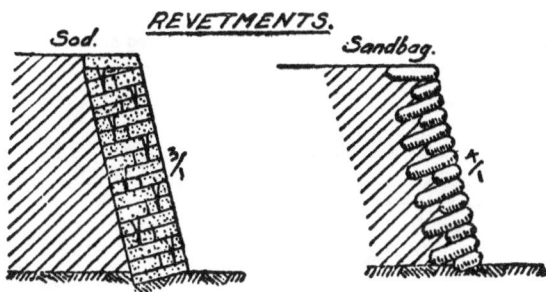

Sandbag

log or plank

Sandbag

Sandbag

Fire Step.

REVETMENTS.

Sod.

Sandbag.

FIG. 17.

REVETMENT ANCHORAGES IN DEEP TRENCHES.

(1) Plate Anchorage

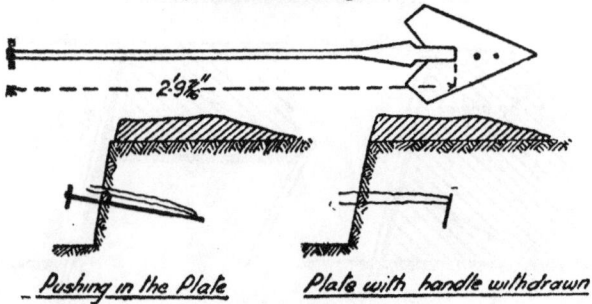

2'9⅞"

Pushing in the Plate   *Plate with handle withdrawn*

(2) Needle.

Detail of Point   9'0"

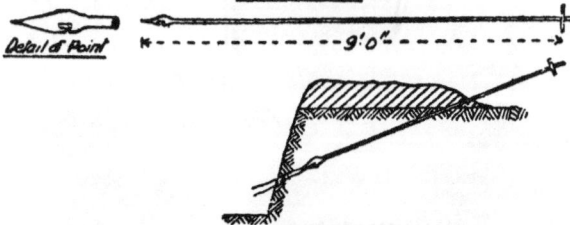

The needle is driven through, wires are then attached and the needle
withdrawn.

(3) Wire in hole filled up with Cement   *(4) Screw Picket*
(See Fig 19)

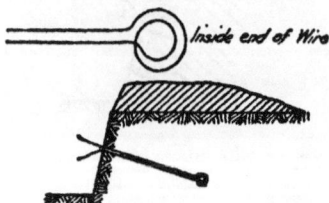

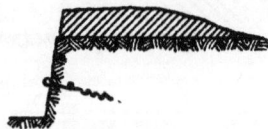

Inside end of Wire

FIG. 18.

COLLAPSIBLE WIRE NETTING GABION.

Wire Netting Omitted.

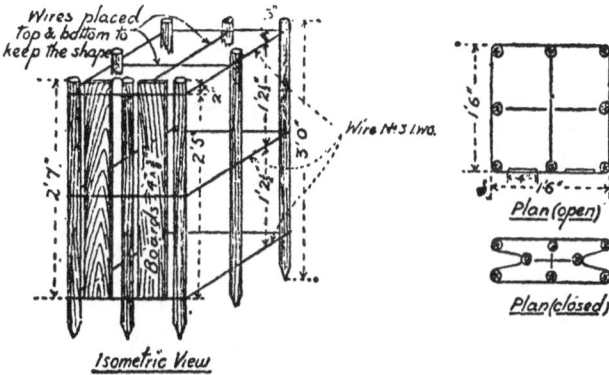

Wires placed Top & bottom to keep the shape

2' 7"

Boards 4"×1"

2' 5"

3' 0"

5"

2"

2½"

2½"

Wire N° 3 I.W.G.

Isometric View

1' 6"

1' 6"

4"

Plan (open)

Plan (closed)

LIGHT COLLAPSIBLE GABION OF CANVAS

Waterproof Canvas

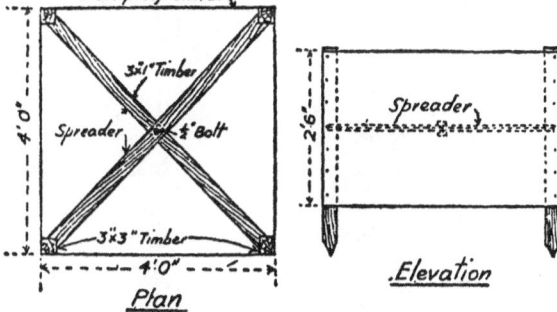

3"×1" Timber

Spreader

½" Bolt

4' 0"

3"×3" Timber

4' 0"

Plan

Spreader

2' 6"

Elevation

EXPANDED METAL GABION.
(Made of sheets 6'×3')

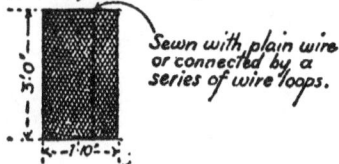

3' 0"

Sewn with plain wire or connected by a series of wire loops.

1' 0"

Fig. 19.

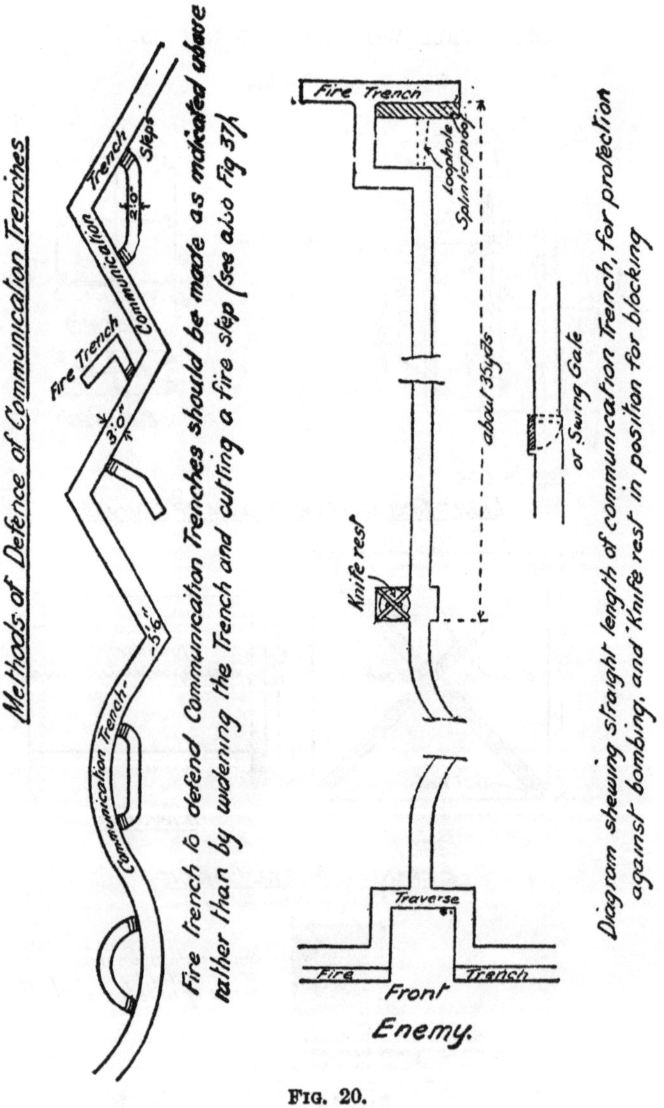
Methods of Defence of Communication Trenches
Communication Trench
Fire Trench
Trench
Steps
2'0"
3'0"
5'6"
Fire trench to defend Communication Trenches should be made as indicated above rather than by widening the Trench and cutting a fire step (see also Fig 37)
Fire Trench
Loophole
Splinterproof
about 35yds
Knife rest
Traverse
Fire
Trench
Front
Enemy.
or Swing Gate
Diagram shewing straight length of communication Trench, for protection against bombing, and Knife rest in position for blocking

FIG. 20.

DEFENCE OF COMMUNICATION TRENCHES.
Trench traced at 1 in 3 to axis in plan.

a. Bullet proof traverse with three loop holes.   *b.* Splinter proof.
c. Fire trench.   *d.* Barbed wire cattle fence.   *e.* Steps.
Or *a* and *b* may be omitted and the legs of the C.T. defended from
the parapet.

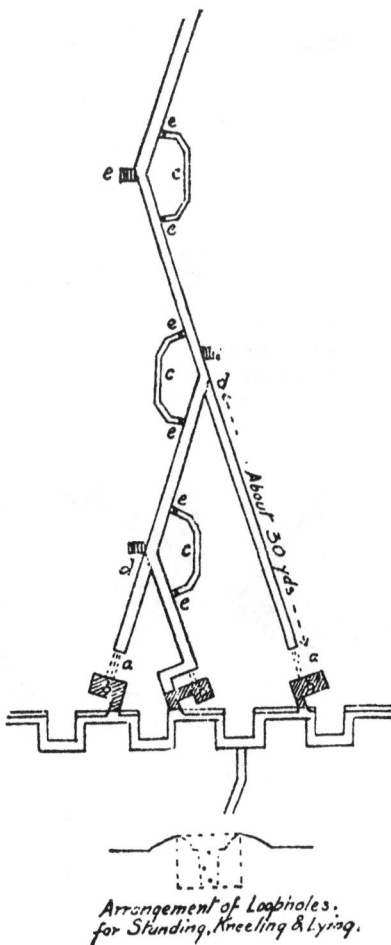

Arrangement of Loopholes.
for Standing, Kneeling & Lying.

FIG. 21.

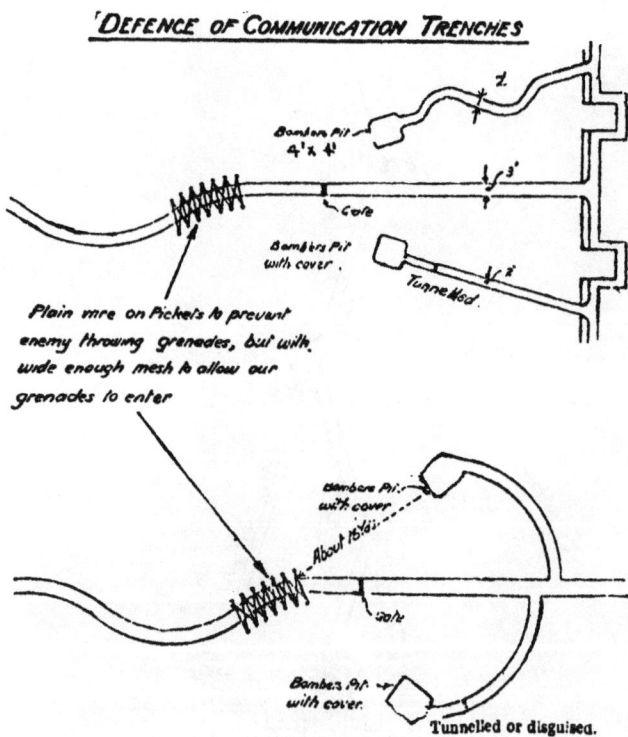

DEFENCE OF COMMUNICATION TRENCHES

Bombers Pit
4' x 4'

Cote

Bombers Pit
with cover.

Tunnelled.

Plain wire on Pickets to prevent
enemy throwing grenades, but with
wide enough mesh to allow our
grenades to enter

Bombers Pit
with cover

About 10 yds.

Hole

Bombers Pit
with cover.

Tunnelled or disguised.

FIG. 22.

CONVENTIONAL SIGNS USED IN PLATES OF WIRE
ENTANGLEMENT.

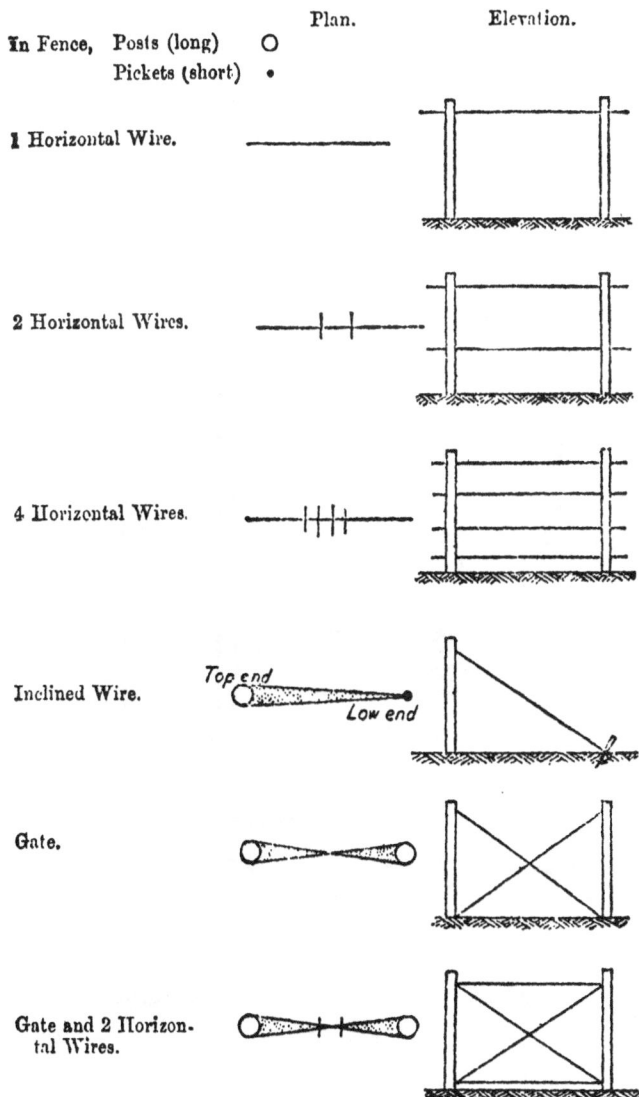

	Plan.	Elevation.
In Fence, Posts (long) ○		
Pickets (short) •		
1 Horizontal Wire.		
2 Horizontal Wires.		
4 Horizontal Wires.		
Inclined Wire.	Top end / Low end	
Gate.		
Gate and 2 Horizontal Wires.		

FIG. 23.

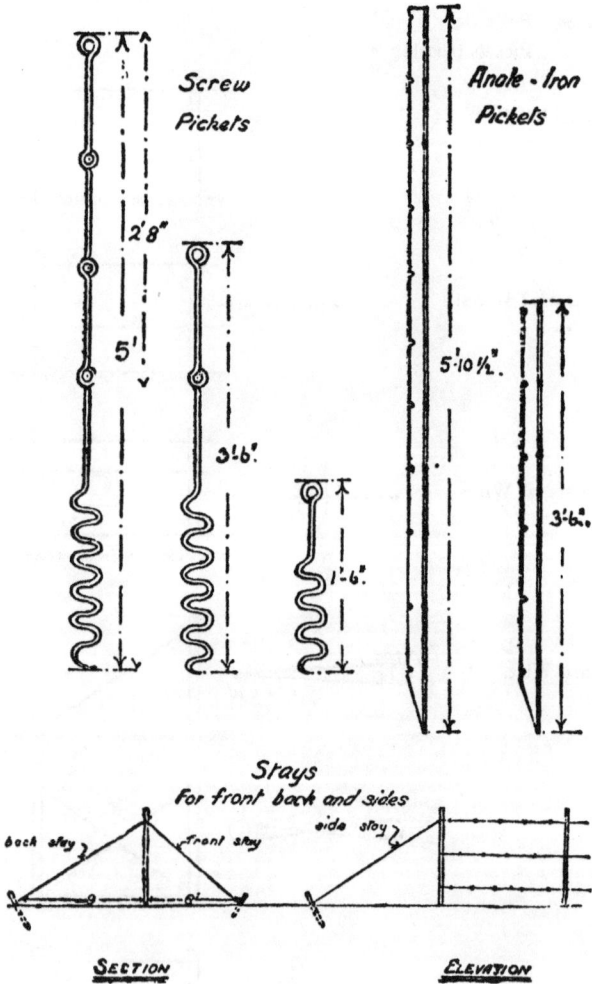

Screw Pickets

2′ 8″

5′

3′ 6″

1′ 6″

Angle - Iron Pickets

5′ 10½″

3′ 6″

Stays
For front back and sides

back stay

front stay

side stay

6′

SECTION

ELEVATION

FIG. 24.

(a) DOUBLE APRON.

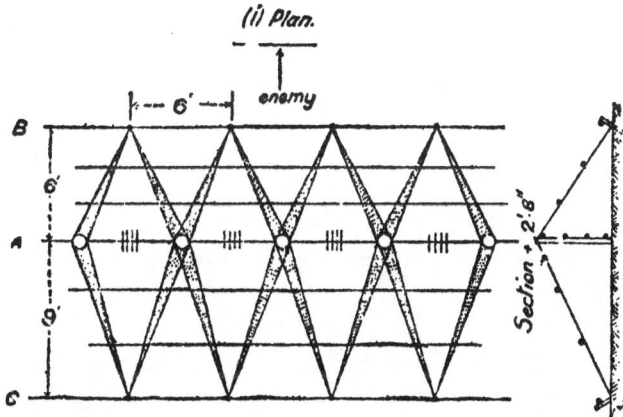

(i) Plan.

enemy

(ii) Arrangement of posts for double width of Entanglement.

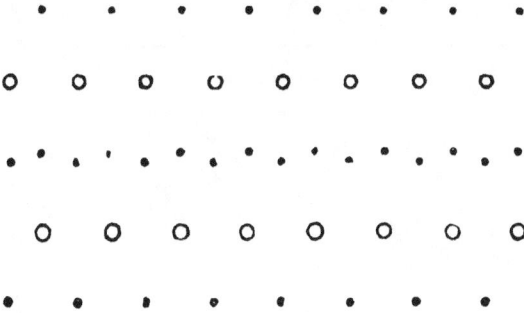

FIG. 25.

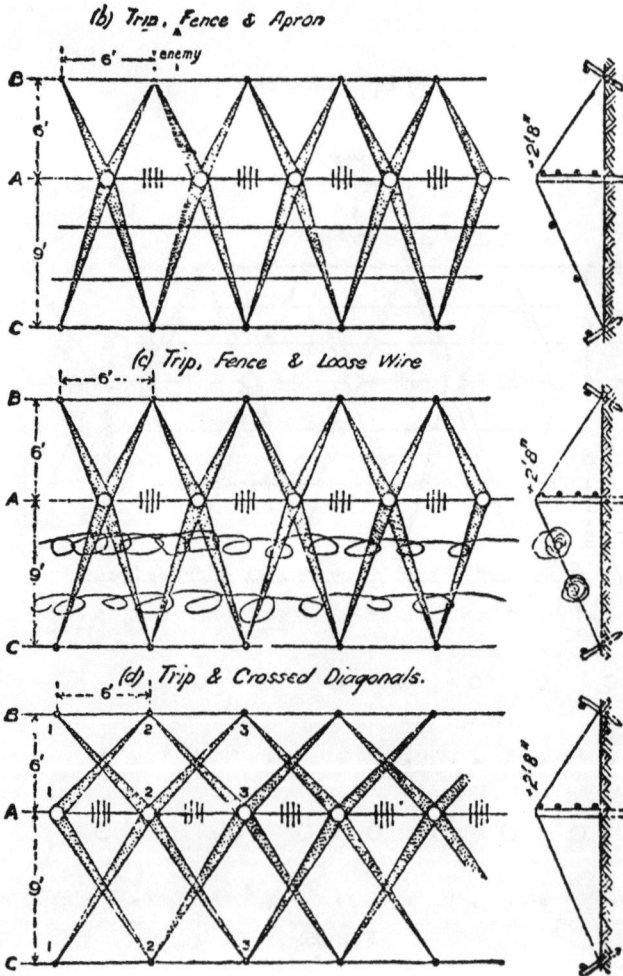

FIG. 26.

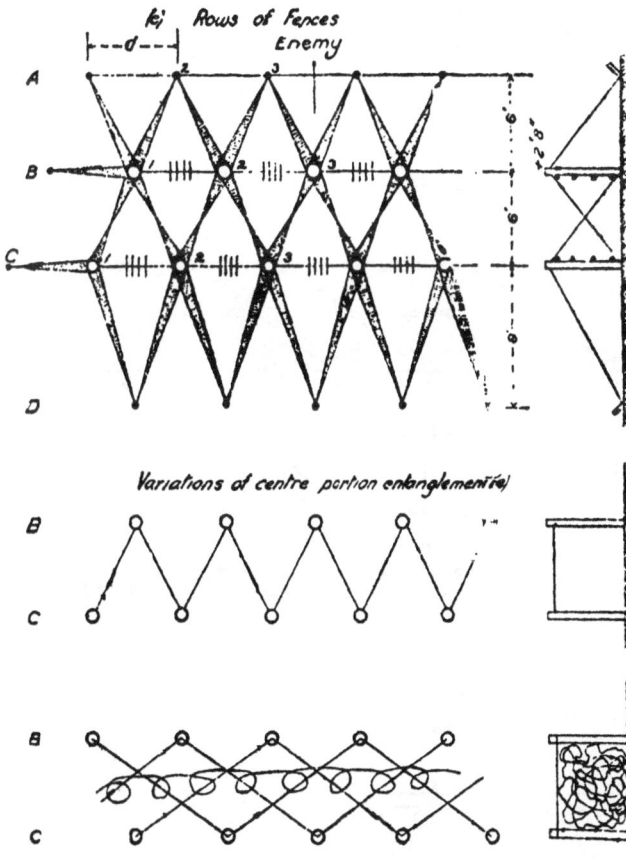

FIG. 27.

Variation of Entanglement (e): Posts opposite each other

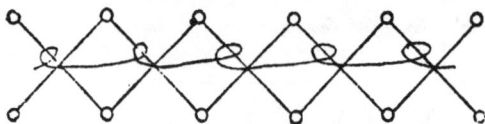

(*f*) Rapid Double Fence.

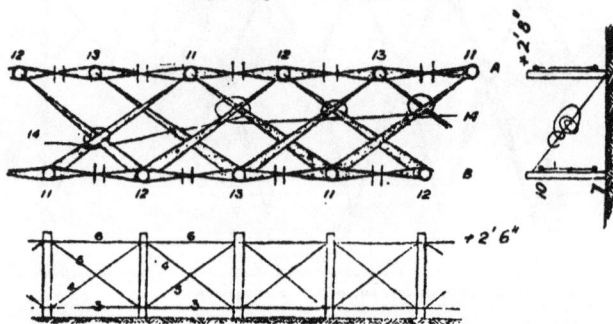

Elevation of A and B.

The numerals show how the Numbers work.
No. 3, 4, 5 and 6 work on Fence A.   No. 7, 8, 9 and 10 on Fence B.

(*g*) Low Wire

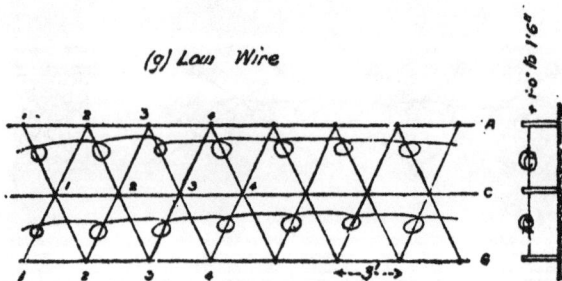

FIG. 28.

(h) Improved Low Wire

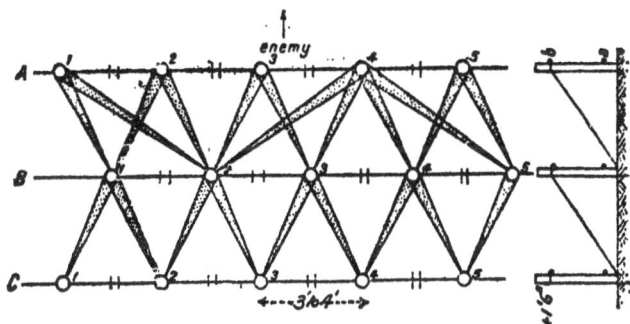

(i) French. Rapid Wire

First method

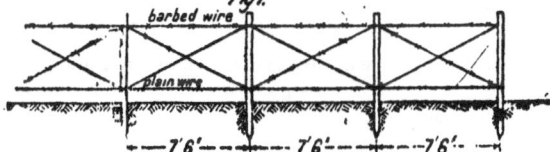

The above fence is made & then rolled up

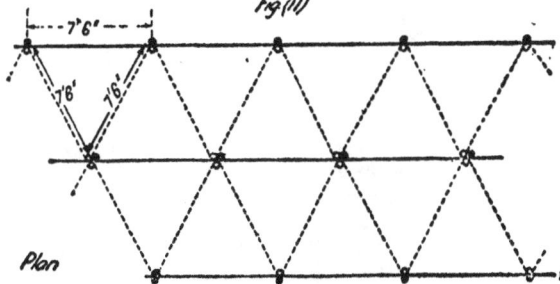

Straight fencing ——— post
zig zag ------- post

The above plan shows how the fences are unrolled & erected

FIG. 29.

(j) FRENCH RAPID WIRE.

Second Method.

Fig. i.	Fig. ii.
Iron Post (angle iron) with wires coiled on.	Wooden Post 3-in. to 4-in. diameter with wires coiled on.

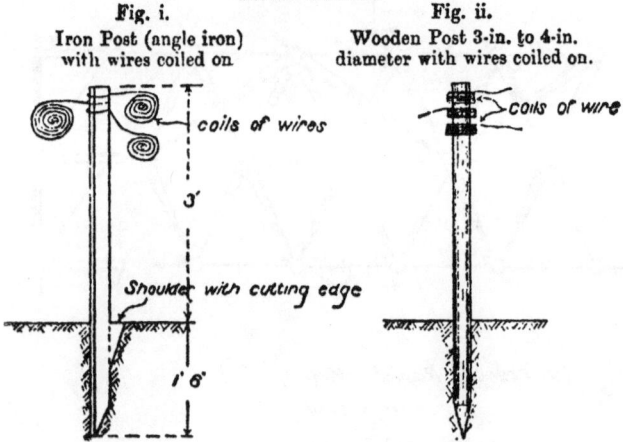

coils of wires

coils of wire

3'

Shoulder with cutting edge

1' 6"

Fig. iii.

The numbers show how the 3 wires on each post are stretched out.

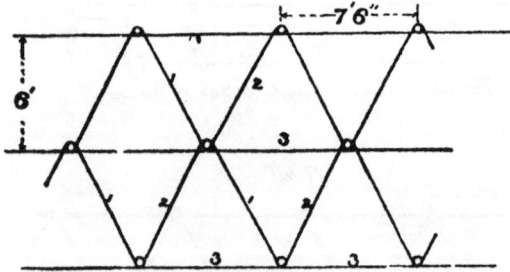

Fig. iv.

Showing arrangement of wire between any pair of posts; the arrows show how the wire is to be uncoiled.

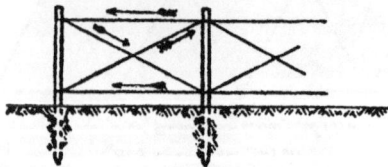

FIG. 29–a.

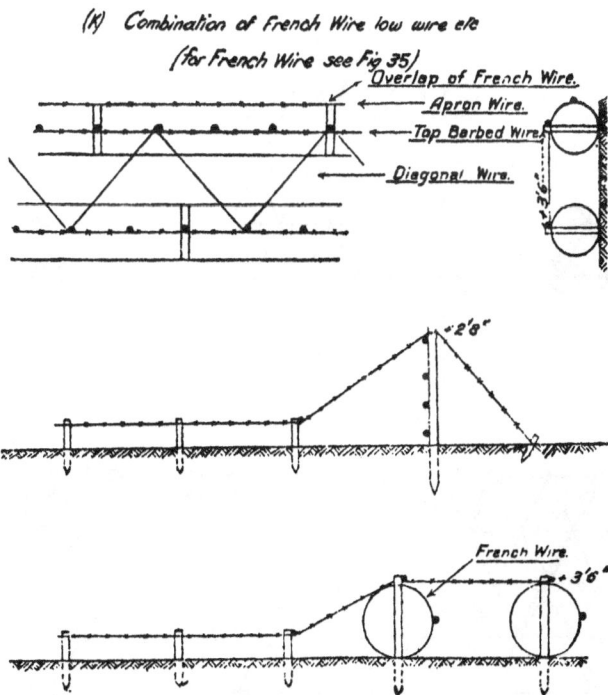

(K) *Combination of French Wire low wire etc*

(for French Wire see Fig 35)

Overlap of French Wire.

Apron Wire.

Top Barbed Wire.

Diagonal Wire.

2'8"

French Wire.

3'6"

FIG. 29b.

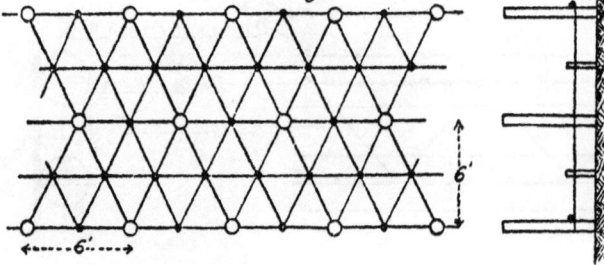

Combination of high & low Wire
(i) First Stage.

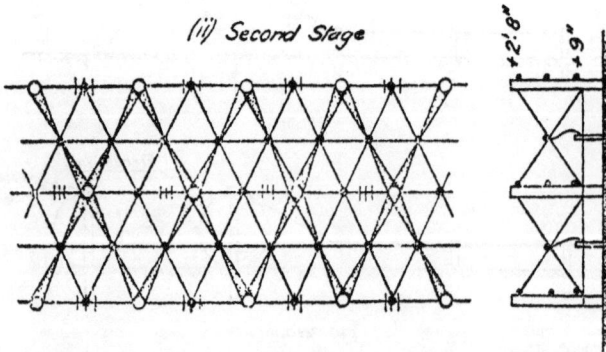

(ii) Second Stage

Fig. 29c.

(m) · Combination of high & Low Wire

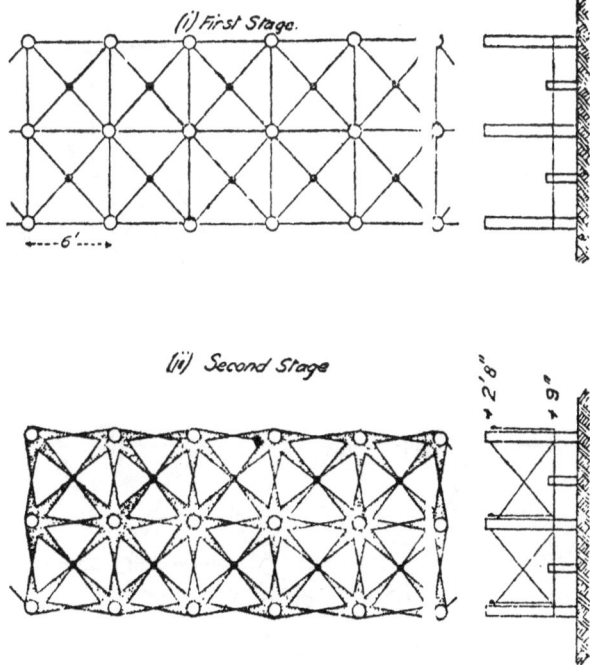

(i) First Stage.

←---6'---→

(ii) Second Stage

FIG. 29d.

(h) Combination of high & low Wire

(i). First Stage

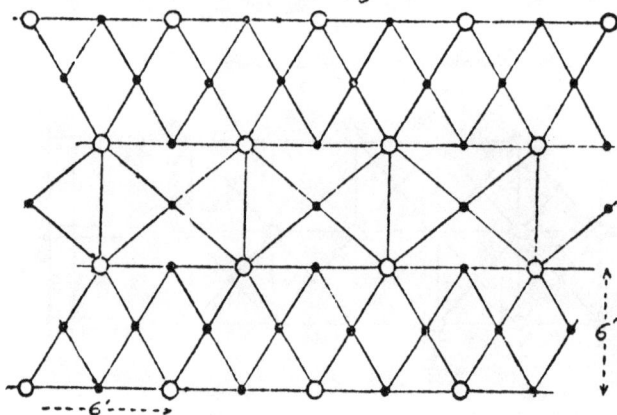

(ii) Second Stage

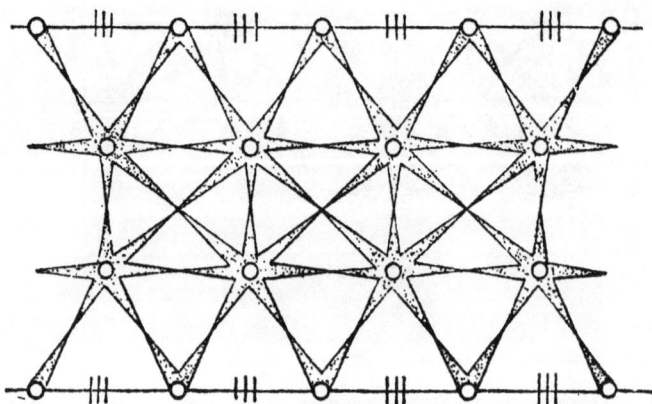

FIG. 29e.

Fig. 30.

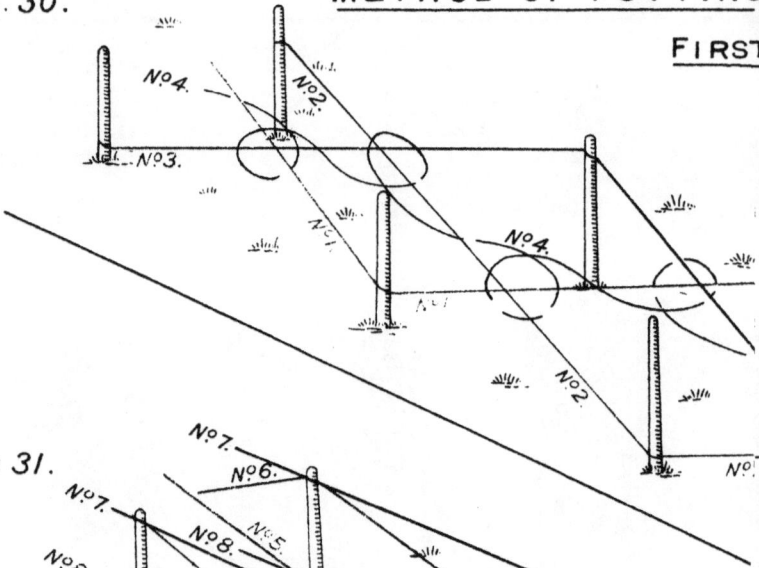

Fig. 31.

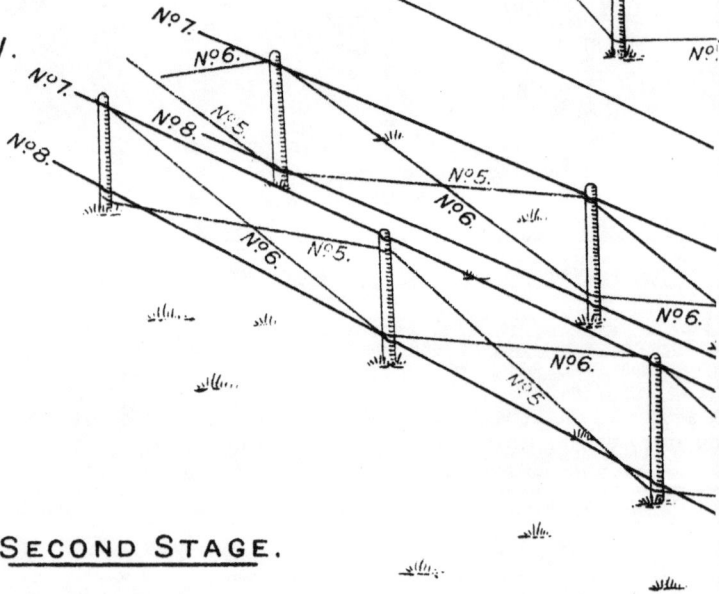

SECOND STAGE.

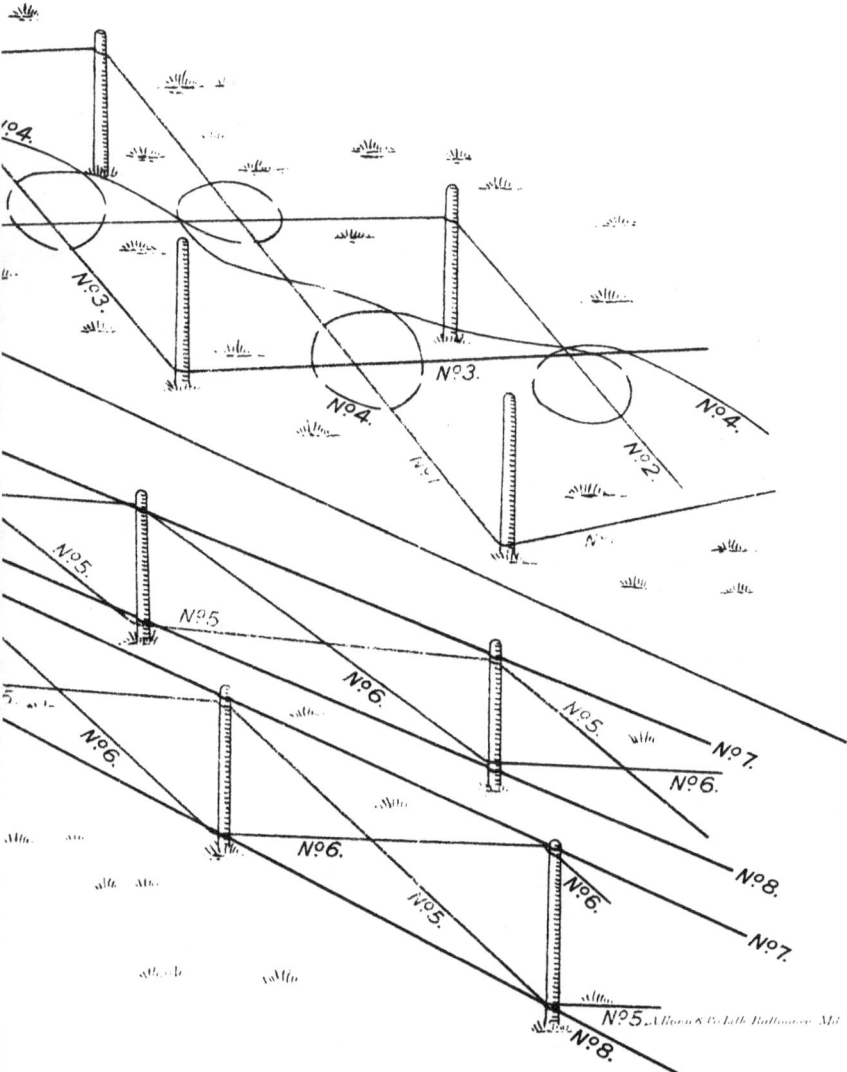

No. 4.
No. 3.
No. 3.
No. 4.
No. 4.
No. 2.

No. 5.
No. 5.
No. 6.
No. 5.
No. 7.
No. 6.
No. 6.
No. 6.
No. 8.
No. 6.
No. 7.
No. 5.
No. 5.
No. 8.

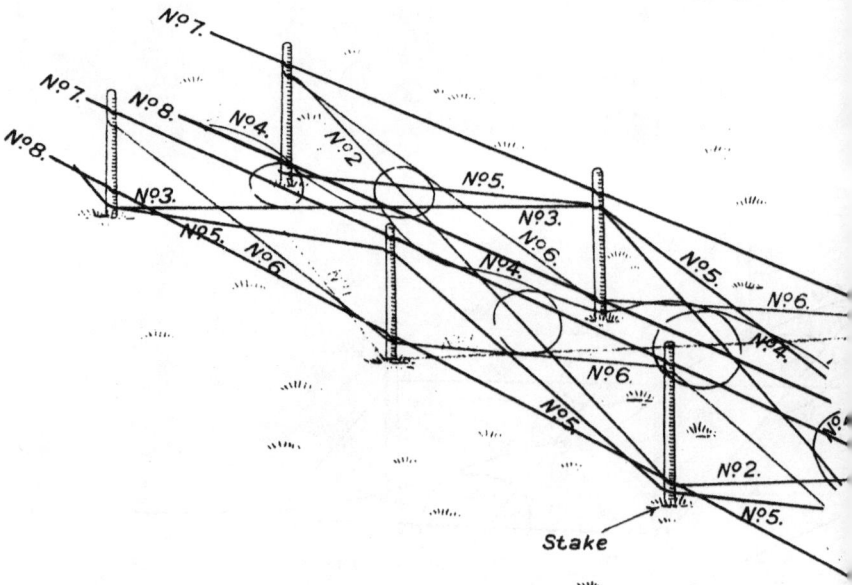

Stake

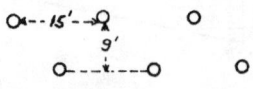

Plan

Setting out of Stakes.

Number of Men Required.

2 to place stakes at proper point (1 each side)
4 „ drive in stakes (2 each side)
2 „ wire Nº 1.
2 „ „ Nº 2.
2 „ „ Nº 3.
2 „ centre wire Nº 4.
4 (2 each side) to wire Nº 5.
4 (" " ") „ „ Nº 6
4 (" " ") „ „ Nº 7
4 (" " ") „ „ Nº 8
30 Total.

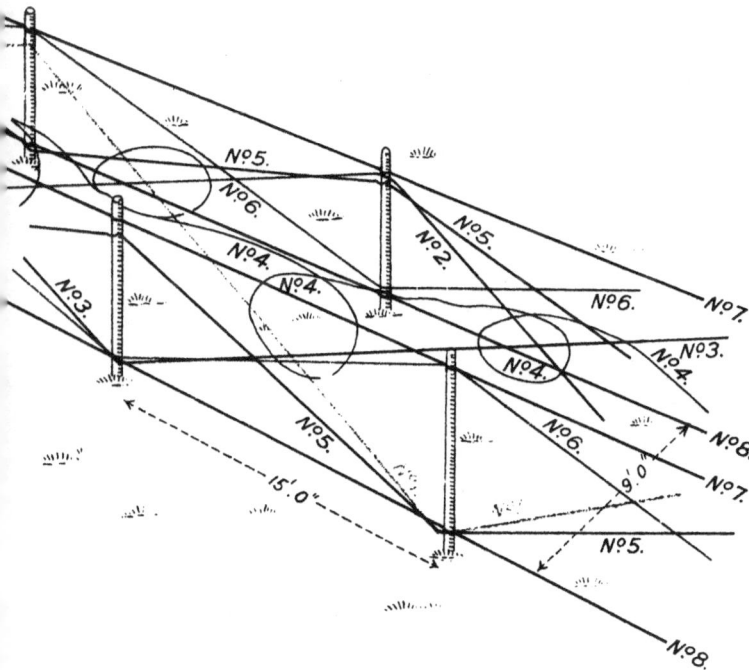

GAPS IN ENTANGLEMENTS.

Not to Scale.

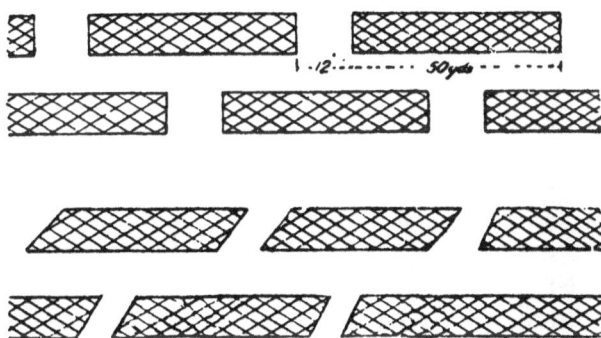

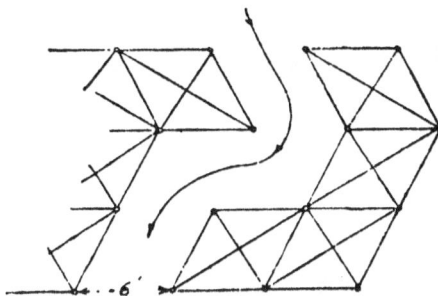

There should be " knife rests " or other obstacles handy for
blocking gaps.

FIG. 33.

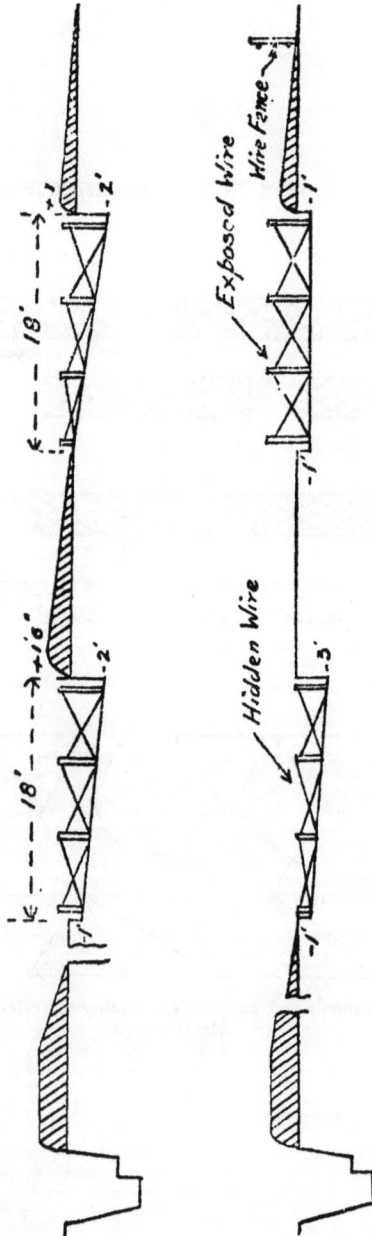

SUNK OR "DUG IN" WIRE ENTANGLEMENTS,
Not to scale.

FIG. 34.

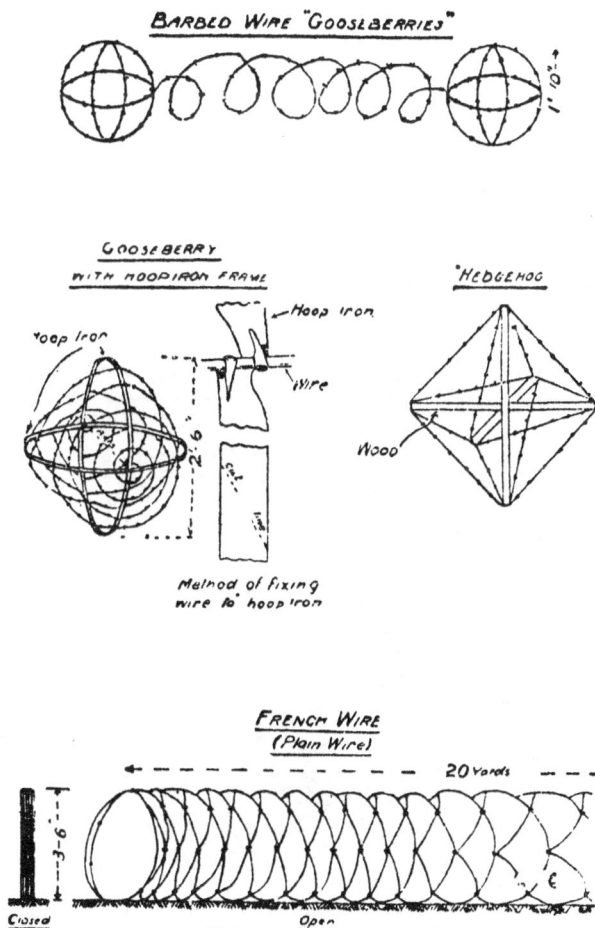

BARBED WIRE "GOOSEBERRIES"

1' 0"

GOOSEBERRY
WITH HOOP IRON FRAME

Hoop Iron

Hoop Iron

Wire

2' 6"

Method of fixing
wire to hoop iron

"HEDGEHOG"

Wood

FRENCH WIRE
(Plain Wire)

20 Yards

3' 6"

Closed   Open

FIG. 35.

Small Knife Rest.

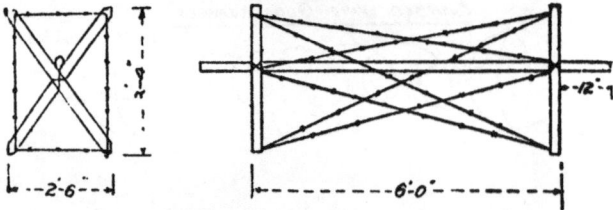

Spiral wire can be added

Large Knife Rest

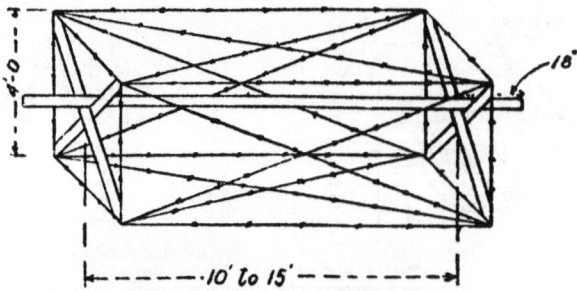

Knife Rest with Iron Framework

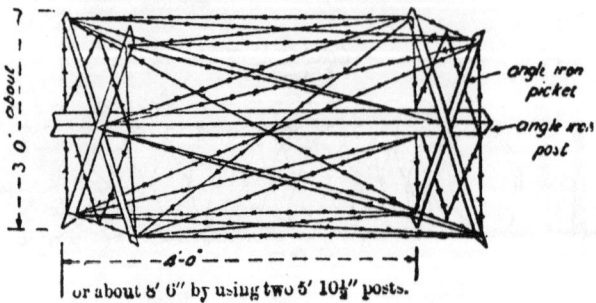

angle iron picket

angle iron post

or about 8′ 6″ by using two 5′ 10½″ posts.

COLLAPSIBLE . PORTABLE ENTANGLEMENT WITH ANGLE IRON ENDS.

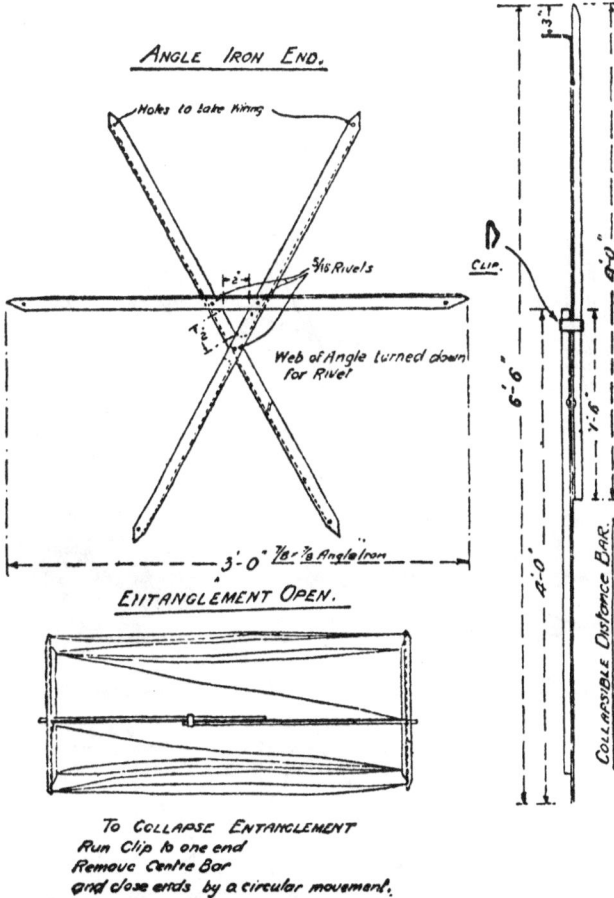

ANGLE IRON END.

Holes to take Wiring

3/16 Rivets

Web of Angle turned down
for Rivet

3'-0" 7/8 or 7/8 Angle Iron

ENTANGLEMENT OPEN.

CLIP.

4'-0"

6'-6"

1'-6"

4'-0"

COLLAPSIBLE DISTANCE BAR.

TO COLLAPSE ENTANGLEMENT
Run Clip to one end
Remove Centre Bar
and close ends by a circular movement.

FIG. 37.

CONCERTINA BARBED WIRE.
(FIRST ARMY PATTERN)

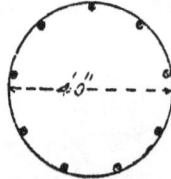

Arrangement of Pickets

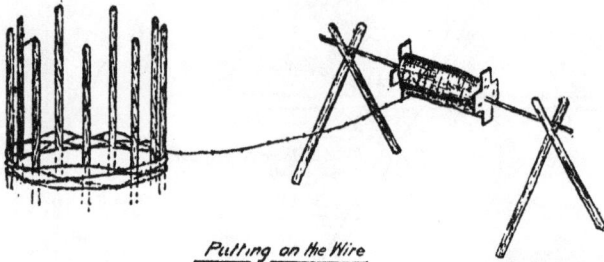

Putting on the Wire

Portion of Web after Binding.

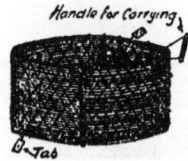

Handle for Carrying

Tab

Finished Coil

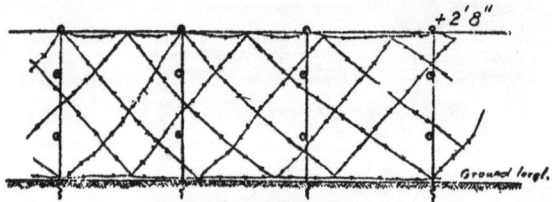

+2'8"

Ground level.

Wire when Erected.

FIG. 38.

SPECIMENS OF SUITABLE COVER AGAINST 5·9-INCH
HOWITZER SHELL FIRE.

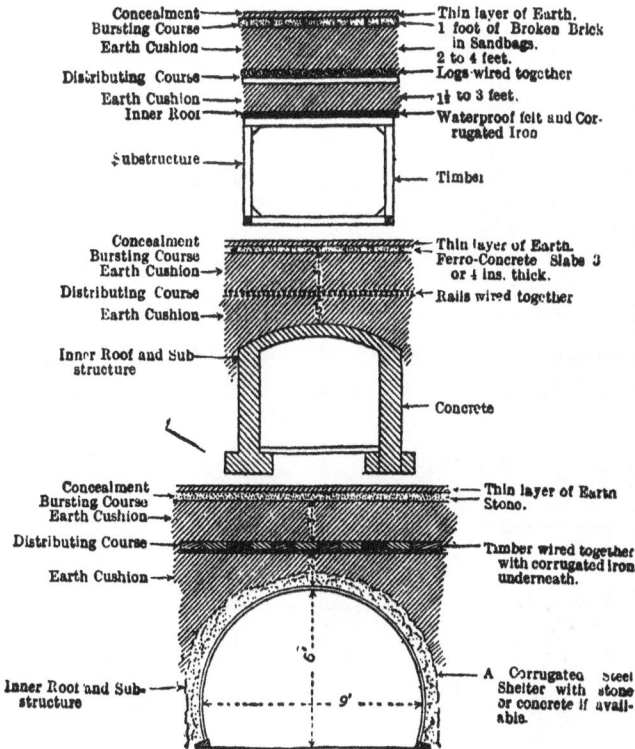

Concealment — Thin layer of Earth.
Bursting Course — 1 foot of Broken Brick in Sandbags.
Earth Cushion — 2 to 4 feet.
Distributing Course — Logs wired together
Earth Cushion — 1½ to 3 feet.
Inner Roof — Waterproof felt and Corrugated Iron
Substructure — Timber

Concealment — Thin layer of Earth.
Bursting Course — Ferro-Concrete Slabs 3 or 4 ins. thick.
Earth Cushion —
Distributing Course — Rails wired together
Earth Cushion —
Inner Roof and Substructure —
Concrete

Concealment — Thin layer of Earth.
Bursting Course — Stone.
Earth Cushion —
Distributing Course — Timber wired together with corrugated iron underneath.
Earth Cushion —
Inner Roof and Substructure — A Corrugated Steel Shelter with stone or concrete if available.

6'
9'

FIG. 39.

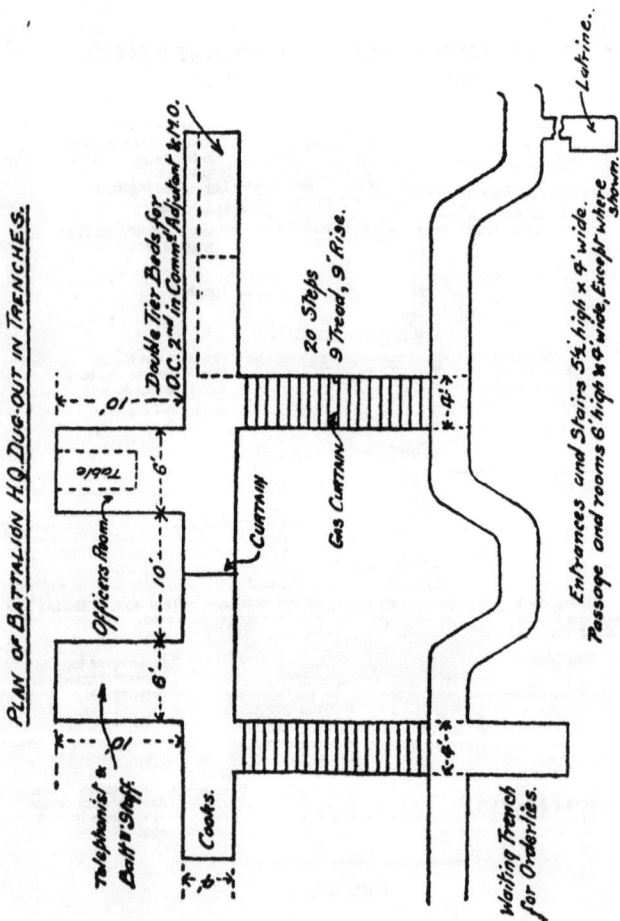

PLAN OF BATTALION H.Q. DUG-OUT IN TRENCHES.

Telephonist & Batt. Staff.

Officers Room.

Table

Double Tier Beds for O.C. 2nd in Comm. Adjutant & M.O.

Cooks.

Curtain

Gas Curtain

20 Steps
9" Tread, 9" Rise.

Latrine.

Entrances and Stairs 5½' high × 4' wide.
Passage and rooms 6' high & 3' wide, Except where shown.

Waiting Trench
for Orderlies.

FIG. 40.

TYPICAL DUG-OUT.

Scale 1 in. = 12 ft.

(For Sections see Fig. 62.)

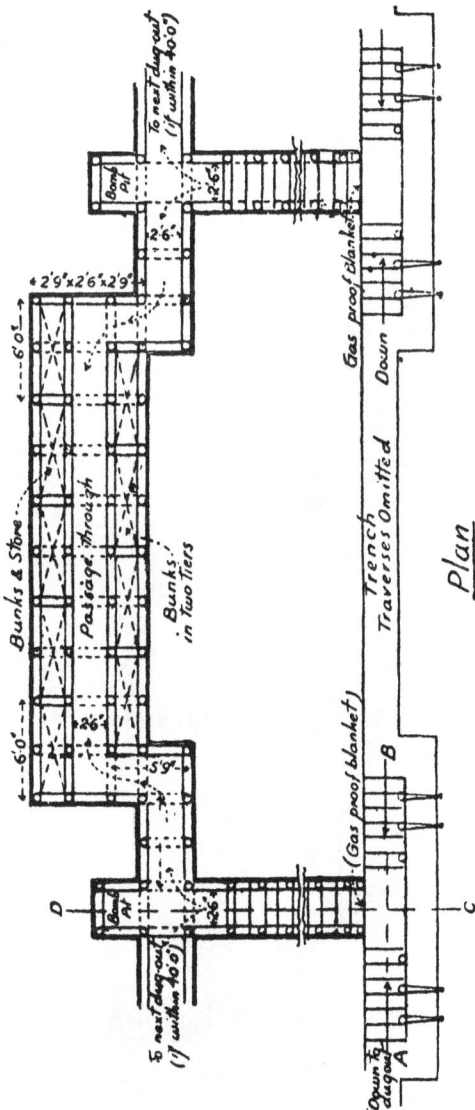

Bomb Pit

To next dugout
(if within 40·0')

2·9"x2·6"x2·9"

6·0'

Bunks & Store

Passage through

Bunks in Two Tiers

6·0'

2·6"

5·9"

Bomb Pit

To next dugout
(if within 40·0')

D

C

B

A

Down to dugout

(Gas proof blanket)

Gas proof blanket

Down

Trench Traverses Omitted

Plan

In certain localities a shaft exit from the rear may be usefully adopted.

FIG. 41.

TYPICAL DUG-OUT.

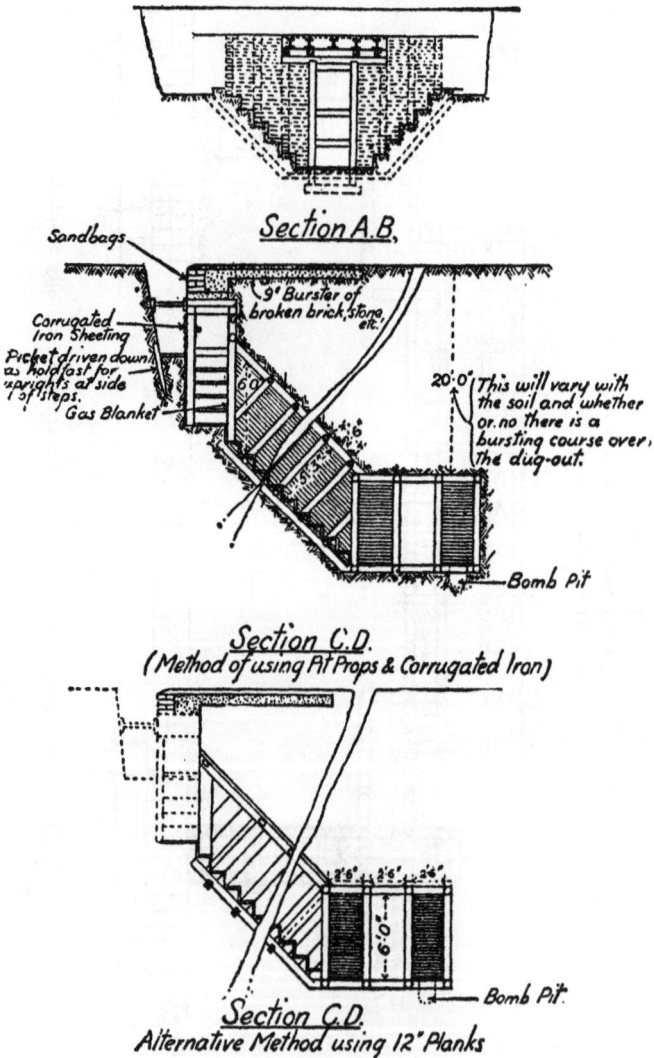

Section A.B.

Sandbags.

9" Burster of broken brick, stone, etc.

Corrugated Iron Sheeting

Picket driven down as holdfast for uprights at side of steps.

Gas Blanket

6'0"

4' 6"

20' 0" This will vary with the soil and whether or no there is a bursting course over the dug-out.

Bomb Pit.

Section C.D.
(Method of using Pit Props & Corrugated Iron)

Bomb Pit.

Section C.D.
Alternative Method using 12" Planks

FIG. 42.

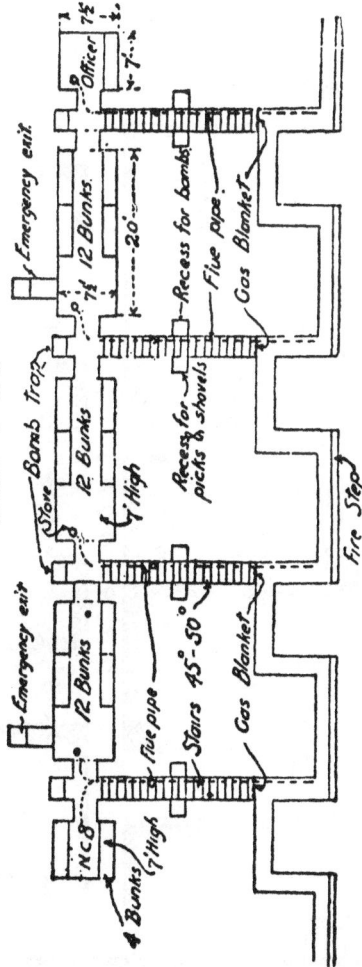

FIG. 43.

DEEP DUG-OUTS. EXAMPLE OF THE LATEST PRACTICE.

CHAMBERS DIRECTLY ON CORRIDOR ON ALTERNATE SIDES (96 MEN).

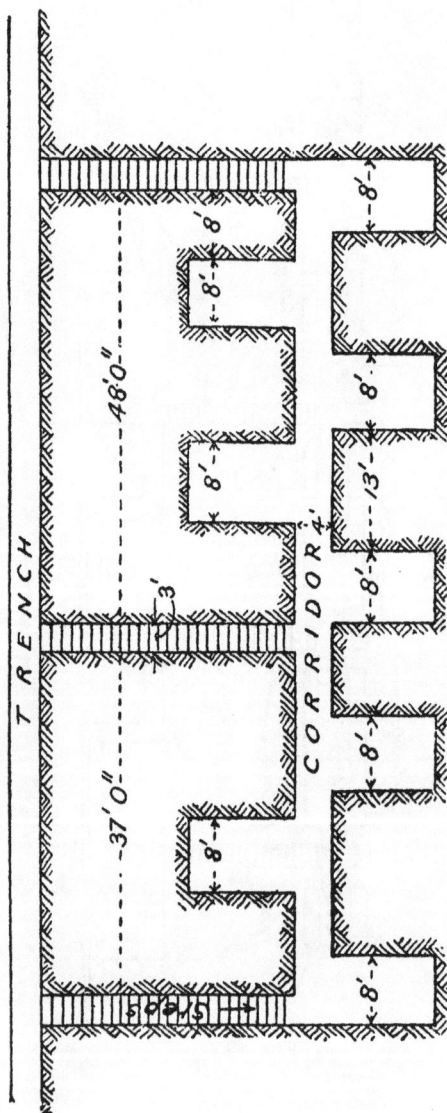

Scale 1 in. = 20 ft.

FIG. 44.

NOTE.—In no case should any side of a pillar have a less width than 12 feet, or a pillar of chalk less than 8 feet. 9 feet being the length of the 5 inch × 3 inch R. S. J., which is an article of store, chambers are usually made of such a width that they can be used for the top sills of the frames.

DEEP DUG-OUT NEAR FRONT LINE, WITH EMERGENCY EXITS TO TRENCH IN REAR.

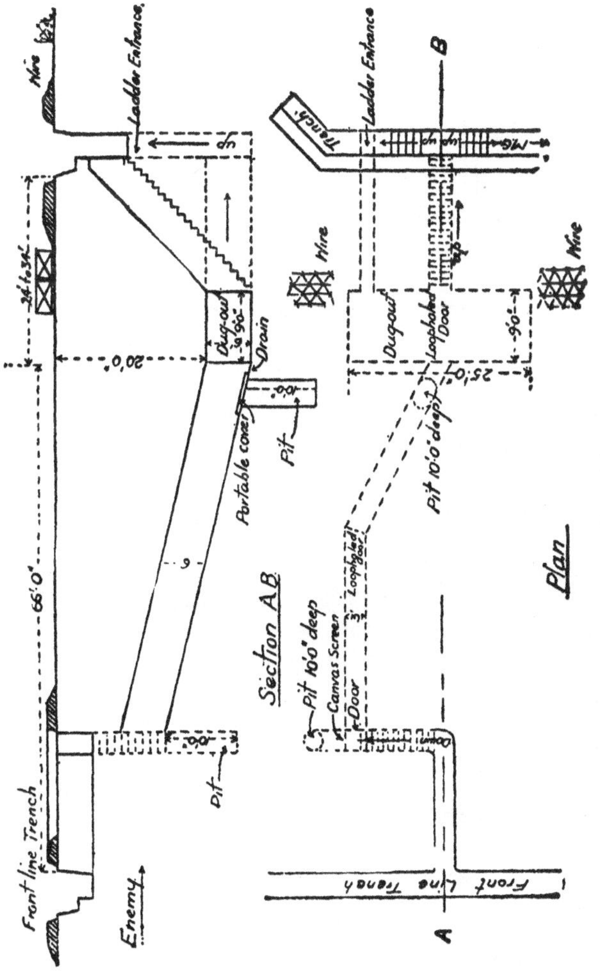

Section AB

Plan

FIG. 64.

FIG. 45.

TYPES OF
SMALL DUG-OUT FRAMES.

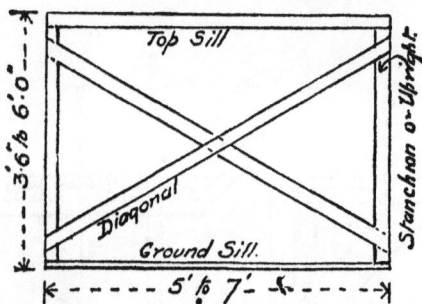

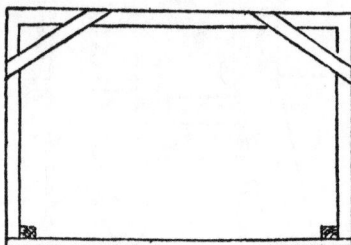

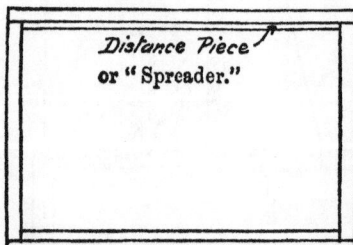

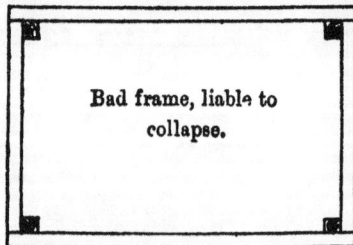

Fig. 46.

TYPES OF
SMALL DUGOUT FRAMES.

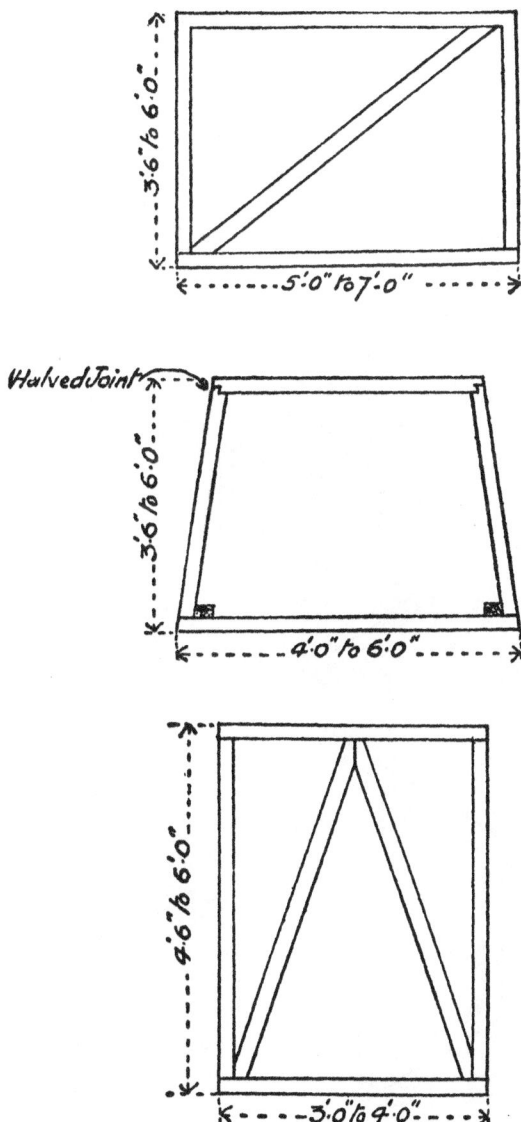

Fig. 47.

TYPES OF
LARGE DUG OUT FRAMES.

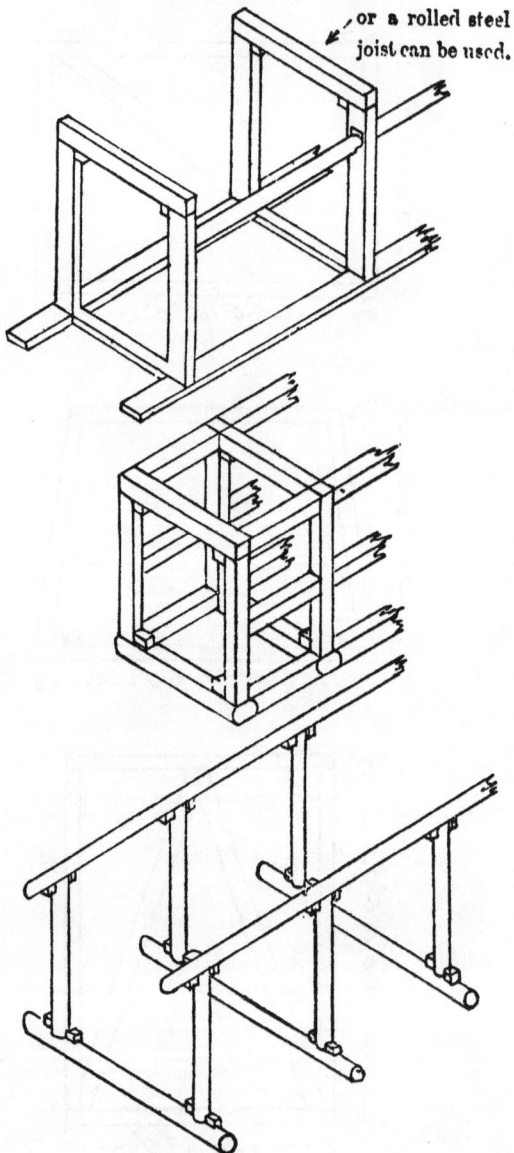

or a rolled steel
joist can be used.

FIG. 48.

Corrugated Steel "Elephant" Shelter (English Pattern)

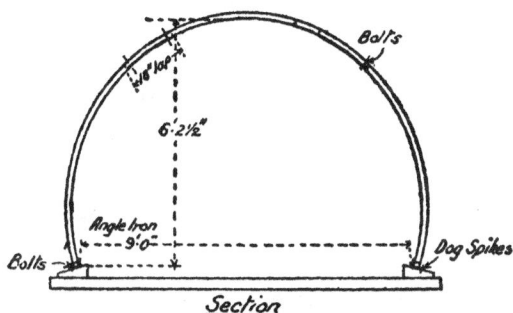

Bolts

6·2½"

Angle Iron
9'·0"

Bolts

Dog Spikes

Section

Each arch is made up of 3 seven foot Corrugated Steel sheets
2ft.3¾ins. wide, bolted together. Ten arches make a shelter 17ft.4.ins
long. Each arch overlaps the next 8¼ins, and is bolted to it.

Corrugated Steel "Elephant" Shelter (French Pattern)

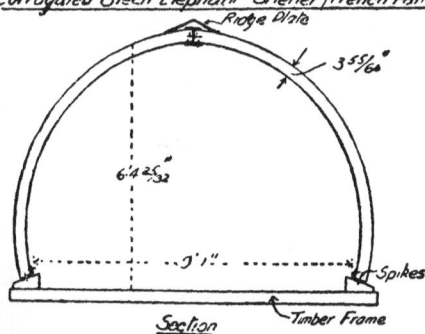

Ridge Plate

3⁵⁵⁄₆₄"

6·4²⁵⁄₃₂"

9'1"

Spikes

Timber Frame

Section

Each arch is made up of two Steel sheets, 3ft 1²⁹⁄₃₂ins wide, locked
together by clamps. Six arches make a shelter 19 feet long. There are three
corrugations 3⁵⁵⁄₆₄ins deep in each sheet, The arches overlap slightly
Scale ¼ in =1ft

FIG. 49.

SMALL CORRUGATED STEEL SHELTER.

(Baby Elephant.)

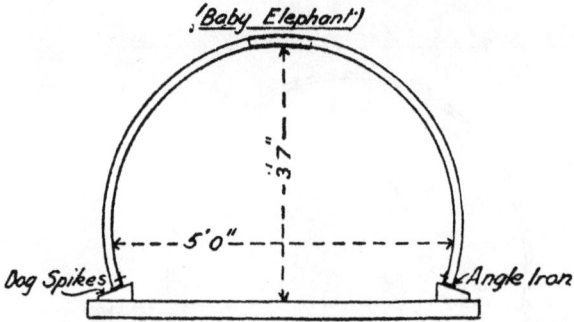

Section

Each arch is made up of two corrugated steel sheets, 2 ft. 3 ins. wide, bolted together. Eight arches form a shelter 14 ft. long. The arches overlap 7½ ins. and are bolted together.

METHOD OF USING HALF ARCH.

(French Pattern.)

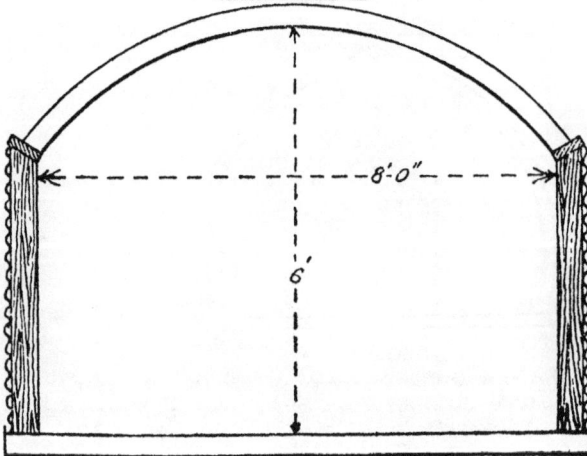

Scale ⅜ in. = 1 ft.

Fig. 50.

MACHINE-GUN EMPLACEMENTS

of minimum dimensions as fixed by Commandant of M.G. School,
November, 1916.

1. EMPLACEMENT WITH OVERHEAD COVER, TO FIRE SITTING.

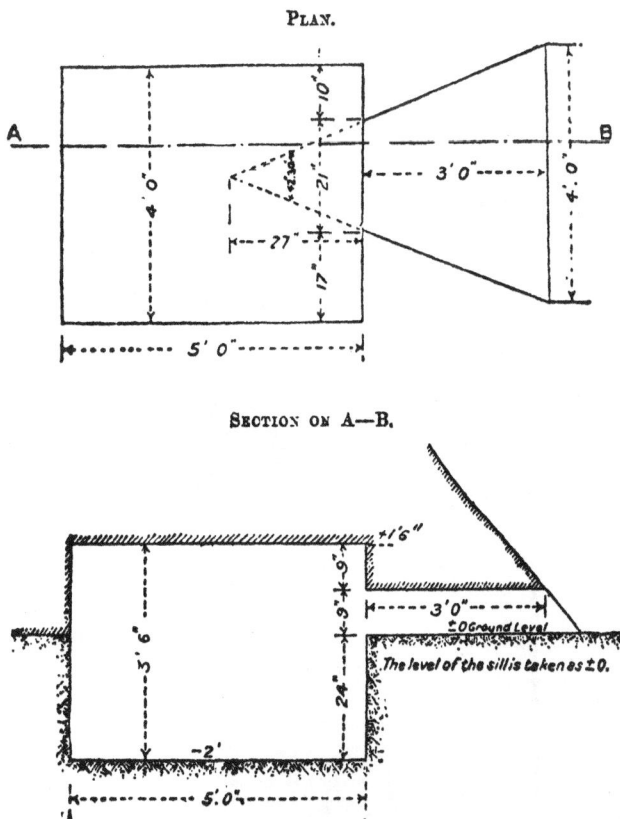

PLAN.

SECTION ON A—B.

FIG. 51.

MACHINE-GUN EMPLACEMENTS

of minimum dimensions as fixed by Commandant of M.G. School,
November, 1916.

2. EMPLACEMENT WITH OVERHEAD COVER, TO FIRE STANDING.

PLAN.

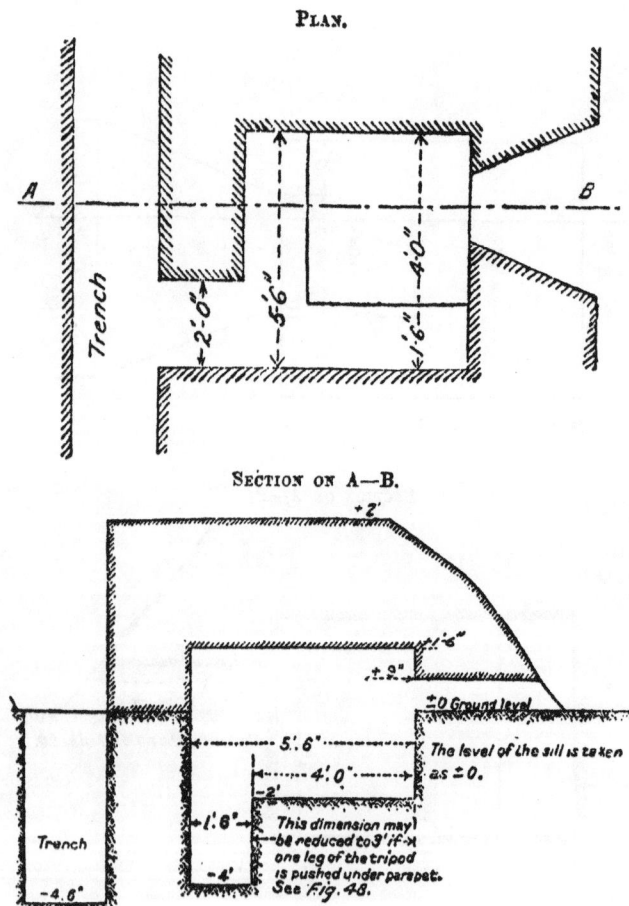

SECTION ON A—B.

FIG. 52.

MACHINE-GUN EMPLACEMENTS

of minimum dimensions as fixed by Commandant of M.G. School,
November, 1916.

8. OPEN EMPLACEMENT, TO FIRE STANDING.

PLAN.

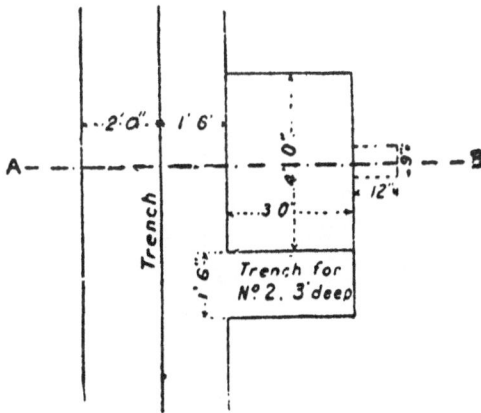

SECTION A—B.

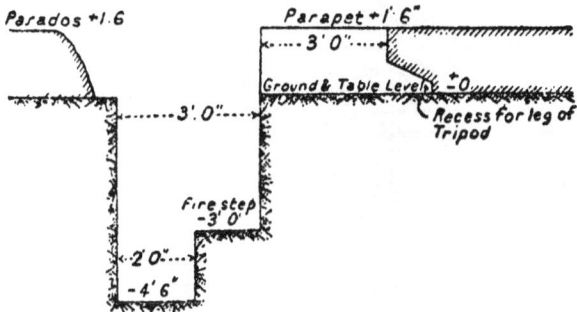

FIG. 53.

MACHINE-GUN EMPLACEMENT.

Scale $\frac{1}{8}'' = 1'$.

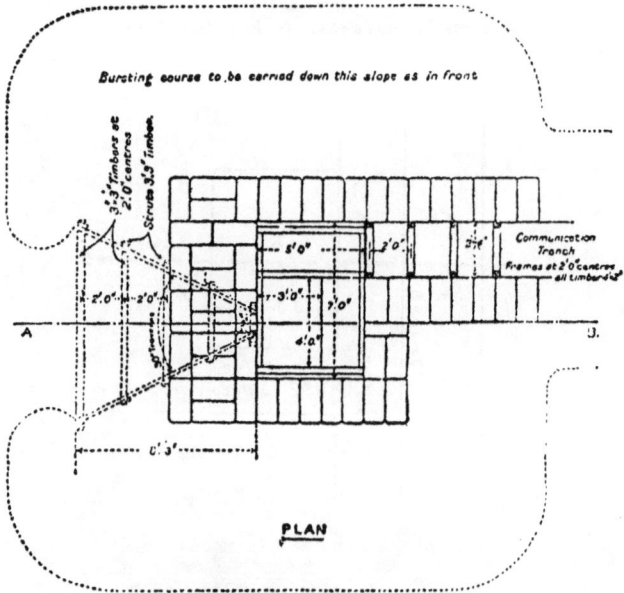

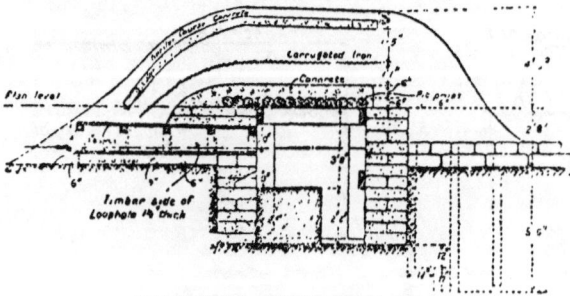

Bursting course to be carried down this slope as in front

PLAN

SECTIONAL ELEVATION ON A—B.

FIG. 54.

CONCRETE MACHINE-GUN EMPLACEMENT.

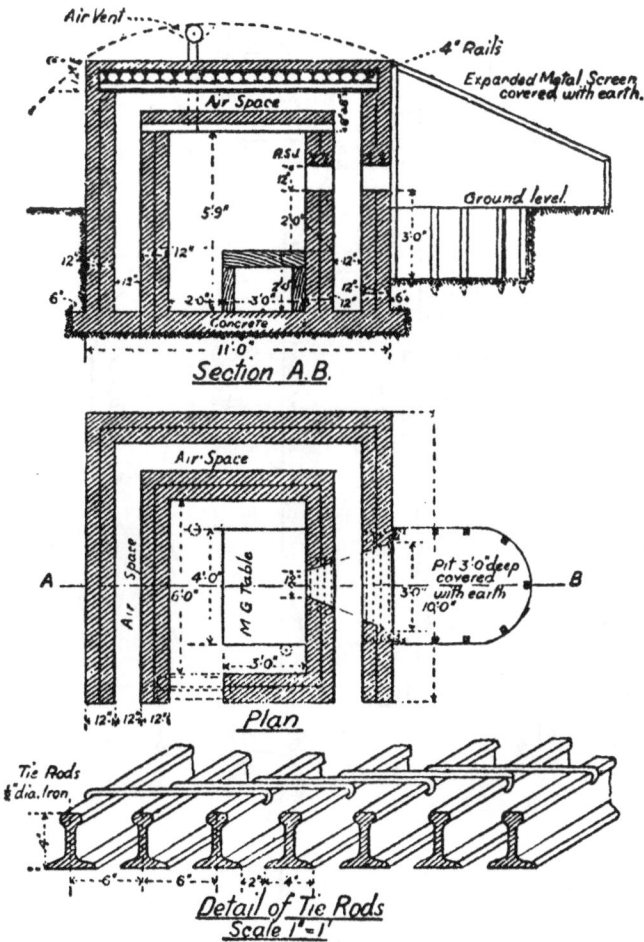

Air Vent

4" Rails

Expanded Metal Screen
covered with earth.

Air Space

R.S.J.

5'9"

Ground level.

12"

12"

12"

6'.

Concrete

11'0"

Section A.B.

Air Space

Air Space

M G Table

A   4'0"

Pit 3'0" deep
covered with earth
10'0"   B

6'0"

3'0"

12" 12" 12"

Plan

Tie Rods
⅝" dia. Iron

6"   6"   2"

Detail of Tie Rods
Scale 1"=1'

FIG. 55.

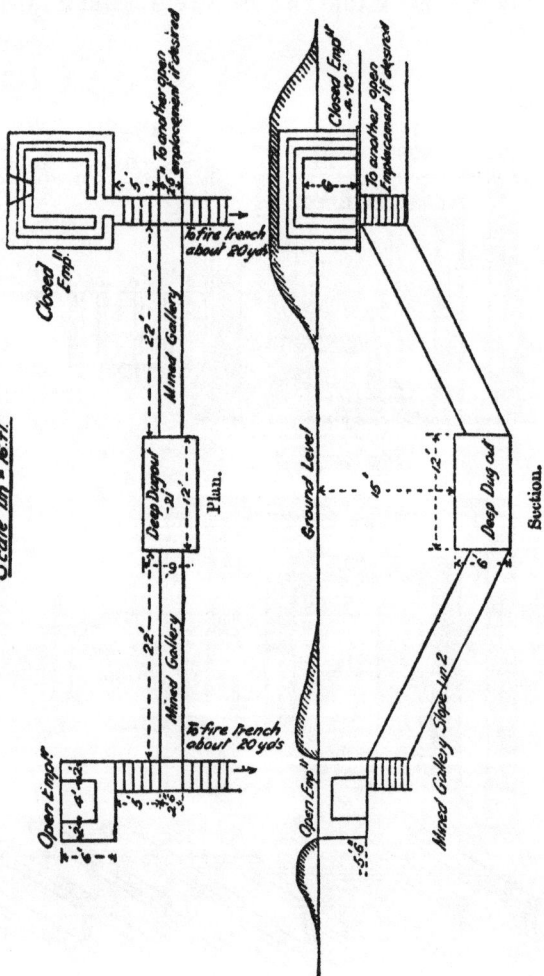

Machine Gun Emplacements
One Open & One Closed
Scale 1in = 16 ft.

Closed Emp.ⁿ

To another open
Emplacement if desired

To fire trench
about 20 yds

Mined Gallery

Deep Dugout

Plan.

Mined Gallery

To fire trench
about 20 yds

Open Emp.ⁿ

Closed Emp.ⁿ

To another open
Emplacement if desired

Ground Level

Deep Dugout

Section.

Open Emp.ⁿ

Mined Gallery Slope 1in 2

Fɪɢ. 56.

MACHINE-GUN EMPLACEMENT IN CELLAR.

Scale $\frac{1}{8\cdot8}'' = 1'$.

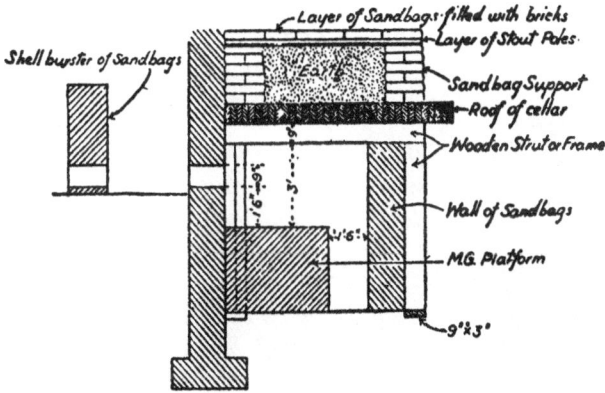

Section

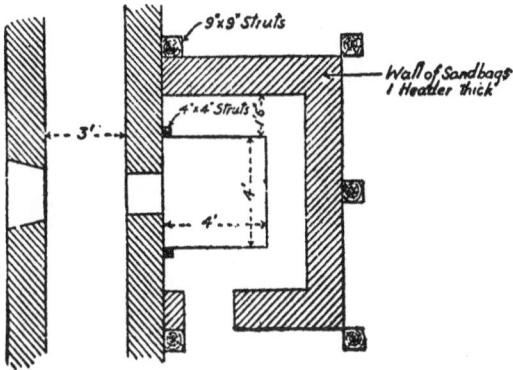

Plan

FIG. 57.

TYPE OF MACHINE GUN EMPLACEMENT WITHOUT PARAPET FOR USE
BEHIND FRONT LINE.

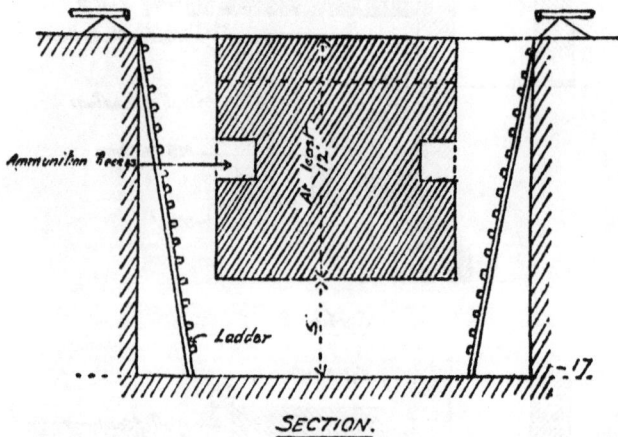

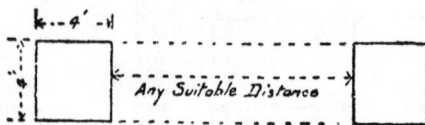

Ammunition Recess

Ladder

SECTION.

PLAN

SHAFTS 40×40 NO PARAPET.
CHAMBER 50×40.
Fig. 58.

LATRINES.

(i) *Deep Latrine off Communication Trench.*

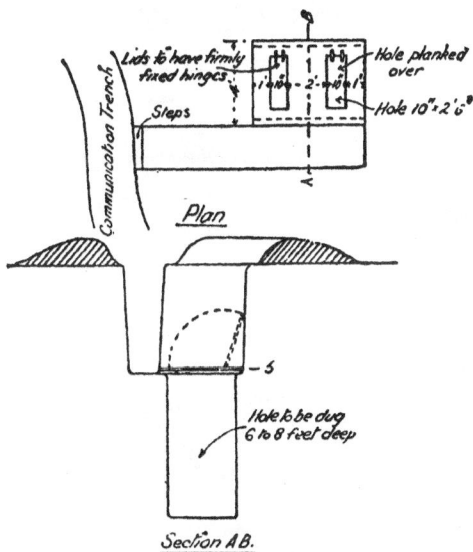

Plan

Section A.B.

(ii) Latrine recess off Trench.

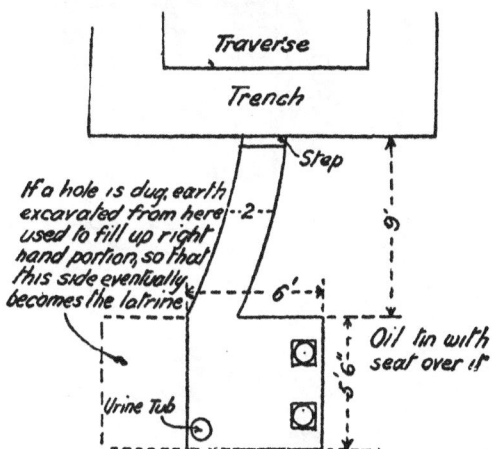

Scale 1″ = 8′.

Fig. 59.

DRAINAGE OF TRENCHES.

Removal of Collected Water.

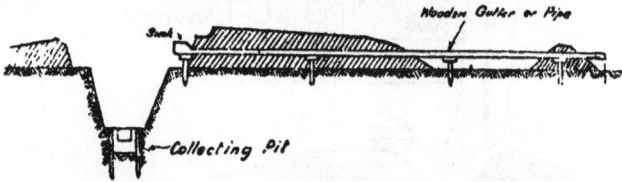

Drainage of Surface Water

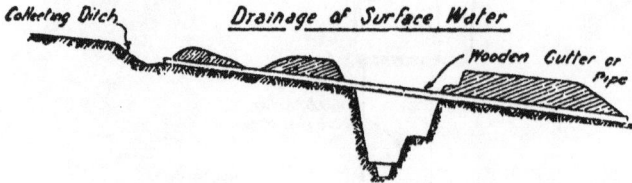

Pumping

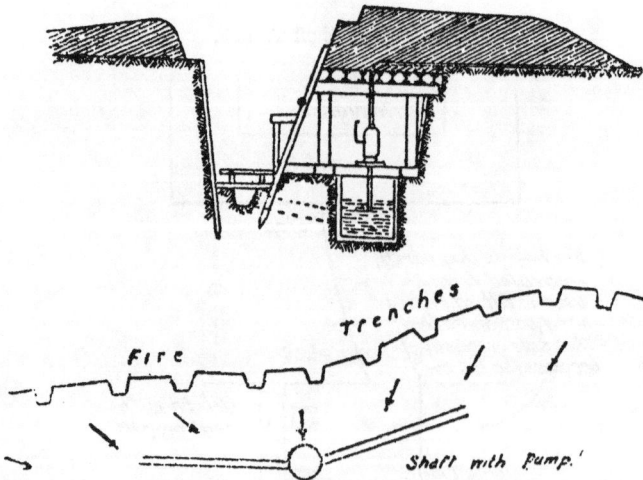

FIG. 60.

DRAINAGE SUMP.

(I.) OFF TRENCH.

Sump hole
Reveted

Slope of ground

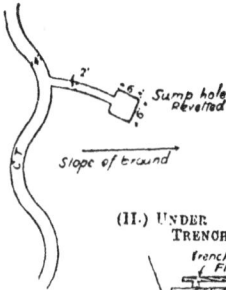

Revetment of Sump hole

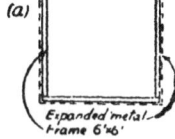

(a)

Expanded metal
frame 6'×6'

(II.) UNDER TRENCH.

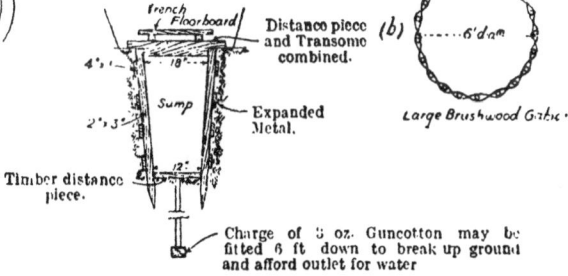

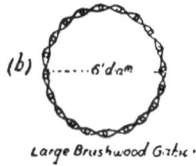

Trench Floorboard

Distance piece
and Transome
combined.

(b)

6' d'am

Large Brushwood Gabic·

Sump

Expanded
Metal.

Timber distance
piece.

Charge of 5 oz. Guncotton may be
fitted 6 ft down to break up ground
and afford outlet for water

Fig. 61.

Sump put under Fire Step.

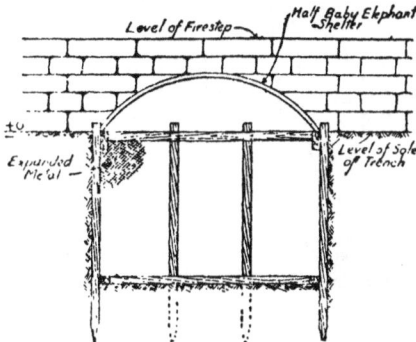

Level of Firestep

Half Baby Elephant
Shelter

Expanded
Metal

Level of Sole
of Trench

Fig. 62.

IMPROVISED WATER LEVEL.

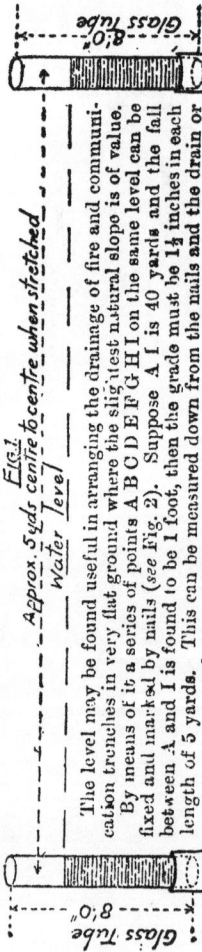

Fig.1

Approx. 5 yds centre to centre when stretched

Water level

Glass Tube 8'0"

Glass Tube 8'0"

The level may be found useful in arranging the drainage of fire and communication trenches in very flat ground where the slightest natural slope is of value.

By means of it a series of points A B C D E F G H I on the same level can be fixed and marked by nails (see Fig. 2). Suppose A I is 40 yards and the fall between A and I is found to be 1 foot, then the grade must be 1½ inches in each length of 5 yards. This can be measured down from the nails and the drain or bottom of the trench arranged accordingly.

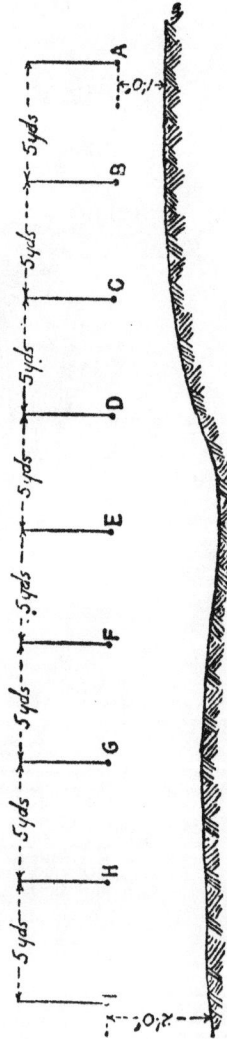

FIG.2.

A B C D E F G H I

5 yds 5 yds 5 yds 5 yds 5 yds 5 yds 5 yds 5 yds

1'0"   2'0"

FIG. 63.

AMMUNITION RECESS WITH AIR SPACE.

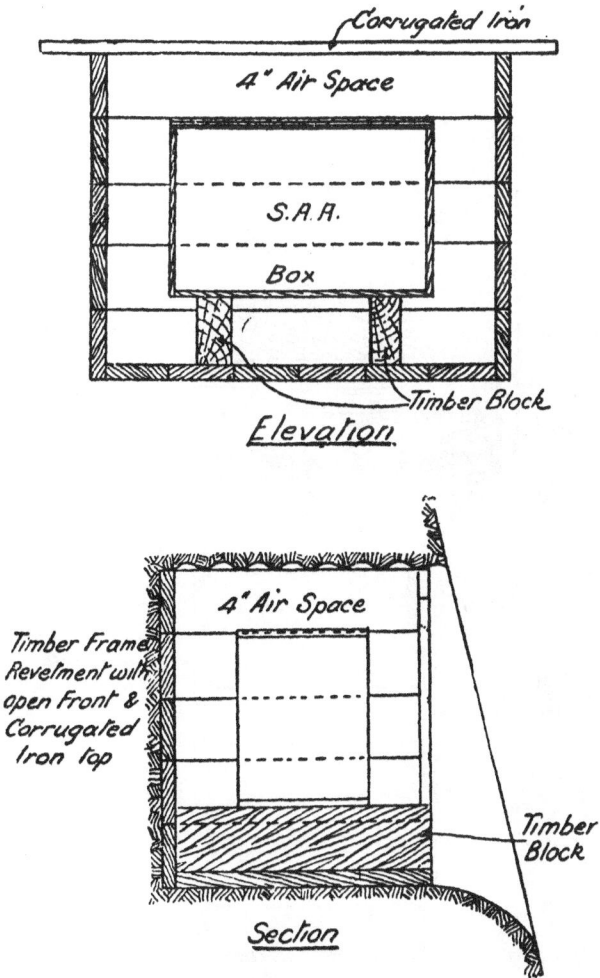

Corrugated Iron

4" Air Space

S.A.A.

Box

Timber Block

Elevation

4" Air Space

Timber Frame Revetment with open Front & Corrugated Iron Top

Timber Block

Section

Fig. 64.

BOMB RECESS.

To hold
{ 16 Boxes of Mills Grenades.
  4 Buckets of Mills Grenades
  100 Rifle Grenades.

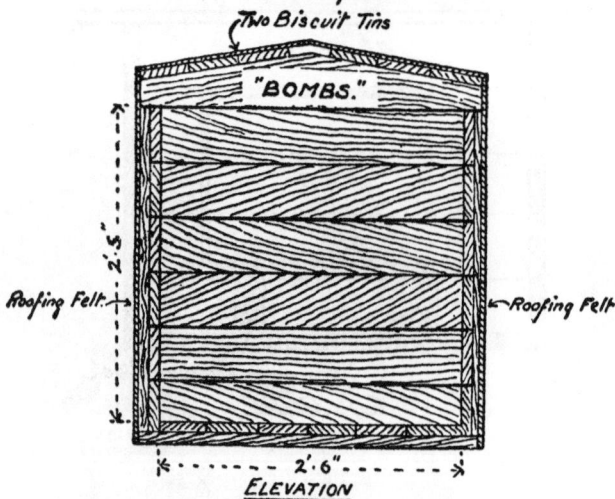

Two Biscuit Tins

"BOMBS."

2'.5"

Roofing Felt.

Roofing Felt

2'.6"

ELEVATION

Two Biscuit Tins

Air Space

Roofing Felt.

All made of
5"x1" Planking.

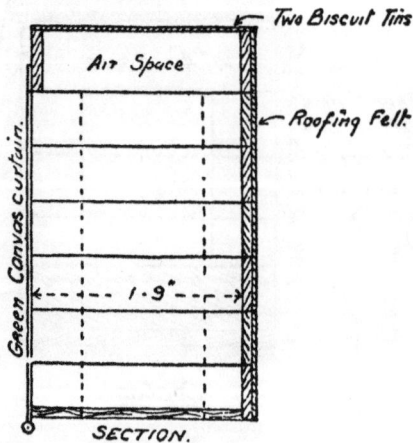

Green Canvas curtain.

1.9"

SECTION.
Fig. 65.

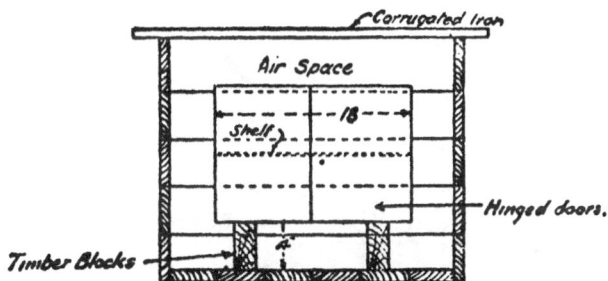

BOMB STORE

To be placed in side of Communication Trench close to Front Line.

Corrugated Iron

Air Space

Shelf

18

Hinged doors.

Timber Blocks

4"

ELEVATION.

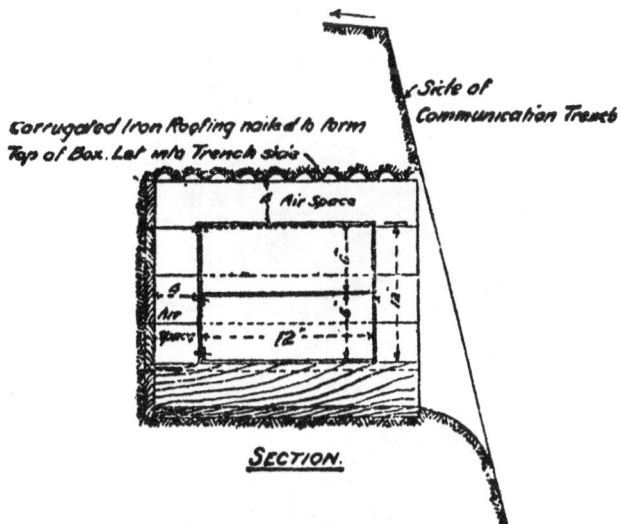

Side of Communication Trench

Corrugated Iron Roofing nailed to form Top of Box. Let into Trench side.

Air Space

6

9
Air
Space

12

SECTION.

Timber Frame Revetment Box Shape.

FIG. 66.

LOOK-OUT BOX WITH SLIDING PLATES
to enable position of spy-hole to be varied.

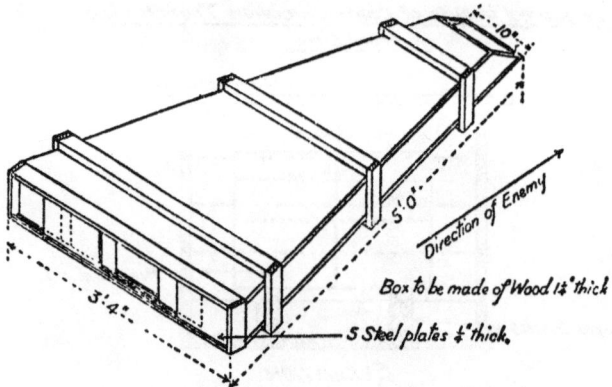

Direction of Enemy

5'0"

3'4"

10"

Box to be made of Wood 1½" thick

5 Steel plates ¼" thick.

MOCK SANDBAG LOOPHOLE MADE OF CEMENT.

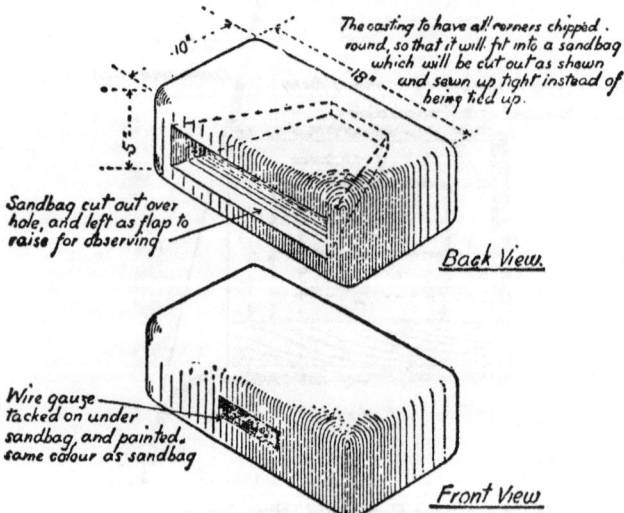

The casting to have all corners chipped round, so that it will fit into a sandbag which will be cut out as shown and sewn up tight instead of being tied up.

10"

18"

5"

Sandbag cut out over hole, and left as flap to raise for observing

<u>Back View.</u>

Wire gauze tacked on under sandbag, and painted same colour as sandbag

<u>Front View</u>

FIG. 67.

SPLINTER AND BULLET PROOF SENTRY POST.

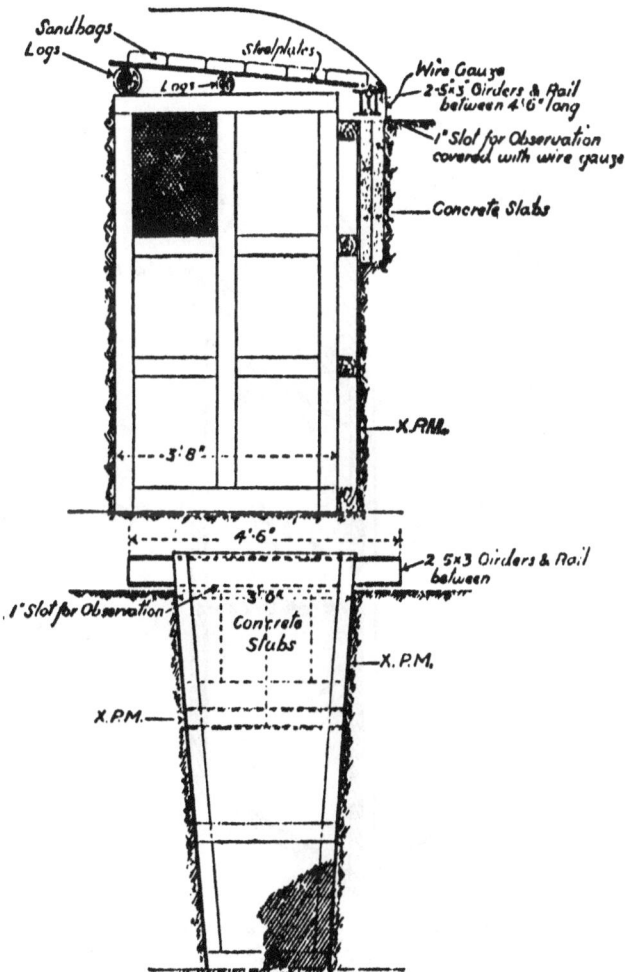

Sandbags
Logs
Logs
steelplates

Wire Gauze
2·5×3ʺ Girders & Rail
between 4ʹ6ʺ long

1ʺ Slot for Observation
covered with wire gauze

Concrete Slabs

X. P.M.

3ʹ 8ʺ

4ʹ 6ʺ

2 5×3ʺ Girders & Rail
between

1ʺ Slot for Observation

3ʹ 0ʺ

Concrete
Slabs

X. P.M.

X. P.M.

This Post can be dug & erected in one night

FIG. 62.

SNIPERS POST.

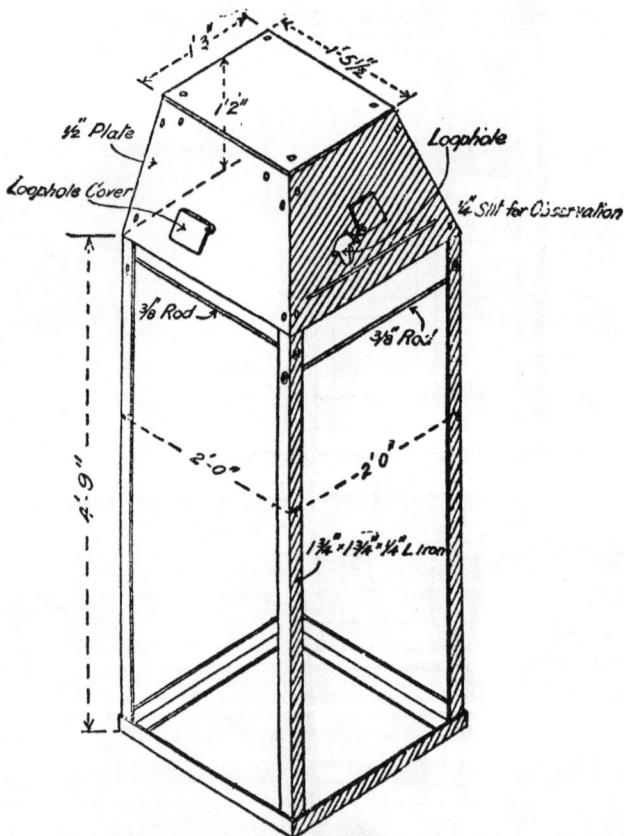

½″ Plate

Loophole Cover

Loophole

¼″ Slit for Observation

1′ 3″

1′ 5½″

2″

⅜″ Rod

⅜″ Rod

4′ 9″

2′ 0″

2′ 0″

1¾″ × 1¾″ × ¼″ L. iron

Made on a framework of 1¾″ angle iron, with 4 loophole shields cut and bolted to it.

FIG. 69.

SNIPERS POST.

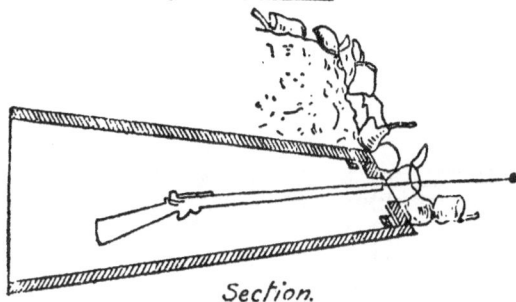

Section.

VIEW FROM FRONT.

As our Front Parapets are covered with tins of all kinds, the tin used to disguise the loophole is very difficult to identify even at 10 yards range.

OBLIQUE LOOPHOLE.

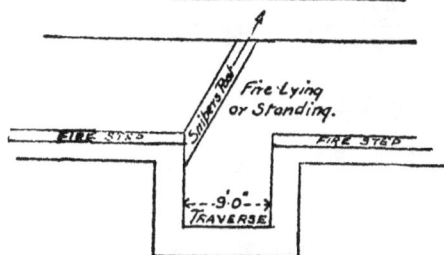

Fire Lying or Standing.

FIRE STEP

FIRE STEP

9.0"
TRAVERSE

Plenty of Dummy Loopholes should be provided.

FIG. 70

ARMOURED SENTRY BOX.

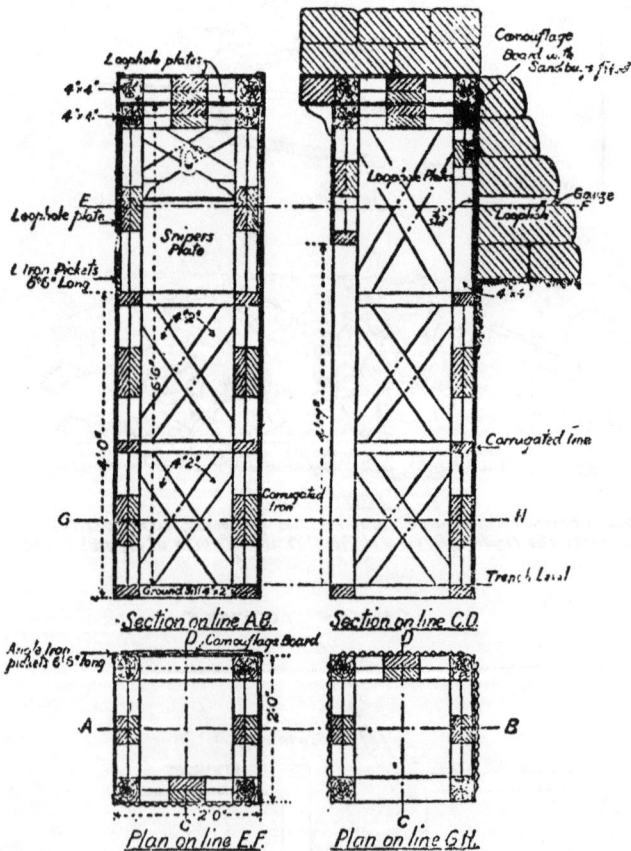

FIG. 71.

METHOD OF UTILIZING ENEMY TRENCHES.
(a) FIRE STEP BEHIND PARAPET OR PARADOS.

The dotted lines show the work to be done.

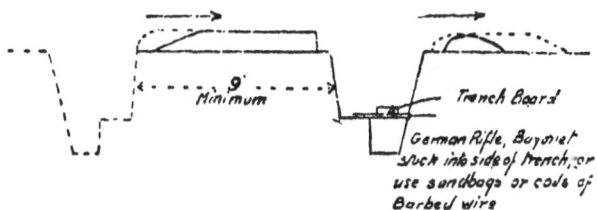

9'
Minimum

Trench Board

German Rifle, Bayonet
stuck into side of trench, or
use sandbags or coils of
Barbed wire

(b) FIRE STEP BEHIND PARADOS

Recesses not nearer
than 3 feet.

(c) BREASTWORK.

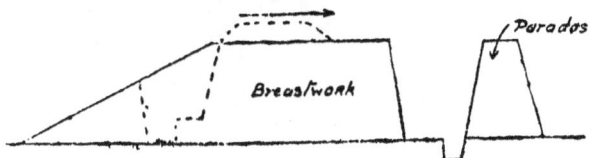

Parados

Breastwork

FIG. 72.

DEFENCE OF CRATERS.

(a) Near Lip Defended.

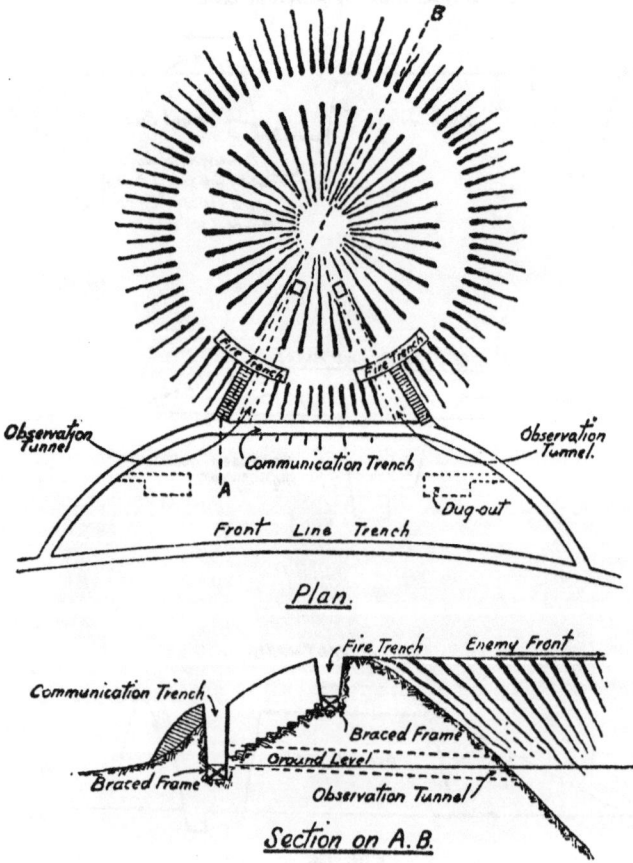

Plan.

Section on A.B.

Fig. 73.

DEFENCE OF CRATERS.

(b) Far Lip Defended.

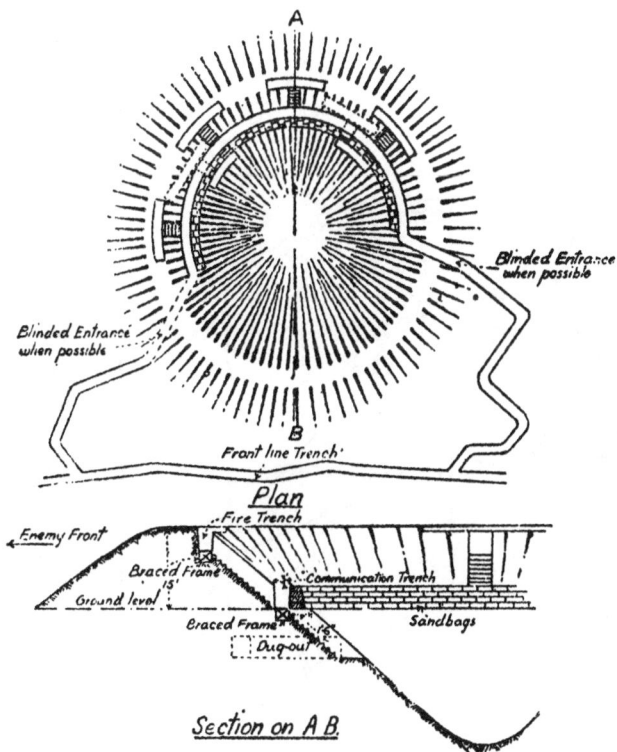

Plan

Section on A B.

Fig. 74.

DEFENCE OF CRATERS.

Showing proposed system of defence by bombing trenches behind craters when no field of fire can be obtained.

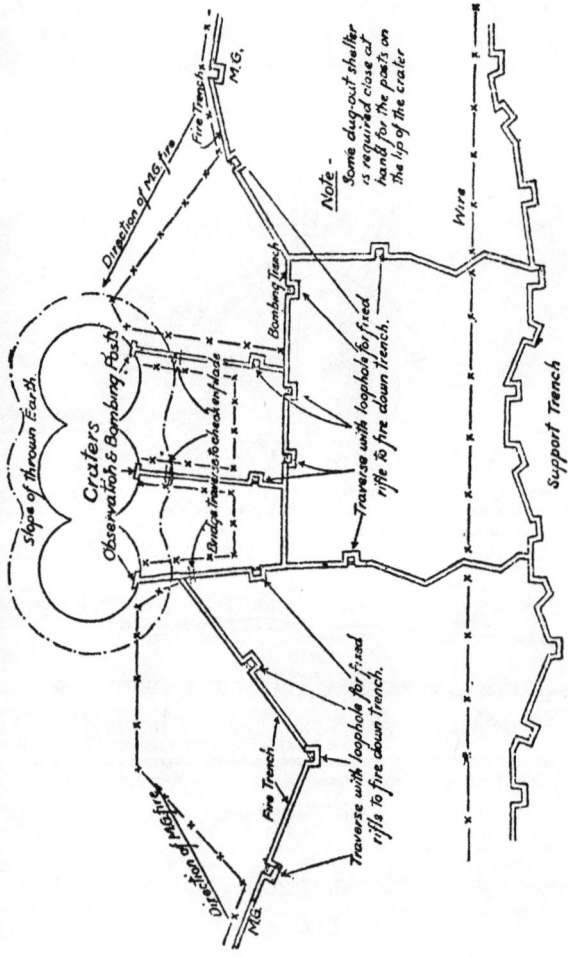

Fig. 75.

DEFENCE OF SHELL CRATERS.

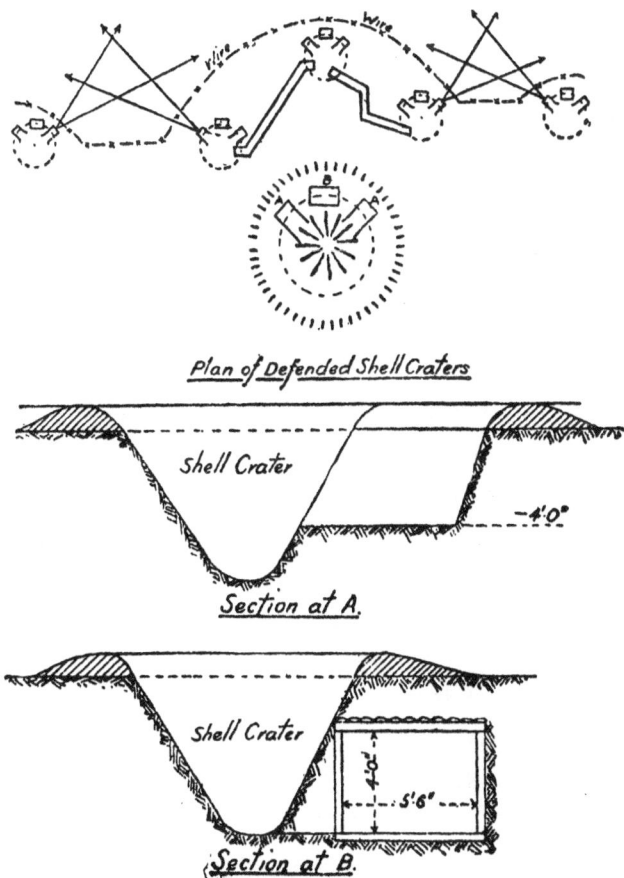

Plan of Defended Shell Craters

Section at A.

Section at B.

FIG. 76.

INDEX.

A.

B.

C.

D.

E.

S.S. 196.]

40/W.O./6971.

[O.B./1008.

DIAGRAMS OF FIELD DEFENCES.

Issued by the General Staff.

CONTENTS.

Note on the general principles of field defences and on the field-works shown in the Plates.

LIST OF PLATES.

GENERAL PRINCIPLES.

It is unnecessary to explain at length the value of Field Defences ; in general they allow of economy of force. Well-sited and well-constructed fire trenches enable a few men to hold on to large areas, because not only is the garrison less exposed to casualties than in the open, but its weakness is concealed ; good communication trenches and subways facilitate supervision, communication and supply ; obstacles delay the enemy and by deflecting him in selected directions give time and opportunity to deal with him, and attempts at their destruction give warning of attack ; shelters and dug-outs, weather-proof, splinter-proof, and shell-proof add in their various degrees to the comfort and security of the men ; camouflage conceals works and the defence organization from air observation, dummy works mislead the enemy and cause him to make wrong dispositions, to overlook the real targets, and to waste ammunition.

There is no mystery about field fortification. It requires no more than tactical skill on the part of the officers who site the works, willing arms, and a knowledge of a few simple types of trenches, wire entanglements, revetments, and shelters on the part of the troops who have to make the works. In siting defences, as in any tactical disposition, every advantage must be taken of the ground ; once occupied, every opportunity must be taken to improve and strengthen them.

No defences in themselves can withstand a determined attack for more than a certain time ; all that can be expected of them is that they will enable a few men to delay the enemy until sufficient forces can be aroused, or brought up from support, reserve, or rest, to deal with the situation. Defences, therefore, must be arranged in depth.

The general principles of the organization of defences will be found in S.S. 210 " The Division in Defence " (supplement to S.S. 135).

The organization will consist of several zones of defence disposed in depth, each of which will take the form of a network of posts and localities sited for mutual support in considerable depth. These posts and localities are to be connected for purposes of command and covered communication on certain portions of the front.

The system should be initiated and developed on the following general lines :—

(a) A line of observation covering the immediate foreground, consisting of a series of groups of shell-holes or of defended posts, gradually improved by the occupants.

Each post should be wired completely round and be suitable for all-round defence. A continuous line of wire should be erected along the entire front, *this being the first work to be done.*

(b) About 150 to 300 yards in rear of (a) will be positions in support, consisting of a series of traversed works for Lewis guns and infantry posts ; continuous wire should be erected along the entire front.

This system is of great importance and follows the wire of (a) above in order of urgency. Its *rôle* is to prevent the penetration of the zone by raiding parties or minor surprise attacks.

(B 15226) Wt. w. 1701—PP3914 1M 9/20 H & S Ltd. G.S. 28

Behind will come the " main defensive system," consisting of defended localities and posts, organized in depth, with the ground between them swept by flanking and cross fire to break up the enemy's attack and provide supporting points for our own counter-attacks.

This system will of course vary with the ground, but might consist of :—

(c) A system of carefully selected M.G. positions skilfully sited in the area between the general line (b) and system (d) below. Rays of M.G. tactical wire should be erected in conjunction with this.

(d) A series of traversed works or localities, constructed and wired on the same principles as (b) and some 1,000 to 4,000 yards in rear of it.

(e) In rear of (d), a system of defended localities completely wired in for all-round defence, with a further system of M.G. positions with tactical wire in the area between (d) and (e). Such localities as are likely to be easily identified must be merged in a trench system. The wire must never be erected in masses, which only attract attention and reveal the position of the posts and localities they protect ; it must be spread in depth and be of irregular trace. (See below ; wire entanglements.)

Where it is decided to connect up posts the following is the order of priority of work in the construction of communication trenches :—

(i) Between (b) and (d).
(ii)   ,,   (a) and (b).
(iii)   ,,   (d) and (e).

The trace of the connecting trenches should be as irregular as is compatible with economy in labour, and any tendency to parallel trenches must be avoided.

Revetment of trenches should be dispensed with when possible by giving berms on both sides, and digging the trenches at easy slopes ; but it must be remembered that some clays will not stand permanently at any slope at all, unless revetted, and that trenches dug in winter require more revetting than those dug in summer.

The construction of deep dug-outs depends upon the skilled labour available. First in order of importance are Brigade and Battalion Headquarters ; then come dug-outs for the M.G. positions in the area between (b) and (d) above, vide (c). Next come dug-outs for troops and for M.G. positions in the area between (d) and (e). Deep dug-outs should never be constructed in advance of the support trench of the front line system. O.P.s, buried cable communications, and deep dug-outs for R.A. are a separate consideration, the two former being constructed as required, and the last by the R.A. with R.E. assistance.

The position of the line of observation will usually, where choice is possible, be chosen so as to cover ground from which good ground artillery observation can be secured. In general, freedom from enemy observation and good communication to the rear should be sought for ; a long field of fire is not of importance : the ground is best swept by cross fire from machine and Lewis guns.

If it is essential to deny the occupation of a hill to the enemy, this result can only be secured by holding the forward slope of the hill in considerable depth, not less than 400 to 500 yards. (See Plate 17.)

In defended localities, according to their size, one or more lines of defence may be prepared ; but, however many there are, each locality should contain at least one strongly organized point to act as a " keep " should the enemy break in. Thus in the defence of a village which is situated on tactically suitable ground, in addition to trenches outside it, buildings should be prepared, from which the roads through it can be blocked by fire. These should be wired in and provided with dug-outs. Such keeps are invaluable, as they prevent the enemy passing on without taking them, and it is difficult for him to attack them with artillery without withdrawing his men. Thus they make it possible to gain time, which is one of the chief aims and objects of field fortification.

DETAILS.

The *trace*, or pattern on the ground, of trenches may be laid out in various ways, but the general line must not be too straight, nor must the particular type employed be such that it contains long straight lengths (30 ft. is a common limit in fire trenches, *see* Plates 1, 14 and 16) ; this is in order to prevent the enemy from enfilading the trenches should he get into them or to any place within range in prolongation of the line. Moreover, the general line should always be irregular so as to provide plenty of flanking fire. Enfilade of particular portions of a fire trench is prevented by leaving mounds of earth (traverses) projecting into it (*see* Plate 1) or making the trace zig-zag, curved, &c. (*see* Plates 14, 15 and 16). These devices serve also to break up a fire trench into compartments and thus limit the effect of a shell. Traverses under present conditions should not be less than 15 ft. thick at ground level, and may be thicker.

The same principles apply to communication trenches (*see* Plate 4), but traverses are rarely made in them as they considerably increase the distance to be travelled by parties moving up and down, and the angles to be passed add to the difficulty of carrying stores, stretchers, &c. Communication trenches must be provided with passing places ; at intervals exit steps on either side should be made.

The correct way for a communication trench to enter and leave a fire or traffic trench is shown in Plate 8 ; it must not go straight across, for one shell at the junction would block it both ways. Main communication should never be run directly into a post or locality, but should connect with a traffic trench leading into it. Plates 9 and 11 indicate a method of defending a communication trench.

The *section* of a fire trench (*see* Plate 2) must be such as to provide 4 ft. 6 in. of cover where the soldier stands to fire (fire step). How much of this is provided by the trench dug, and how much by the parapet of earth thrown up, will depend on the site and nature of the ground. The parapet should not be less than 4 ft. 6 in. thick, and the top of it must be so sloped that every firer can use his rifle effectively on the front ground line of the wire in front of him, and has as extended field of fire in front of that as the ground permits. Below the fire step is a passage at a lower level with about 7 ft. of cover. Communication trenches (*see* Plate 4) will only have fire steps in certain parts where required for defence.

Both fire and communication trenches must be wide ; narrow deep trenches under present conditions are death traps, as they collapse under bombardment and bury the men in them, unless specially strutted, and this prevents easy movement in them (*see* Plate 5) ; for mere protection a trench just sufficiently wide and deep to conceal a man lying is preferable.

The same general principles apply to the selection and arrangement of shell-holes as defences. (*See* Appendix and Plates 33 and 34.)

Drainage must receive immediate attention even in fine weather if there is no natural fall to carry off water. Sumps (pits) dug a short distance from the trench with a channel leading to them is a simple means of drainage. (*See* Plate 7.) Trenches must not be undercut to make a drainage

3

channel, for this will only cause them to fall in. Sumps should never be provided where drainage to lower ground can be arranged.

Trenches should be *trench-boarded* as soon as possible, as the passage of men up and down them soon cuts up the natural surface, and, except on specially hard ground, the bottom of the trench soon becomes an impassable slough.

The *fire step* must be revetted (that is, have some material placed against it to prevent it from falling down) as soon as possible.

This is best done by the use of planks, hurdles, corrugated iron or brushwood supported by short revetting frames (Plate 3). If these frames are not available, they will have to be replaced by pickets, but this is not such a good arrangement, owing to the difficulty of anchoring them back. They may, however, be strutted apart across the floor of the trench, as shown on Plate 22. The trench boards should then be supported on these struts.

It is not desirable in new trenches to use revetments above the fire step, as they only add to the difficulty of clearing the trench if it is knocked in; the ground is best left at its natural slope. Exception must usually be made in the case of high parapets or breastworks. (*See* Plate 23.) It must not be overlooked that though steep sides may stand when trenches are first cut in fine weather, they rapidly collapse in bad weather, and particularly after a thaw.

For *repairs* of trenches sandbag revetments are suitable; they should, however, be used sparingly, and rarely in new work. The sandbags must be properly built and bonded. (*See* Plate 6, where some of the various wrong ways of using sandbags are shown.) Repairs can easily be carried out without them. If the sides of a trench have fallen in, the first step is to throw back the berm. This can only be done by men working on the top. The next step is to slope the trench from the top at the slope at which it may be expected to stand, and then to remove the earth from the bottom, throwing it well clear of the berm. It is quite useless to remove the earth from the bottom first, and for the men at the bottom of the trench to attempt to work from the bottom upwards. Widening the bottom of a trench without removing the earth well clear of the top, and keeping the sides at a proper slope, is one of the chief causes of the collapse of trenches, and of the useless work which is continuously being done throughout the winter.

Posts usually consist of short lengths of trench, or groups of shell-holes. *Supporting points* are posts designed for a particular purpose. Their trace should be of the simplest form consistent with the proposed strength of garrison, the natural features of the ground and ability to bring fire in all directions. They also may be formed by organizing a group of shell-holes. Both posts and supporting points should, as a rule, be wired all round, and in such a way as not to mark their position clearly on an air photograph.

The erection of *wire entanglements* is dealt with in S.S. 177," Instructions on Wiring." Several belts about 6 yards across, with 30 yards interval between them, are better than one wide belt. The belts should be parallel neither to each other nor to the fire trench. Gaps should be left for the passage of patrols, with " knife rests " or " concertinas " ready to block them; and, where the tactical situation demands, there should be wide ones for the passage of counter-attacks. The belts of wire can be made to overlap and thus cover the gaps. Wire should invariably be sited to conform to the position of the machine and Lewis guns so that these enfilade the front of it. Consequently, the siting of the wire should follow, and not precede the selection of site for machine guns and posts. Care must be taken that their position is not given away by it. Obstacles must not be so close to the parapet that fire directed on them would involve

4

the destruction of trenches and wire simultaneously if the enemy begins wire cutting, or that the trenches can be bombed from outside of the wire,* nor so far off that they cannot be watched. They should be covered, if possible, from ground observation and fire by placing them in hollows or by " digging in " in wide shallow trenches, but it is essential that the ground line of obstacles should be covered by fire. It is impossible to conceal belts of wire from aeroplane observation ; it is sometimes advisable therefore to erect a few simple fences in addition to the ordinary belts of wire in order that the obstacle may come as a surprise to the enemy.

Shelter may be merely weather-proof, or splinter-proof or shell (5·9 in. or heavier) proof. The last may consist of 3 ft. 6 in. to 5 ft. of concrete, or be a mixed roof, as shown on Plate 28. Such cover requires very strong supports, which take engineer skill to make. Splinter-proof cover can easily be erected. It is sufficient to provide 18 to 24 in. of earth lying on planks, corrugated iron, &c., but even the supports of this must be strong and secured from being driven in sideways. (*See* Plates 18, 19 and 20.) It is a mistake to use more than 24 in. of earth in splinter-proof cover, as it merely serves to bury the occupants of a shelter if it is hit by a shell ; nothing less than 18 ft. of hard chalk or 24 ft. of loam or clay is 5·9 in. proof, though probably 5 ft. of chalk with a bursting course of concrete slabs would be effective protection from a single hit.

Illustrations are given (Plates 29 and 30) of *mined dug-outs and subways* for use of Infantry. Water will usually percolate into all forms of dug-outs ; if not kept properly dry by pumping or baling, there is always a danger of their collapsing.

It will often be desirable to conceal the fact that certain works are being constructed ; the place of the excavation can be covered by *Camouflage* (*see* Plate 25), under which men can work. The camouflage should be made to cover all the work, including the spoil. The sides of the camouflage must be sloped gently to the ground to avoid dark shadows. The use of camouflage is also shown in Plates 26 and 27. For screens *see* S.S. 180, " Notes on Screens."

For notes on camouflage *see* S.S. 206. Principles and Practice of Camouflage.

No illustrations of *slab roads, tracks or tram-lines* are given in the diagrams, as their construction is the business of the R.E. and Pioneer Battalions, assisted by what infantry can be spared. Communications are, however, intimately connected with defence ; without good ones it may be impossible to hold a position, and the appreciation of the question as to what infantry labour should be devoted to defences pure and simple, and what to assist in constructing and maintaining communications may be of great importance.

EXECUTION OF TRENCHES.

New trenches must be made to fit in properly with the general scheme of defence ; the best way of ensuring this is to mark their proposed site on a trench map first, and then to correct this alignment by reconnaissance on the ground.

Before work is begun the ground must be carefully reconnoitred and the trench sited and taped out. It is of great advantage if the trench is dug to a few inches by selected men before large working parties are set to work ; the excavation can then be done by any sort of labour, and with less supervision. The work should then be divided into sections, and officers who know the ground made responsible for each section.

---

* The outer edge of the furthest belt of wire should not be nearer than 60 yards from our parapet.

Night work is generally necessary in the forward zone, but work on dark nights is most unremunerative and wasteful. Good results can be obtained only when superintending officers are thoroughly acquainted with the ground.

Every officer and man must be told what is required before going on to the actual ground. A sketch of the trench should be issued with the orders.

Officers and platoon sergeants must have a rough sketch of the section of the trench to be constructed. They must each have a measuring rod, and, where the work entails gauging slopes, they must have an improvised field level. These can be made by Battalion Pioneers, and should be kept in Battalion Stores. Templets (outlines of the section of the trench made of light pieces of wood) are useful to show clearly what is to be done and to ensure, by fitting them into the trench, that the right section is being dug

The working parties are told off according to the length of each section for which a superintending officer is responsible. They should work at two paces (5 ft.) extension ; two men, one with a pick and one with a shovel, may be made responsible for 10 ft. of trench.

There are various methods of filing on to the work; two in general use are given below.

First method.—The leading man halts as he arrives at his place and the others pass behind him, each halting as the beginning of his task is marked ; this method is the quickest, but it causes the men to bunch and is unsuitable for work under fire.

Second method.—The leading man goes right through to the far end of the work and the remainder space themselves out behind him along the line of the work. The commander of the party then checks and corrects their intervals, starting from the leading man and working backwards. This method takes slightly longer, but the men are always well extended.

The superintending officer paces along the tape, or along the side of the trench, and the man marks the place where his foot comes down with his pick or shovel ; this indicates the flank of his task.

A trench must always be dug to the full width from the outset ; one of the main causes of bad trench construction is the tendency to dig only a portion of the width, but deeper than the proper task.

Nothing indicates the standard of discipline and the morale of a Division more clearly than the work done on a defensive front.

Officers and men must realise that good work stimulates interest, and consequently tends to keep up morale, and that a good trench system economises men and minimises losses. There is, perhaps, nothing more demoralising to Infantry than taking over badly constructed and badly kept trenches, except actually constructing and keeping them badly.

NOTE.—The plates are arranged in order of importance from the point of view of instruction. Plates 1—7 should be mastered first.

APPENDIX.

SHELL HOLE POSITIONS.

In heavily shelled ground the quickest way to dig in on a captured objective is to occupy and improve the cover afforded by the shell holes. At the end of an attack the troops will be taking cover in scattered shell holes, and will be more or less disorganized. It is the duty of their officers to decide what line is to be held, to select suitable groups of shell holes, and to reorganize their men.

Positions should be organized in depth and should be so arranged as to afford mutual support by flanking fire. Lewis guns are particularly suitable for this type of defence. The men of each section should be kept together in a group of holes under the section commander. Later these holes can be improved as described below.

It is almost impossible to conceal organized shell holes from low-flying aircraft, and they are very easily detected on air photographs. They can, however, be concealed from ground observation, if care is taken not to throw up any fresh earth or to disturb the lip of the holes; any excavated earth must be dumped in neighbouring holes.

Plates 33 and 34 show various methods of improving the selected holes and of connecting groups of holes to form section posts.

In the water-logged soil of Flanders fresh shell holes are drier and easier to work in than old ones, but in dry soil the sides of old holes are more settled and will stand better.

Drainage, though a difficult problem, is of vital importance. Small shell holes may be connected by drains to deeper holes, or it may only be possible to dig a sump in the bottom of each hole, covering it with a length of duckboard or a shell basket.

Plate 1.

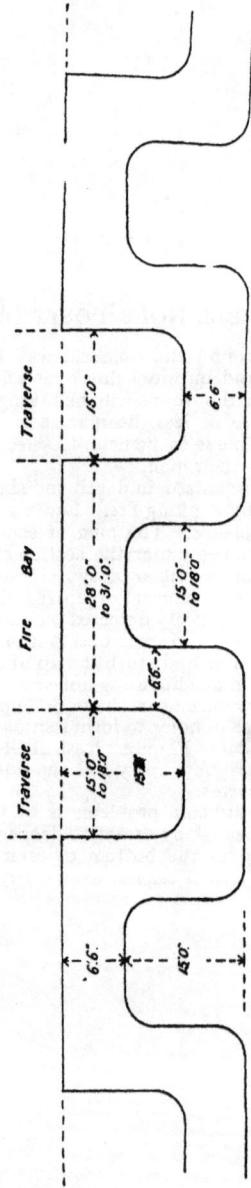

NORMAL TRACE.
(FOR SECTION SEE PLATE 2.)

Traverse   Fire   Bay   Traverse

15'·0"
to 18'·0"

28'·0"
to 31'·0"

15'·0"
to 18'·0"

15'·0"

6'·6"

6'·6"

6'·6"

15'·0"

The upper line should be marked out by tapes and
if possible also the lower one

Plate 2.

NORMAL SECTION OF FIRE TRENCH.

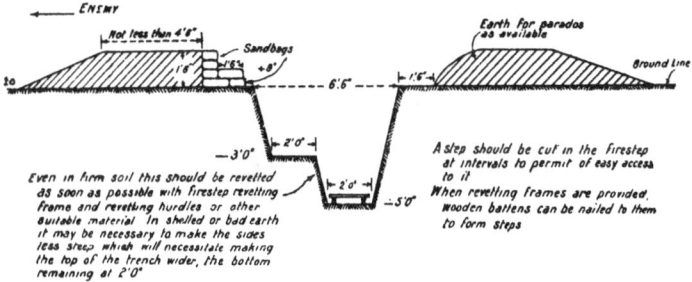

Enemy

Not less than 4'6"

Sandbags

Earth for parados as available

Ground Line

1'6"   1'6"   +8"

6'6"

1'6"

to

—3'0'   2'0"

2'0"

—5'0'

Even in firm soil this should be revetted as soon as possible with firestep revetting frame and revetting hurdles or other suitable material. In shelled or bad earth it may be necessary to make the sides less steep which will necessitate making the top of the trench wider, the bottom remaining at 2'0"

A step should be cut in the firestep at intervals to permit of easy access to it.
When revetting frames are provided, wooden battens can be nailed to them to form steps

ORDER OF WORK.

Enemy

Sandbag revetted as soon as possible

Ground line

1'6'   6'6'   1'6'

+o

I

—3'0'   II

2'0"   III

—5'0'

I and II may be combined as the first task

All excavations from FIRST TASK to be put on parapet Excavations from SECOND and THIRD tasks to be divided between parapet, parados and traverses

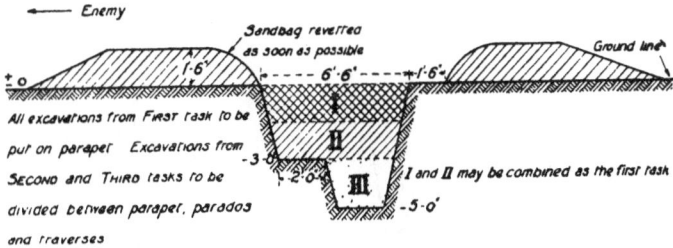

FINAL SECTION of TRENCH
WITH DOUBLE BERM AND REVETTING FRAME
(For Details of Revetting Frame see Plate 3)

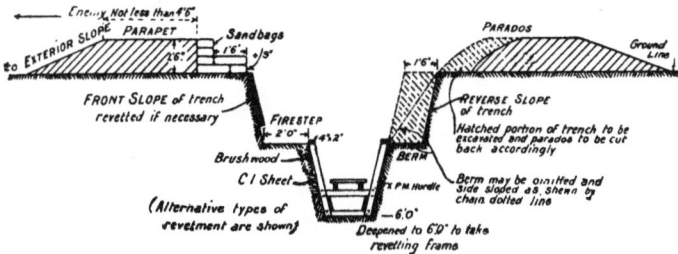

Enemy, Not less than 4'6"

EXTERIOR SLOPE   PARAPET   Sandbags

PARADOS

to   2'6'   1'6"   +3"

Ground Line

FRONT SLOPE of trench revetted if necessary

1'6'

FIRESTEP

2'0"   4'2"

REVERSE SLOPE of trench

Hatched portion of trench to be excavated and parados to be cut back accordingly

Brushwood

BERM

C I Sheet

x PM hurdle

Berm may be omitted and side sloped as shewn by chain dotted line

(Alternative types of revetment are shewn)

—6'0'

Deepened to 6'0" to take revetting frame

Plate 3.

SHORT REVETTING FRAME

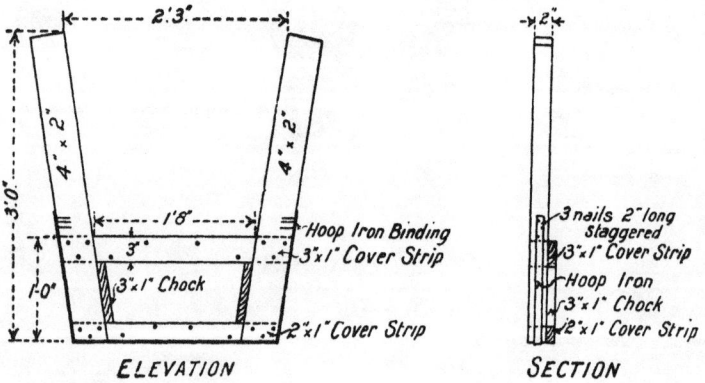

ELEVATION   SECTION

Plate 4.

NORMAL COMMUNICATION TRENCH SECTIONS.

TYPE IN GOOD GROUND WITHOUT DOUBLE BERMS

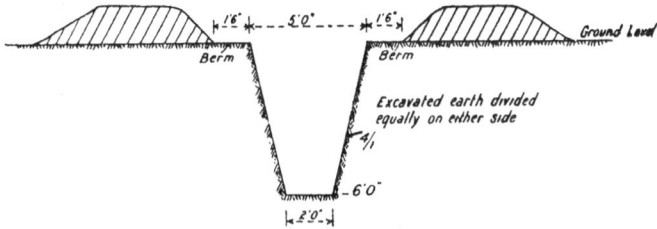

TYPE IN INDIFFERENT GROUND

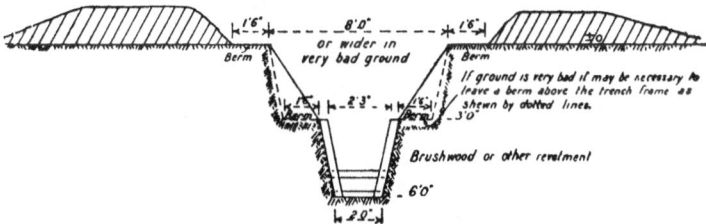

NOTE : C.T⁸ should be firestepped on either side as necessary for defence
Exit steps should be provided at intervals

TYPE OF TRACE FOR COMMUNICATION TRENCH

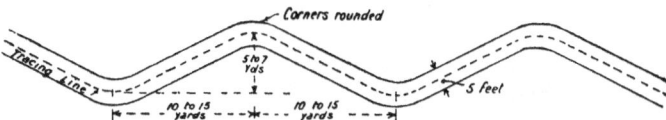

The bends in the trench must conform to the ground so as to get the best advantage in cover, but roughly, the distance between bends should not be more than 15 yards up to the support trenches, and not more than 10 yards between support and fire trenches

Plate 5.

SHELL SLITS.
TO GIVE QUICK IMPROVISED SHELTER

UNSTRUTTED

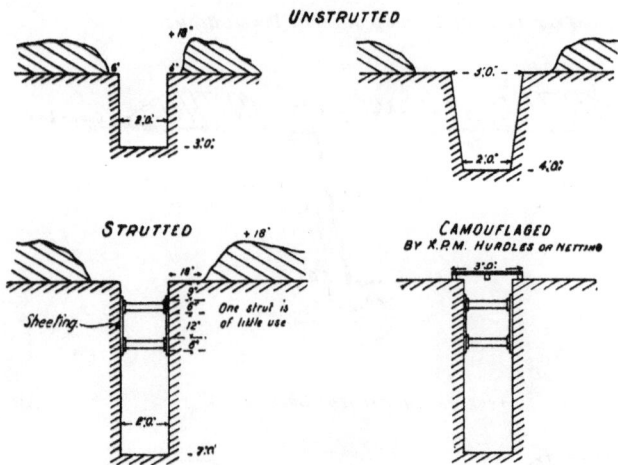

STRUTTED

CAMOUFLAGED
BY X.P.M. HURDLES OR NETTING

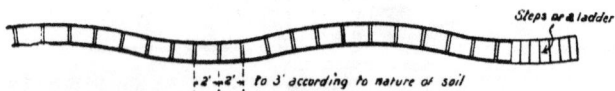

PLAN OF STRUTTED TRENCH

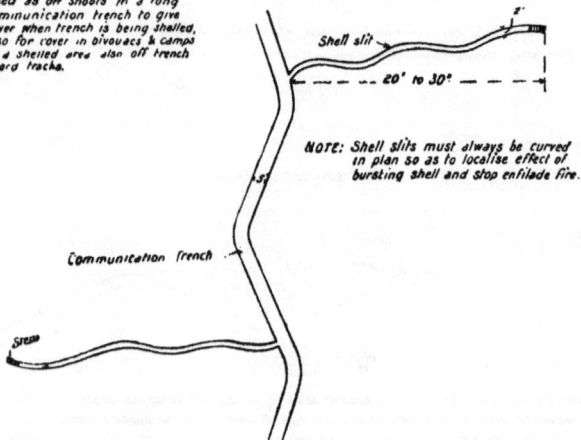

Steps or a ladder

2' + 2' + to 3' according to nature of soil

Used as off shoots in a long communication trench to give cover when trench is being shelled, also for cover in bivouacs & camps in a shelled area also off trench board tracks.

Shell slit

20' to 30'

NOTE: Shell slits must always be curved in plan so as to localise effect of bursting shell and stop enfilade fire.

Communication trench

Steps

Plate 6.

SANDBAG   REVETMENT

ELEVATION

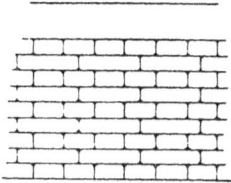

CORRECT

SECTION

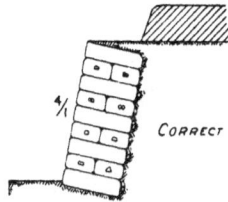

$\frac{4}{1}$

CORRECT SECTION

Foundation should be cut at right angles to slope and always brought to a solid bottom

Parapet

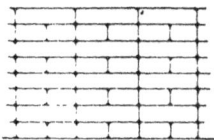

WRONG (JOINTS NOT BROKEN)

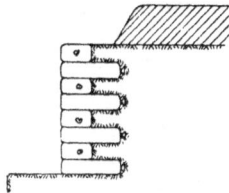

WRONG (VERTICAL)

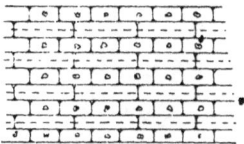

WRONG (SEAMS AND CHOKED ENDS OF BAGS OUTWARDS)

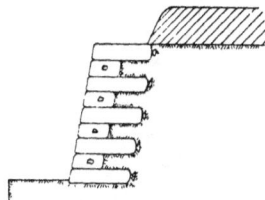

WRONG (BAGS NOT AT RIGHT ANGLES TO SLOPE)

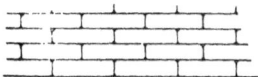

WRONG (ALL STRETCHERS AND NO HEADERS)

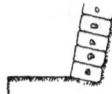

13

Plate 7.

TYPE OF SUMP.

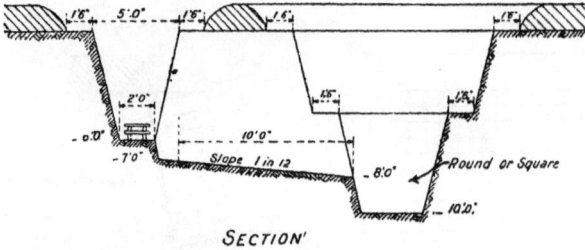

SECTION

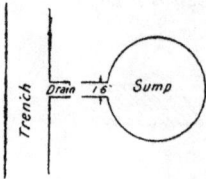

PLAN

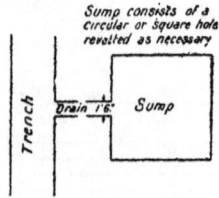

Sump consists of a circular or square hole revetted as necessary

PLAN

NOTE: Sumps should never be put in where drainage out to lower ground can be arranged

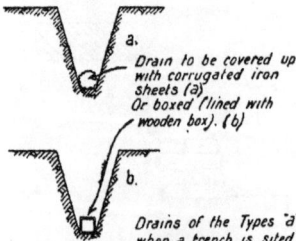

Drain to be covered up with corrugated iron sheets (a)
Or boxed (lined with wooden box). (b)

Drains of the Types 'a' & 'b' can be used when a trench is sited on sloping ground sufficient to ensure the flow of water as below.

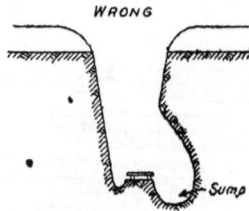

WRONG

Sump

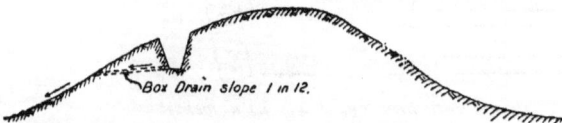

Box Drain slope 1 in 12.

Plate 8.

COMMUNICATION TRENCHES.

CROSSING A FIRE TRENCH.

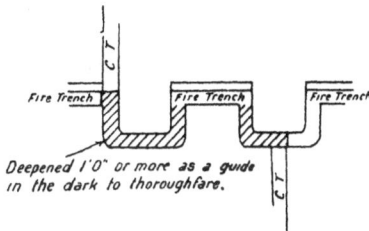

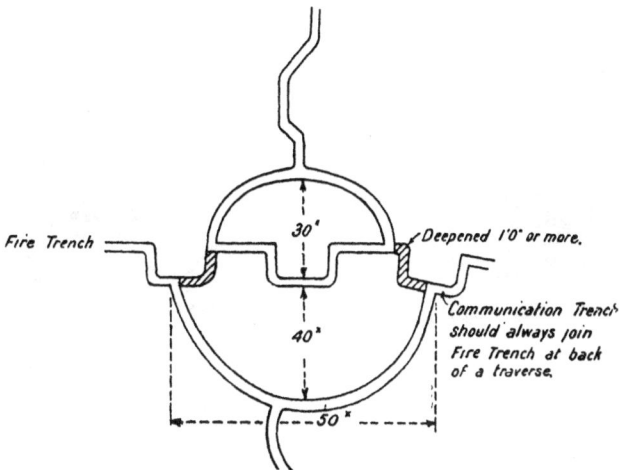

Fire Trench   Fire Trench   Fire Trench

C.T.

C.T.

Deepened 1'0" or more as a guide
in the dark to thoroughfare.

Fire   Trench

C.T.

C.T.

WRONG.

Fire Trench

30"

40"

50"

Deepened 1'0" or more.

Communication Trench
should always join
Fire Trench at back
of a traverse.

ALTERNATIVE METHOD.

15

Plate 9.

DIAGRAMMATIC SKETCH OF PORTION OF FRONT LINE
AND SUPPORT LINE WITH COMMUNICATION TRENCH.

(Advanced Posts and Wiring omitted.)

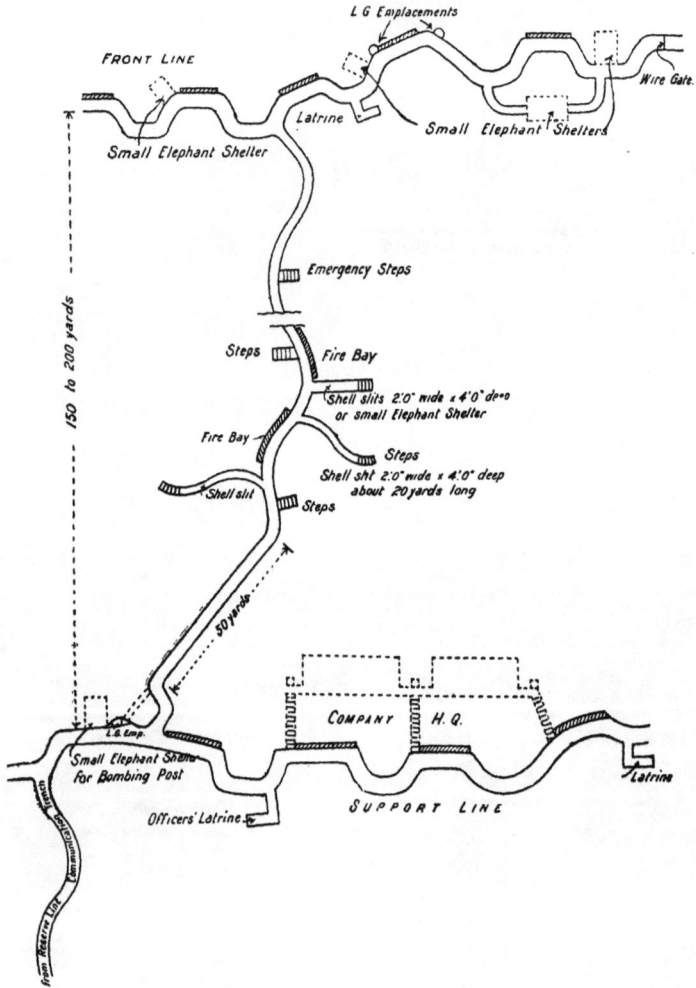

L G Emplacements

FRONT LINE

Wire Gate.

Latrine

Small Elephant Shelters

Small Elephant Shelter

Emergency Steps

Steps

Fire Bay

Shell slits 2'0" wide x 4'0" deep
or small Elephant Shelter

Fire Bay

Steps

Shell slit 2'0" wide x 4'0" deep
about 20 yards long

Shell slit

Steps

150 to 200 yards

50 yards

COMPANY   H. Q.

L.G. Emp.

Small Elephant Shelter
For Bombing Post

Latrine

Officers' Latrine

SUPPORT LINE

from Reserve Line

Communication Trench

16

Plate 10.

SECTION OF A DEFENSIVE SYSTEM

(Showing Vickers Gun Defences.)

No Lewis Guns shown.

Wiring omitted.

Thickened portions of the line show actual portions of the trenches held.

(1) Forward Vickers Guns are shown in yellow.

(2) Rear Vickers Guns in green.

(3) Where a Vickers Gun fires direct the actual band of fire which it can place is marked by thickening the line in colour.

(4) S.O.S. Targets are all in red and each Vickers Gun or Battery can fire as marked from the outset, turning on to its direct target as soon as necessary.

(5) Batteries of 4 Vickers Guns each are numbered A, B, C, D.

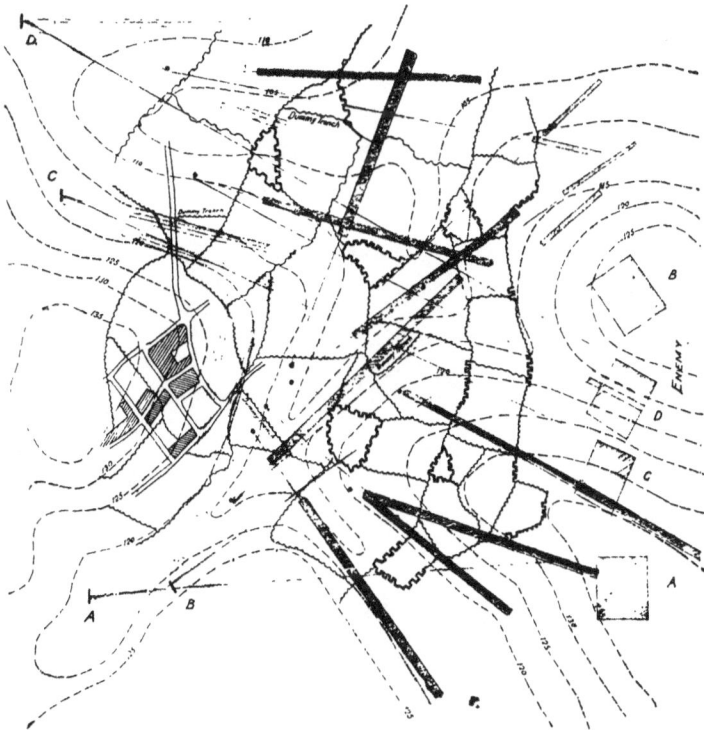

SCALE.

Plate 11.

Methods of Defence of Communication Trenches

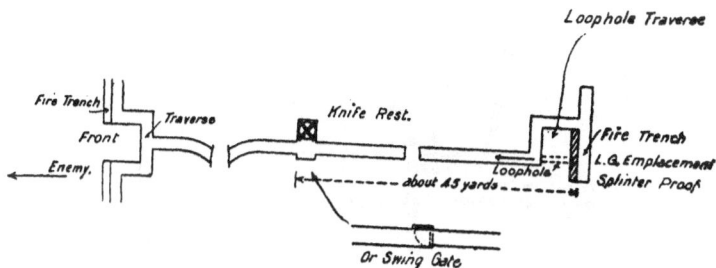

Loophole Traverse

Fire Trench

Front

Traverse

Knife Rest.

Enemy.

Fire Trench

L.G. Emplacement

Loophole

Splinter Proof

about 45 yards

Or Swing Gate

Diagram shewing straight length of Communication Trench, for protection against bombing and knife rest in position for blocking.

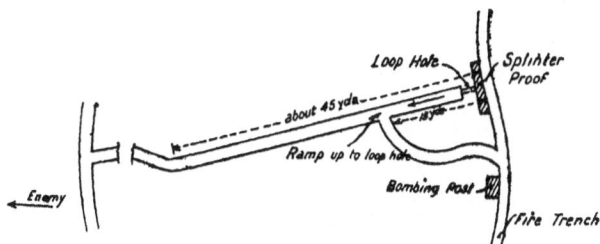

Loop Hole

Splinter Proof

about 45 yds.

Ramp up to loop hole

Bombing Post

Enemy

Fire Trench

ALTERNATIVE METHOD

Plate 12.

LATRINES.

DEEP LATRINE off C.T.

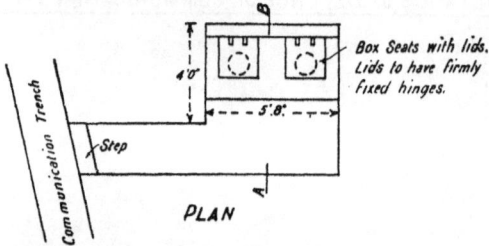

Box Seats with lids.
Lids to have firmly
Fixed hinges.

4'0"

5'8"

Communication Trench

Step

PLAN

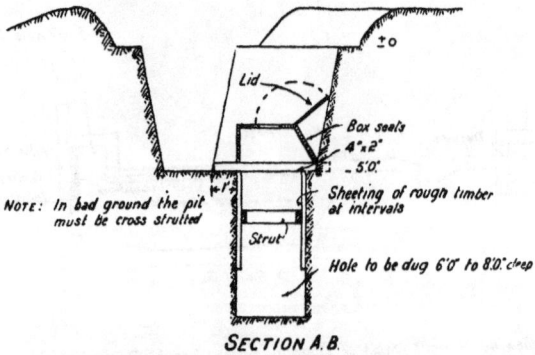

Lid

Box seats
4"x2"

5'0"

Sheeting of rough timber
at intervals

NOTE: In bad ground the pit
must be cross strutted

Strut

Hole to be dug 6'0" to 8'0" deep

SECTION A.B.

LATRINE RECESS off TRENCH (BUCKET SYSTEM)

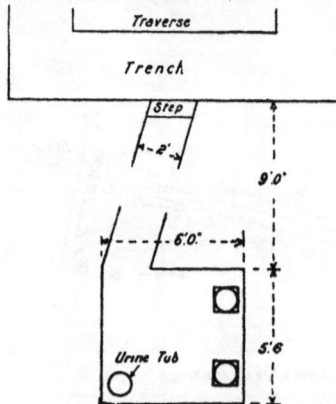

Traverse

Trench

Step

2'

9'0"

6'0"

5'6"

Urine Tub

Plate 13.

MACHINE GUN EMPLACEMENT
OF MINIMUM DIMENSIONS.

OPEN EMPLACEMENT TO FIRE STANDING

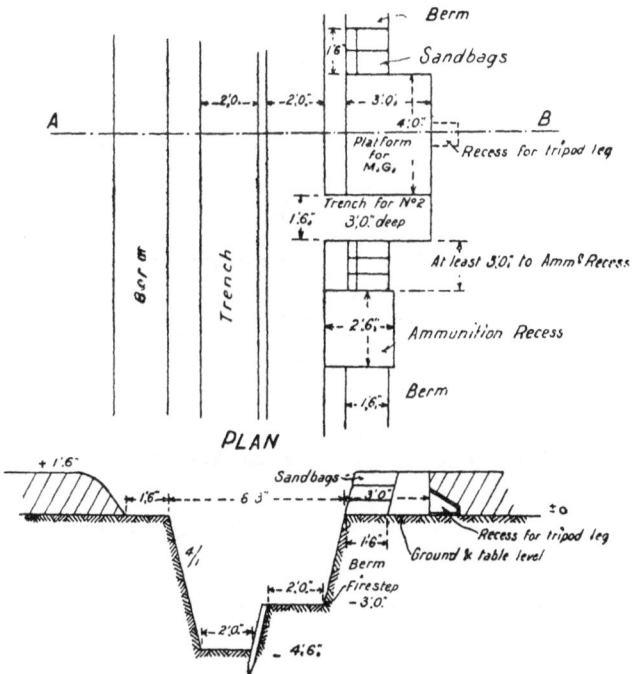

Berm

Sandbags

1'6"

A — 2'0" — 2'0" — 3'0' — 4'0" — B

Platform for M.G.

Recess for tripod leg

Trench for Nº2
1'6" 3'0" deep

At least 3'0" to Ammº Recess

Borm

Trench

2'6"

Ammunition Recess

Berm

1'6"

PLAN

+ 1'6"

Sandbags

1'6" — 6 3" — 3'0'

±o

Recess for tripod leg

1'6"

Ground & table level

Berm

4/1

2'0" Firestep − 3'0"

2'0"

4'6"

SECTION A. B.

NOTE: Dugout or Small Elephant Shelter for Crew must be close at hand.

Plate 14.

TRACE OF TRENCHES.

FIRE TRENCH
Showing application of normal trace to the ground.

FORWARD TRAVERSE TO EXISTING LINE

This island traverse provides a separate traffic route but is liable to draw fire.

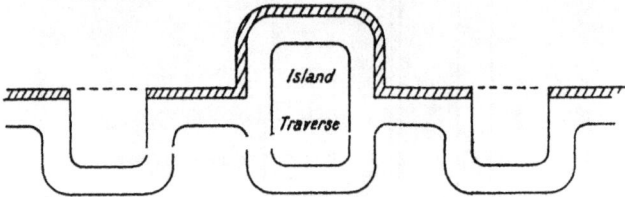

Island

Traverse

WAVY FIRE OR COMMUNICATION TRENCHES.

WRONG.

As it can be enfiladed, the general direction being too straight.

CORRECT

This principle should also be used for duckboard tracks on mud flats.

Plate 15.

ALTERNATIVE
TRACE OF TRENCHES.

ZIG - ZAG.

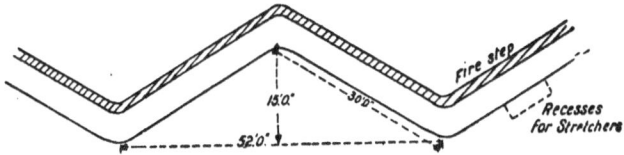

15'0"   30'0"   fire step

52'0"   Recesses
for Stretchers

Provision should be made for loopholed traverses to defend long lengths of Dog leg and Zig-zag.

T. HEAD.

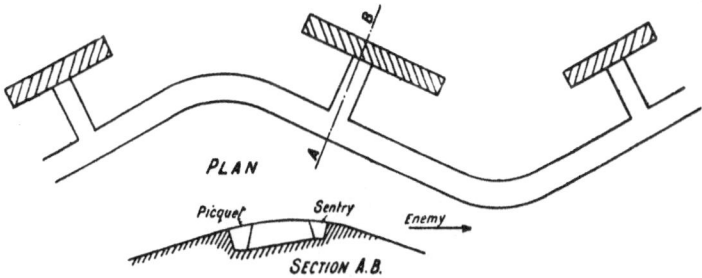

PLAN

Picquet   Sentry   Enemy →

SECTION A.B.

T. Heads should only be used in well concealed positions. such as wooded slopes or when the ground is so broken that proper field of fire cannot be obtained from trench itself. Also for sap heads for observation when trench is sited on reverse slope as in Section A B. The objection to them is that they show in an aeroplane photograph where the trench is prepared for defence.

OCCASIONAL FORWARD TRAVERSE
Provides a good position for a snipers post or position for a machine gun for flanking fire

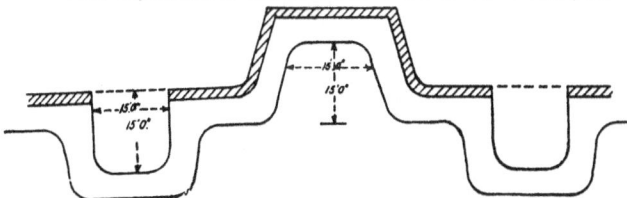

15'0"   15'0"   15'0"   15'0"

21

Plate 16.

Plate 16.

ALTERNATIVE
TRACE OF FIRE TRENCHES.

FOR USE IN SPECIAL CASES (CHIEFLY DEPENDING ON THE GROUND)

ALTERNATIVE NORMAL TYPE OF FIRE TRENCH

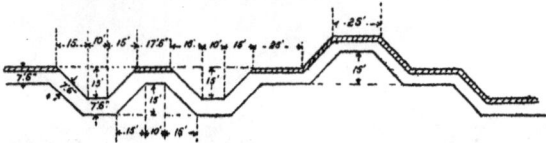

This type of trench is harder to lay out but makes communication especially carriage of stretchers, easier

CURVED WITHOUT TRAVERSES
A traversed trench is the better
but takes longer to dig

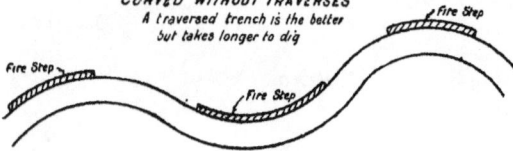

Fire Step

Fire Step

Fire Step

DOG LEGS

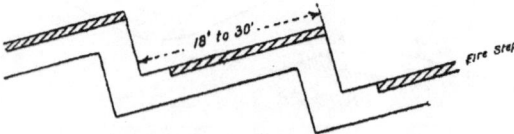

18' to 30'

Fire Step

EXAMPLE OF USE OF DOG LEGS.

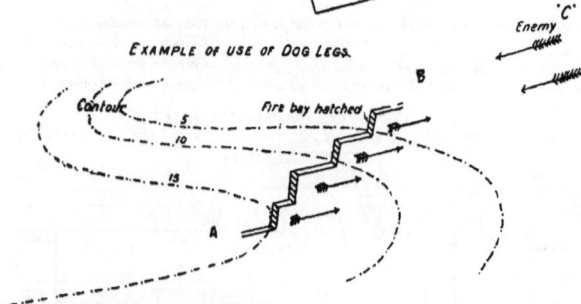

Contour

Fire bay hatched

B

Enemy

'C'

A

A.B. is the general direction in which it is necessary to site a trench down a slope that is enfiladed by the enemy from 'C'.
This trench should be dog legged as shewn

Plate 17.

SITING OF TRENCHES.

FIG. I. Example of a good reverse slope position; our artillery covers the front and leaves no dead ground.
Our infantry position is hidden from direct enemy observation and sweeps with its fire the immediate front of the trenches

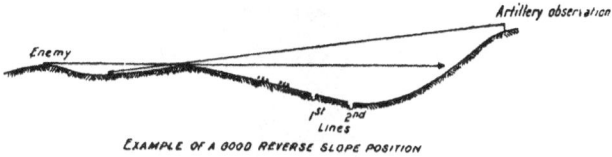

Artillery observation

Enemy

1st 2nd
Lines

EXAMPLE OF A GOOD REVERSE SLOPE POSITION

FIG 2 Unless the crest and front slope of the most advanced hill is held, the enemy's trenches are completely screened from our observation. This position therefore compels the siting of our 1st and 2nd lines on the forward slope. The 3rd line which would be the line of main resistence is on reverse slope, screened from enemy observation and possessing sufficient though limited field of fire (The line of main resistence MUST be screened from direct enemy observation to enable it to be held under bombardment; length of field of fire is secondary)

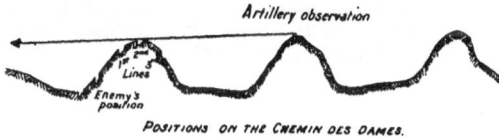

Artillery observation

1st 2nd
Lines
Enemy's position

POSITIONS ON THE CHEMIN DES DAMES.

FIG 3. Here the front line must be held to deny observation from it by the enemy. In this case the forward slope must be held as far forward as possible to compel the enemy to retire to the other side of the valley, and thus secure the hill by a position in depth.

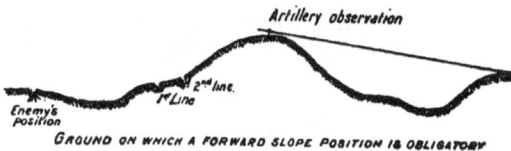

Artillery observation

2nd line.
1st Line
Enemy's position

GROUND ON WHICH A FORWARD SLOPE POSITION IS OBLIGATORY

23

Plate 18.

SMALL CORRUGATED STEEL SHELTERS.
(*Baby Elephant*).

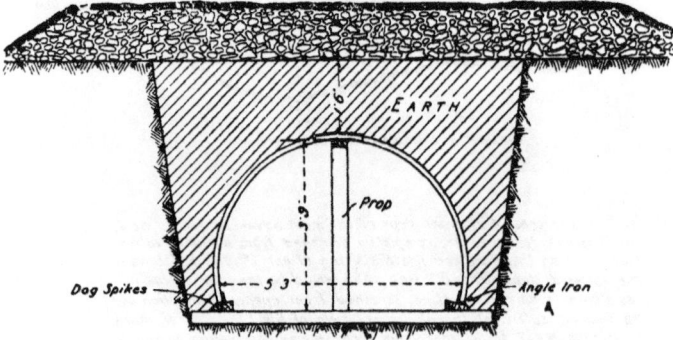

EARTH

Prop

Dog Spikes

Angle Iron

Section.

Each arch is made up of two corrugated steel sheets 2 ft. 9 in. wide bolted together.   Five arches form a shelter 12 ft. 9 in. long.   The arches overlap 3 ins. and are bolted together.

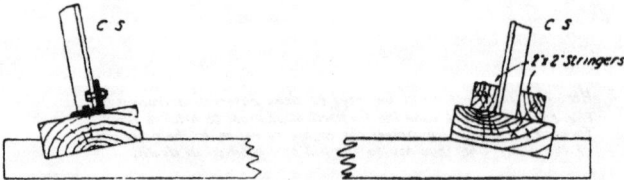

C S

C S

2"x 2" Stringers

Alternative Details at A.

With " L " Iron.   *Without " L " Iron (Latest Pattern).*

24

Plate 19.

SIMPLE WEATHER-PROOF SHELTERS.

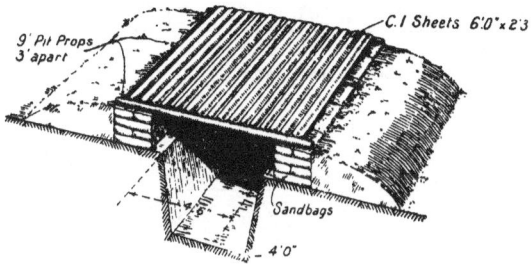

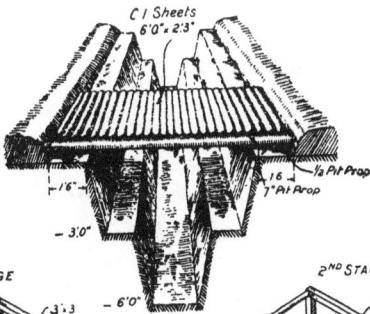

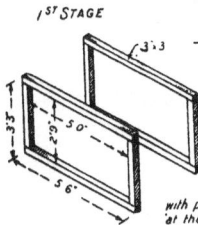

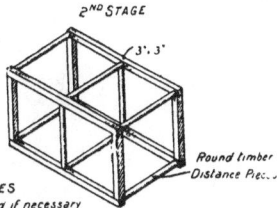

9' Pit Props
3' apart

C.I Sheets 6'0"x 2'3

Sandbags

4'0"

C I Sheets
6'0"x 2'3

1'6"

½ Pit Prop

1'6"

7" Pit Prop

3'0"

1ST STAGE

3'·3

6'0"

2ND STAGE

3'·3'

3'3

5'0"

2'9"

5'6"

Round timber
Distance Piec...

TIMBER FRAMES
with planks or C I over, and if necessary
at the sides which can be used in place
of small Elephant Shelters ¡ See Plate 22¡

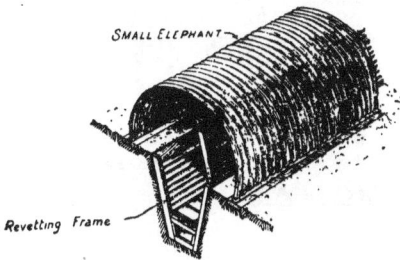

SMALL ELEPHANT

Revetting Frame

Plate 20.

SPLINTER PROOF SHELTERS.

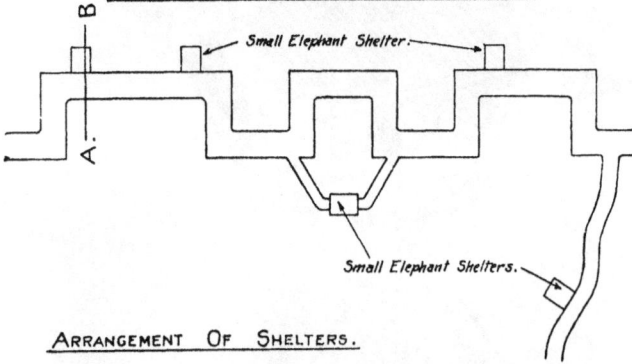

B

A.

Small Elephant Shelter.

Small Elephant Shelters.

ARRANGEMENT OF SHELTERS.

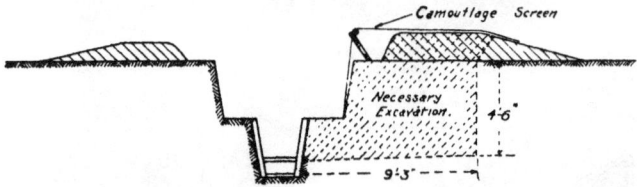

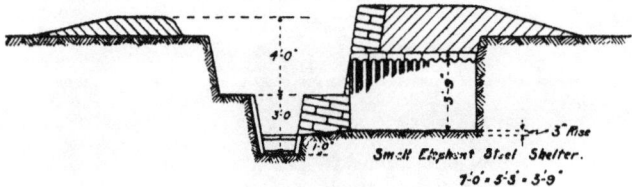

Camouflage Screen

Necessary Excavation.

4'-6"

9'-3"

4'-0"

3'-0"

5'-9"

1'-0"

3" Rise

Small Elephant Steel Shelter.
7'-0" × 5'-3" × 5'-9"

SECTION A.B.

Plate 21.

ANCHORAGES IN BREASTWORKS.

NOTE: All anchorages should be held back by at least 5 double strands of binding wire twisted together

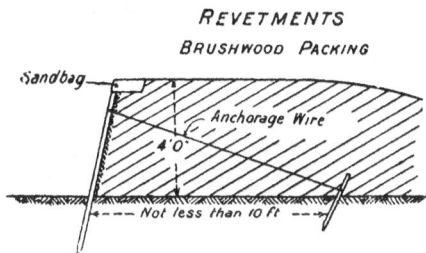

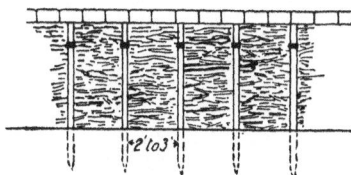

REVETMENTS
BRUSHWOOD PACKING

Sandbag

Anchorage Wire

4'0"

-- Not less than 10 ft --

SECTION
(RIGHT METHOD)

NOTE:-
Anchorage pickets and wires must be placed in position before the earth is thrown up.
In ordinary trenches, to get a straight pull in the anchorage wire a groove must be cut for it in the parapet

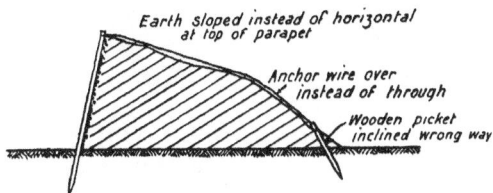

2'to 3'

ELEVATION

Earth sloped instead of horizontal at top of parapet

Anchor wire over instead of through

Wooden picket inclined wrong way

SECTION
(WRONG METHOD)

Plate 22.

METHOD OF REVETMENT WITHOUT REVETTING FRAME

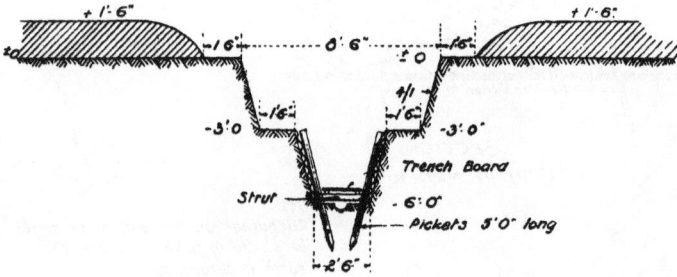

+ 1'·6"

±0   -1'·6"   6'·6"   -1'·6"   ±0

4/1

-3'·0"   -1'·6"   -3'·0"

Trench Board

Strut   -6'·0"

Pickets 5'·0" long

-2'·6"

Trench board laid on trestles 3'0" apart where soil is too soft for
central drain to stand.

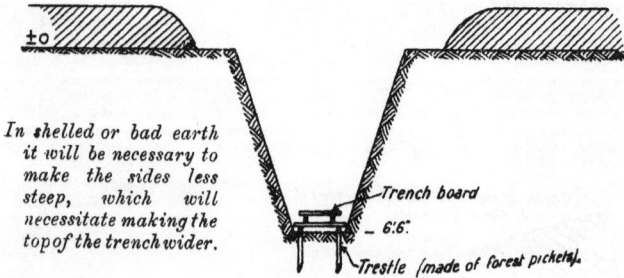

±0

In shelled or bad earth
it will be necessary to
make the sides less
steep, which will
necessitate making the
top of the trench wider.

Trench board

-6'·6"

Trestle (made of forest pickets).

Plate 23.

SECTIONS OF FIRE TRENCH

SECTION OF BREASTWORK IN WET SOIL

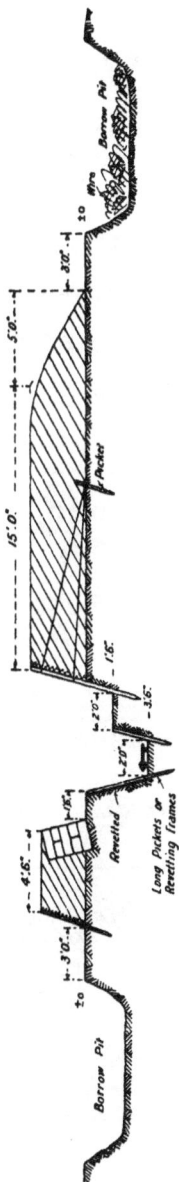

NOTE:- Care must be taken that the borrow pit is not commenced within 3 ft. of where the toe of the completed breastwork will reach

When fire bays are required for immediate use the employment of gabions or boxes filled with earth to form a revetment permits this to be done, giving the maximum of protection in the minimum of time.

Plate 24.

SNIPER'S POST.

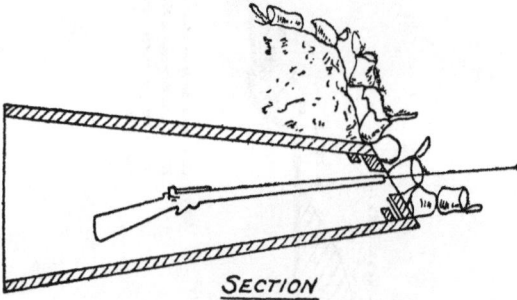

SECTION

VIEW FROM FRONT.

As our front Parapets are covered with tins of all kinds, the tin used to disguise the loophole is very difficult to identify even at 10 yds range.

OBLIQUE LOOPHOLE.

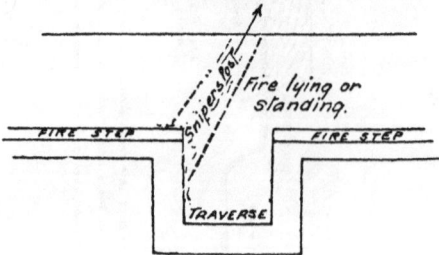

Snipers post · Fire lying or standing.

FIRE STEP · FIRE STEP

TRAVERSE

Plenty of Dummy Loopholes should be provided.

Plate 25.

CONCEALMENT OF TRENCHES.

Painted transparent canvas—stretch tightly over trench and parapet. All traces of work must be covered and edges of canvas broken with turf, etc., to avoid regular outline.

This shows concealment of defences already dug. Where as is generally the case it is desired to conceal the making of the work, the canvas should be stretched over the site, raised a little if necessary, on timber laid on the ground, and all excavation carried out underneath it. All or part of the spoil can be concealed by removing it in sandbags, etc, to hollows or old trenches near.

31

Plate 26.

Examples of the Use of Unarmoured Portable O.P. in Shell Holes and Parapets of Trenches.

Side view

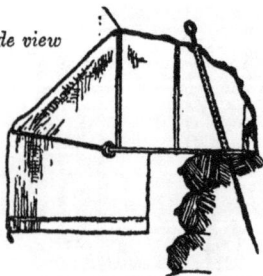

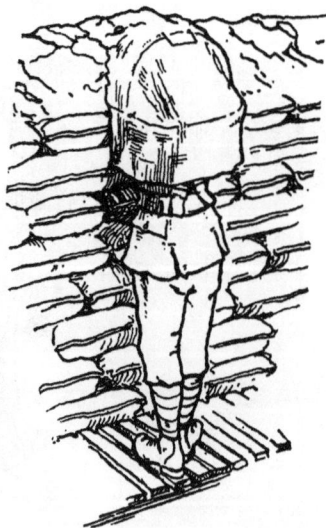

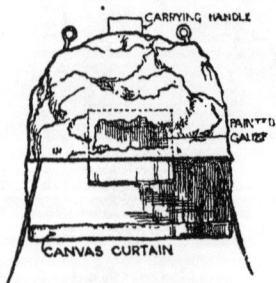

CARRYING HANDLE

PAINTED GAUZE

CANVAS CURTAIN

Plate 27.

Examples of the Use of Portable Armoured O.Ps. in Trenches for Sentries.

Armoured Sandbag O.P.

Hood of Painted Transparent Canvas used for Scouts or looking over Parapets.

Armoured Turf O.P.

Plate 28.

SPECIMEN OF SUITABLE COVER.
Proof against 5·9" Shells.

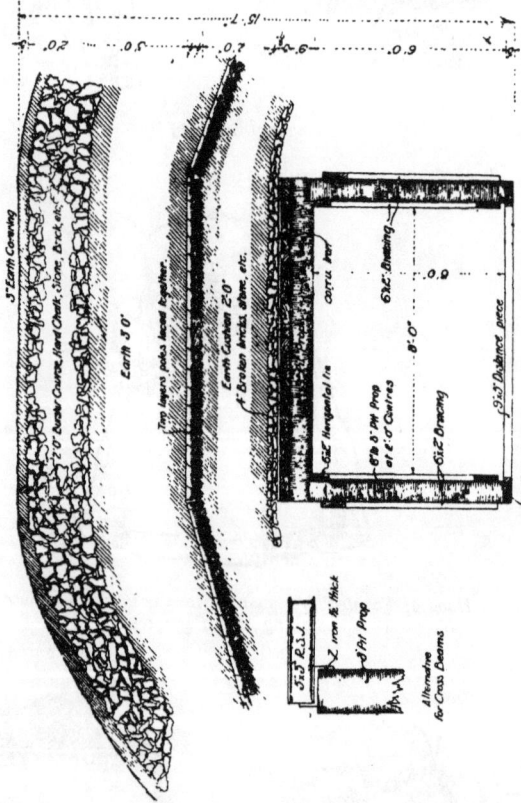

SCALE OF FEET.

Cross Section.

Plate 29.

TYPES OF DUGOUTS.

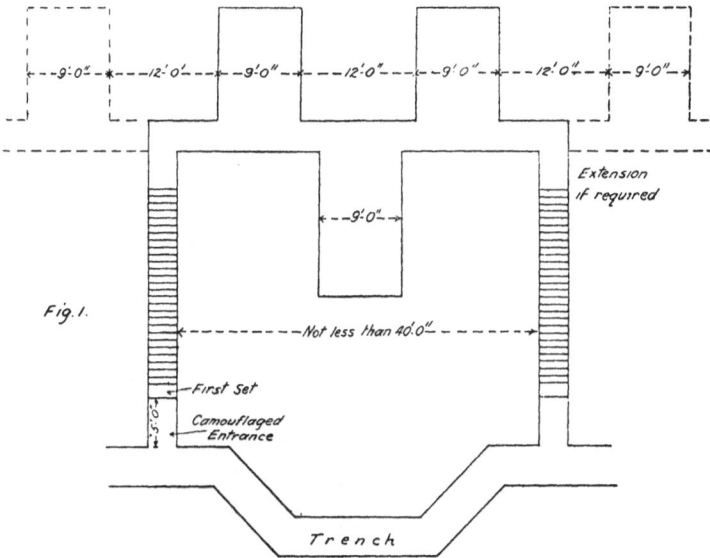

Fig. 1.

Extension if required

9'0"

Not less than 40'0"

First Set

Camouflaged Entrance

Trench

Type A

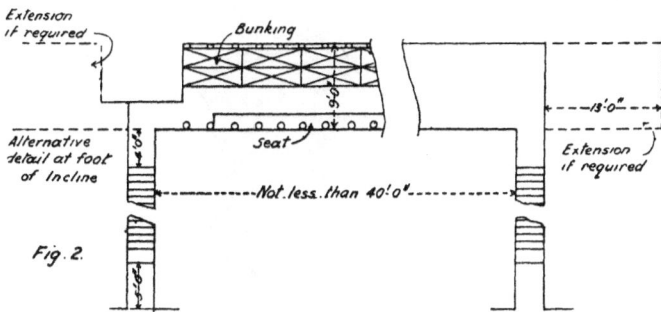

Extension if required

Bunking

Alternative detail at foot of Incline

Seat

Not less than 40'0"

Extension if required

13'0"

Fig. 2.

Type B

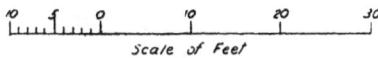

Scale of Feet

35

Plate 30.

— Subways —

Typical Arrangement of Galleries and Accessory Dugouts

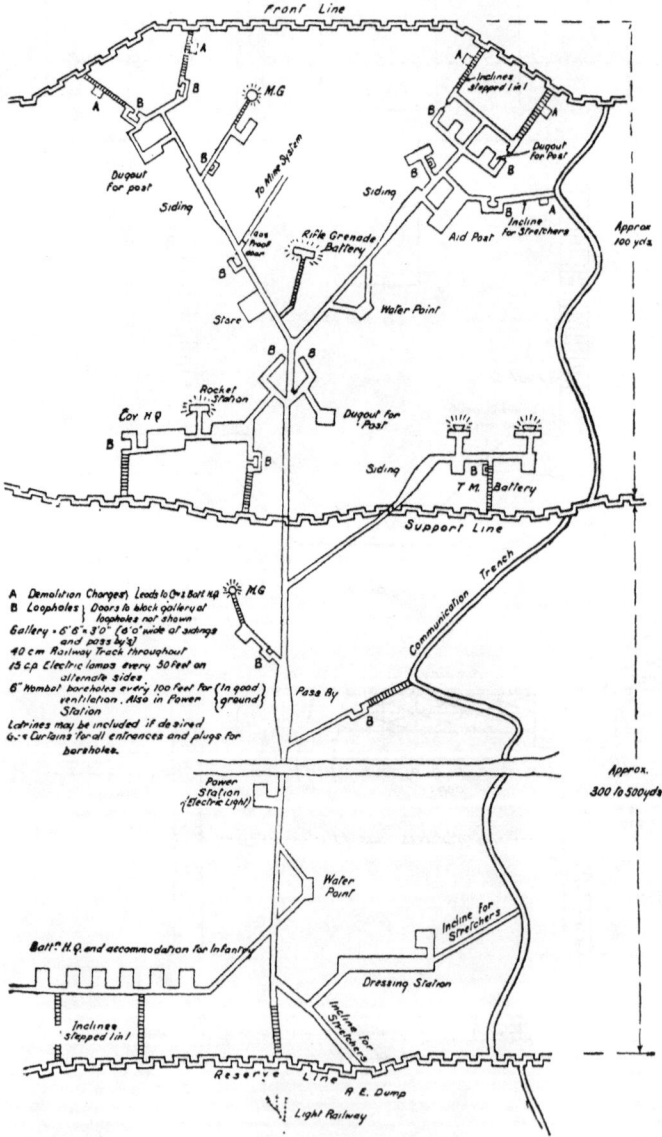

A Demolition Charges) Leads to C $\times$ s Batt H.Q
B Loopholes) Doors to block gallery at
        loopholes not shown
Gallery - 6'6"x 3'0" (6'0" wide at sidings
      and pass bys)
40 cm Railway Track throughout
15 c.p. Electric lamps every 50 feet on
    alternate sides
6" Nombat boreholes every 100 feet for (In good
    ventilation. Also in Power {ground }
    Station
Latrines may be included if desired
Gas Curtains for all entrances and plugs for
    boreholes.

36

Plate 31.

DEFENCE OF CRATERS.

NEAR LIP DEFENDED

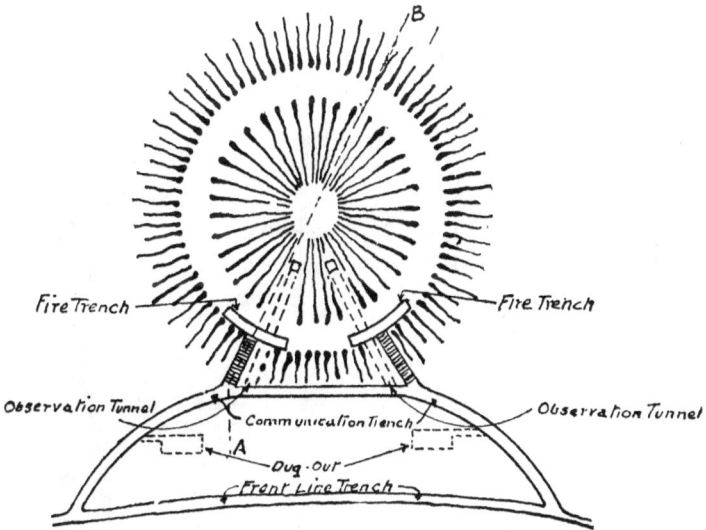

Plan

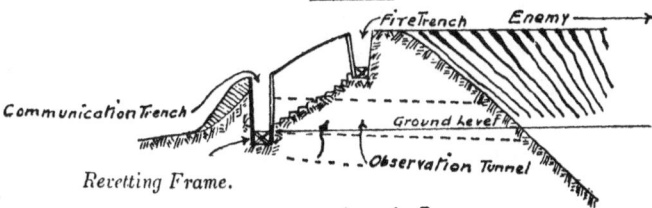

Section A.B.

Plate 32.

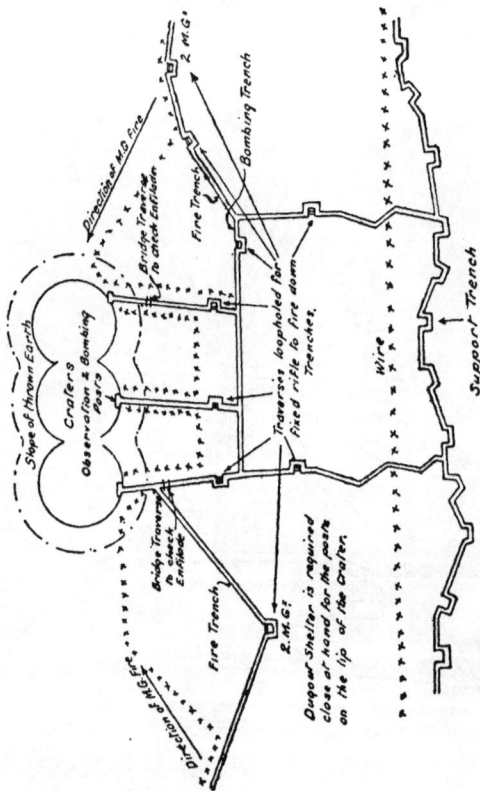

DEFENCE OF CRATERS

BY BOMBING TRENCHES WHERE THERE IS NO FIELD OF FIRE.

Direction of fire

2 M.G.

Bombing Trench

Bridge Traverse to check Enfilade

Fire Trench

Slope of thrown Earth

Craters
Observation & Bombing Posts

Bridge Traverse to check Enfilade

Traverse loopholed for fixed rifle to fire down Trenches.

Fire Trench

Dug-out Shelter is required close at hand for the posts on the lip of the craters.

2 M.G.

Direction of M.G.

Wire

Support Trench

38

Plate 33.

ARRANGEMENT OF SLIT TRENCHES.
(To provide Cover).

Fig. 1.

No excavated earth to show above ground level.

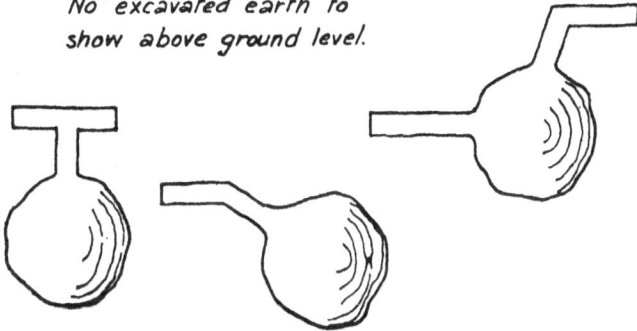

SHELL HOLE POSITIONS.

Fig. 2.

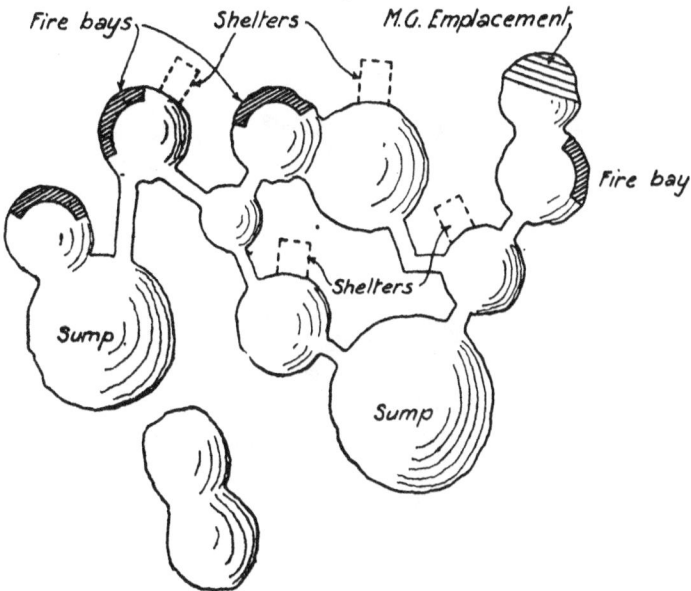

Plate 34.

IMPROVEMENTS TO SHELL HOLES.

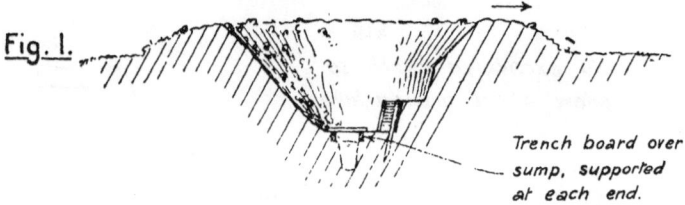

Fig. 1.

Trench board over sump, supported at each end.

Fig. 2.

Lip of shell hole not to be disturbed.

SECTION

Weather proof cover for lewis gun and crew. Gun fires from top of shelter.

All excavated earth to be dumped in neighbouring holes.

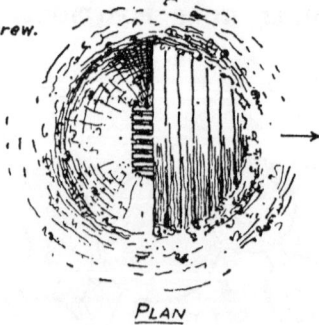

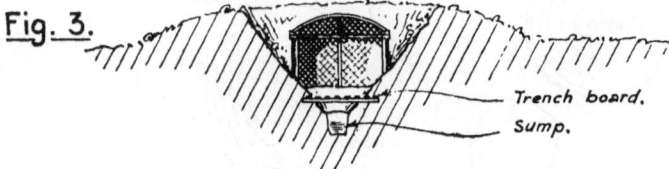

PLAN

Fig. 3.

Trench board.
Sump.

Showing shelter let into side of shell hole, roof of curved sheets of C.I.

www.ingramcontent.com/pod-product-compliance
Lightning Source LLC
Chambersburg PA
CBHW022005090426
42741CB00007B/904